DANIEL

Books in the PREACHING THE WORD Series:

JEREMIAH AND LAMENTATIONS:
From Sorrow to Hope
by Philip Graham Ryken

MARK, VOLUME ONE:
Jesus, Servant and Savior

MARK, VOLUME TWO:
Jesus, Servant and Savior

LUKE, VOLUME ONE:
That You May Know the Truth

LUKE, VOLUME TWO:
That You May Know the Truth

JOHN:
That You May Believe

ACTS:
The Church Afire

ROMANS:
Righteousness from Heaven

EPHESIANS:
The Mystery of the Body of Christ

COLOSSIANS AND PHILEMON:
The Supremacy of Christ

1 & 2 TIMOTHY AND TITUS:
To Guard the Deposit

1 and 2 Timothy by R. Kent Hughes

Titus by Bryan Chapell

HEBREWS, VOLUME ONE:
An Anchor for the Soul

HEBREWS, VOLUME TWO:
An Anchor for the Soul

JAMES:
Faith That Works

THE SERMON ON THE MOUNT:
The Message of the Kingdom

Unless otherwise indicated, all volumes are by R. Kent Hughes

PREACHING THE WORD

DANIEL

The Triumph of God's Kingdom

Rodney Stortz

R. Kent Hughes, General Editor

CROSSWAY BOOKS

A DIVISION OF
GOOD NEWS PUBLISHERS
WHEATON, ILLINOIS

Daniel

Copyright © 2004 by Elizabeth B. Stortz

Published by Crossway Books
    a division of Good News Publishers
    1300 Crescent Street
    Wheaton, Illinois 60187

Cover banner by Marge Gieser

Art Direction: David LaPlaca

First printing, 2004

Printed in the United States of America

Scripture taken from the *Holy Bible: New International Version®*. Copyright © 1973, 1978, 1984 by International Bible Society. Used by permission of Zondervan Publishing House. All rights reserved.

The "NIV" and "New International Version" trademarks are registered in the United States Patent and Trademark Office by International Bible Society. Use of either trademark requires the permission of International Bible Society.

Scripture quotations marked NRSV are taken from the New Revised Standard Version, copyright © 1989 by National Council of Churches.

Library of Congress Cataloging-in-Publication Data
Stortz, Rodney D., 1950–2003
   Daniel : the triumph of God's kingdom / Rodney D. Stortz ; R. Kent Hughes, general editor.
     p. cm. — (Preaching the word)
   Includes bibliographical references and index.
   ISBN 1-58134-550-X (alk. paper)
    1. Bible. O.T. Daniel—Commentaries. I. Hughes, R. Kent. II. Title.
III. Series.
BS1555.53.S76   2004
224'.507—dc22   2003019028

RRD		13	12	11	10	09	08	07	06	05	04
15	14	13	12	11	10	9	8	7	6	5	4	3	2	1

*This book is dedicated to my three daughters
whose love for the Lord Jesus has
made their parents' hearts overflow with great joy.
Thank you for walking in the truth like Daniel did
even when the way was difficult.*

*"I have no greater joy than to hear that my
children are walking in the truth."*
(3 John 4)

The God of heaven will set up a kingdom that shall never be destroyed . . . it shall stand forever.
(Daniel 2:44)

Table of Contents

A Word to Those Who Preach the Word

There are times when I am preaching that I have especially sensed the pleasure of God. I usually become aware of it through the unnatural silence. The ever-present coughing ceases, and the pews stop creaking, bringing an almost physical quiet to the sanctuary — through which my words sail like arrows. I experience a heightened eloquence, so that the cadence and volume of my voice intensify the truth I am preaching.

There is nothing quite like it — the Holy Spirit filling one's sails, the sense of his pleasure, and the awareness that something is happening among one's hearers. This experience is, of course, not unique, for thousands of preachers have similar experiences, even greater ones.

What has happened when this takes place? How do we account for this sense of his smile? The answer for me has come from the ancient rhetorical categories of *logos*, *ethos*, and *pathos*.

The first reason for his smile is the *logos* — in terms of preaching, God's Word. This means that as we stand before God's people to proclaim his Word, we have done our homework. We have exegeted the passage, mined the significance of its words in their context, and applied sound hermeneutical principles in interpreting the text so that we understand what its words meant to its hearers. And it means that we have labored long until we can express in a sentence what the theme of the text is — so that our outline springs from the text. Then our preparation will be such that as we preach, we will not be preaching our own thoughts about God's Word, but God's actual Word, his *logos*. This is fundamental to pleasing him in preaching.

The second element in knowing God's smile in preaching is *ethos* — what you are as a person. There is a danger endemic to preaching, which is having your hands and heart cauterized by holy things. Phillips Brooks illustrated it by the analogy of a train conductor who comes to believe that he has been to the places he announces because of his long and loud heralding of them. And that is why Brooks insisted that preaching must be "the bringing of truth through personality." Though we can never *perfectly*

embody the truth we preach, we must be subject to it, long for it, and make
it as much a part of our ethos as possible. As the Puritan William Ames
said, "Next to the Scriptures, nothing makes a sermon more to pierce, than
when it comes out of the inward affection of the heart without any affecta-
tion." When a preacher's *ethos* backs up his *logos*, there will be the pleasure
of God.

Last, there is *pathos* — personal passion and conviction. David Hume,
the Scottish philosopher and skeptic, was once challenged as he was seen
going to hear George Whitefield preach: "I thought you do not believe in
the gospel." Hume replied, "I don't, but *he does*." Just so! When a preacher
believes what he preaches, there will be passion. And this belief and requi-
site passion will know the smile of God.

The pleasure of God is a matter of *logos* (the Word), *ethos* (what you
are), and *pathos* (your passion). As you *preach the Word* may you experience his smile — the Holy Spirit in your sails!

R. Kent Hughes
Wheaton, Illinois

Preface

When Daniel had finished writing his book, he was confused and exhausted. He said, "I heard, but I did not understand" (Daniel 12:8a). Then he asked the Lord, "What will the outcome of all this be?" (v. 8b). In other words, "How will this all come together in the end?"

The Lord replied, "Go your way, Daniel, because the words are closed up and sealed until the time of the end [or the last days]." The words of the prophecy were sealed. The Lord would give no more prophecy about the future to Daniel, and he would not explain it anymore "until the time of the end." We know from Acts 2:17 that "the last days" began at the time of the death, resurrection, and ascension of Jesus Christ.

The Apostle John tells us of an interesting event in Heaven in those days, described in Revelation 5:1-5. The Lamb who had been slain was standing beside the throne. In the right hand of Him who sat on the throne was a scroll with writing on both sides and sealed with seven seals. John wept, because he thought there was no one worthy to open the seals and explain the prophecies found inside.

Then the elders said to John, "Do not weep! See, the Lion of the tribe of Judah, the Root of David, has triumphed. He is able to open the scroll and its seven seals." When he does so, the prophecies of Revelation 6 — 22 are revealed. They both explain in greater detail the things Daniel was asking about and add new prophecies about the return of Christ. The scroll of Daniel was unsealed by the Lamb through the writings of the New Testament.

This commentary on Daniel will use the light of the New Testament to unseal the scroll of Daniel in order to give a clearer understanding of his prophecies. By God's grace and through the help of his Holy Spirit, you will not be as confused and exhausted when you finish this book as Daniel was when he finished writing it the first time.

Throughout this commentary and the pages of Scripture the God of Daniel is revealed to us. He is a God who loves his people and is in sovereign control over all the events of this world. He is concerned about our holiness and our fears; so he shows us how he worked in Daniel, and he tells us about our future.

THE AUTHOR

The book claims to have been written by Daniel (Daniel 10:21). Also, Ezekiel recognizes Daniel as a historical figure:

> *Even if these three men — Noah, Daniel and Job — were in it, they could save only themselves by their righteousness, declares the Sovereign LORD. . . . as surely as I live, declares the Sovereign LORD, even if Noah, Daniel and Job were in it, they could save neither son nor daughter. They would save only themselves by their righteousness. (Ezekiel 14:14, 20)*

Daniel documents the dates of the beginning of his book and the dates when he received each of the prophecies. If these dates are a lie and Daniel did not receive these prophecies between 605 B.C. and 536 B.C., then how can we believe anything else written in the book? Jesus trusted the content of the book of Daniel, for he quoted it in Matthew 24:15.

THE HISTORICAL BACKGROUND

Before studying the book of Daniel, knowing some of the key people and the key dates of the history of Israel will be helpful.

1010-970 B.C.	King David rules over the united kingdom.
970-930 B.C.	King Solomon rules over the united kingdom.
966 B.C.	The Temple of the Lord is dedicated in Jerusalem.
930 B.C.	The Kingdom of Israel is divided into North and South.
740-681 B.C.	**Isaiah** warns of the coming judgment against Israel.
722 B.C.	Fall of the Northern Kingdom (**Isaiah dies—681** B.C.).
626-585 B.C.	**Jeremiah** warns of coming judgment against Judah.
606 B.C.	**Daniel** taken captive to Babylon.
597 B.C.	**Ezekiel** taken captive to Babylon.
586 B.C.	Fall of the Southern Kingdom (**Jeremiah dies—585** B.C.).
539 B.C.	Fall of Babylon to Persians.
536 B.C.	Cyrus decrees that the Jews can return to Jerusalem (70 years from the taking of the first captives in 606 B.C.).
530 B.C.	**Daniel dies.**
516 B.C.	Temple rebuilt (70 years from its destruction in 586 B.C.).

CHAPTER OVERVIEW

Before studying this commentary on the book of Daniel, knowing the overview of the content of Daniel will be helpful for getting the big picture. We don't want to lose sight of the forest as we study the trees. Note in particular that the focus of the prophecies is limited in scope. Daniel does not prophesy about many different things, but rather about three main things that are repeated several times. He prophesies the first coming of the Messiah, the coming of Antiochus Epiphanes, and the second coming of the Messiah.

Each prophecy relates to one of these three. Both times the Messiah enters our world it will be preceded by a severe time of persecution for God's people. The first time the Messiah came was preceded by the coming of Antiochus Epiphanes. The second time the Messiah comes will be preceded by the coming of the Antichrist.

You will notice the cyclical nature of Daniel's apocalyptic literature. He first speaks of the Antichrist; then he introduces Antiochus. Next he tells us more about Antiochus before he tells us more about the Antichrist. Then Daniel switches the order one last time as he asks a question about the Antichrist, followed by one last question about Antiochus.

If the reader will keep these three main characters in mind — Antiochus, Messiah, and Antichrist — the prophecies of Daniel will be much easier to understand.

Now take a look at this brief overview of the book, noting the references to the three main characters.

DANIEL 1	Daniel and his three friends: men of conviction	Nebuchadnezzar II
*DANIEL 2	Nebuchadnezzar's dream of the statue of the four kingdoms	
	• Head of Gold:	Babylon (636-536 B.C.)
	• Chest and arms of silver:	Persia (536-333 B.C.)
	• Belly and thighs of bronze:	Greece (333-146 B.C.)
	• Legs of iron with feet of iron and clay:	Rome (146 B.C.-400 A.D.)

THE MESSIAH COMES THE FIRST TIME
THE KINGDOM OF GOD ENTERS OUR WORLD

DANIEL 3	Daniel's three friends: men of faith	Nebuchadnezzar II
DANIEL 4	The conversion of Nabonidus	Nebuchadnezzar III
DANIEL 5	The handwriting on the wall	Belshazzar
DANIEL 6	Daniel in the lions' den	Darius the Mede
*DANIEL 7	Daniel's prophetic zoo of four kingdoms	Belshazzar (553 B.C.)
	• Lion	Babylon (636-536 B.C.)
	• Bear	Persia (536-333 B.C.)
	• Leopard	Greece (333-146 B.C.)
	• Beast	Kingdom of Antichrist

ANTICHRIST PREDICTED
THE MESSIAH COMES THE SECOND TIME
THE KINGDOM OF GOD COMES IN ITS FULLNESS

*DANIEL 8	Daniel's vision of the ram and goat	Belshazzar (550 B.C.)
	• Ram	Persia (536-333 B.C.)
	• Goat	Greece (333-146 B.C.)

ANTIOCHUS PREDICTED

1

No Compromise

DANIEL 1:1-25

$\mathbf{D}$r. Bryan Chapell tells a story of the wife of a full-time student at Covenant Seminary. Like the wives of many seminarians, Karen was earning money to keep her husband in school and food on the table. In her case, Karen made her living as a quality-control inspector for a major pharmaceutical company.

One day, through faulty procedures, the automated machines produced a large order of syringes that became contaminated and therefore failed inspection. Karen reported the problem to her boss, but he quickly computed the costs of reproducing the order and made a "cost-effective" decision. Because so much money would be lost in replacing the syringes, the boss ordered Karen to sign the inspection clearance despite the contamination. She refused, but this did not get her off the hook.

Because of certain federal regulations, only Karen could sign the clearance forms. If Karen did not sign, the syringes could not be marketed. The boss urged and threatened, but Karen would not budge. The impasse between Karen and her superior led to a visit from the company president. He also computed the costs of reproduction and issued his decision: The forms must be signed. Karen would have the weekend to think over whether or not she would sign the clearances. The president told her that if she was still determined not to sign the forms on Monday, her job would be in jeopardy.

In fact, much more than Karen's job would be in jeopardy. This was her only means of income, and it was a well-paying job, not easily replaced. Randy's education and their family's future were severely endangered. The hopes, dreams, and career plans of many years could be shattered as a result of the choice that had to be made in the next two days. When Dr. Bryan Chapell, the seminary's president, told this story, he concluded with the following words: "For this young couple, all the theological jargon and doctrinal instruction about consecration, righteousness, and holiness suddenly came down to this one concrete decision: Could they afford to remain undefiled from the contamination the world of business practicalities urged Karen to approve?"[1] What would you do?

This couple's predicament is similar to what God's people have faced in all ages. The first chapter of Daniel well illustrates that there have always been *pressures* on God's people to compromise their holiness. As the chapter unfolds we will also see how important the *preparation* to pursue holiness is. The chapter concludes with the demonstration of the *power* of personal holiness.

THE PRESSURE TO COMPROMISE HOLINESS (1:3-8)

The pressure that we all face was experienced by Daniel and his three friends. Daniel sets the stage to describe this pressure applied by the king in verses 3, 4:

> *Then the king ordered Ashpenaz, chief of his court officials, to bring in some of the Israelites from the royal family and the nobility — young men without any physical defect, handsome, showing aptitude for every kind of learning, well informed, quick to understand, and qualified to serve in the king's palace.*

These were top-notch young men from the royal family and nobility in Israel. According to *Jerome's Commentary on Daniel*, Rabbinic tradition holds that Daniel, Hananiah, Mishael, and Azariah were descendants of King Hezekiah, based on Isaiah 39:7.[2] In that verse Isaiah speaks these words to King Hezekiah: "And some of your descendants, your own flesh and blood who will be born to you, will be taken away, and they will become eunuchs in the palace of the King of Babylon."

Daniel was probably in his early teens when he was taken captive, because he was still alive seventy years later when the captivity ended. Perhaps Daniel was thirteen to sixteen years old when he was taken captive around 606 B.C. Ashpenaz, a member of the pagan royal court, began to apply pressure on these teenagers. We and our children experience some of the same pressures.

There is pressure to change our thinking (1:4b): "He was to teach them the language and literature of the Babylonians."

Imagine the influence these pagan Babylonian teachers had on these teenagers. The Babylonians' literature promoted their worldview, their view of man, their view of God, their view of sin, and their view of redemption, which were all directly opposed to everything these young teens had been taught and believed while in Israel.

Through archaeological evidence Tremper Longman III concludes that undoubtedly one of the subjects Daniel and his friends would have been taught was the Babylonian art of divination.[3] They learned how to make predictions by interpreting unusual terrestrial and celestial phenomena and by examining sheep livers. In Mesopotamia, omens were considered the primary way by which the gods revealed their will and intentions. When powerful communicators keep telling you the same thing over and over again, it is hard not to be influenced. But these methods of divination would all be diametrically opposed to what these young men had been taught from God's Word. Daniel probably knew these words of Isaiah:

> When men tell you to consult mediums and spiritists, who whisper and mutter, should not a people inquire of their God? Why consult the dead on behalf of the living? To the law and to the testimony! If they do not speak according to this word, they have no light of dawn. (Isaiah 8:19, 20)

Though Daniel and his friends went through the classes, they apparently resisted the pressure to change their thinking. This can be seen through the historical accounts of these young men in the chapters to follow.

The pressure on Christians to change their thinking today comes from the print media, movies, and television as well as from teachers. For example, we have all experienced the pressure of our society trying to change our thinking about homosexuality, calling it an alternate lifestyle. Books, even on the elementary level, teach children about "Heather who has two mommies." They teach children that this is a good alternative. God calls it both shameful and a perversion in Romans 1:26, 27:

> Because of this, God gave them over to shameful lusts. Even their women exchanged natural relations for unnatural ones. In the same way the men also abandoned natural relations with women and were inflamed with lust for one another. Men committed indecent acts with other men, and received in themselves the due penalty for their perversion.

In some cases the world has succeeded in changing our thinking on such subjects.

In his sermon on Romans 1:24-32, R. Kent Hughes said, "A mainline denomination's magazine carried an admonishment that said essentially this: Homosexuality should be accepted as a variant lifestyle — the homosexual relationship is neither unnatural, sinful, nor sick."[4]

We need to stand firm and resist the pressure. Be encouraged that Daniel and his three teenage friends stood firm against the Babylonian attempts to change their thinking. We will see what these Jewish teenagers and their parents did to prepare to withstand the pressure, because it is not easy. Christian, though the forces against you are great, take heart, stand firm, and dare to be a Daniel.

There is pressure to change our worship (1:6, 7).

Among these were some from Judah: Daniel, Hananiah, Mishael and Azariah. The chief official gave them new names: to Daniel, the name Belteshazzar; to Hananiah, Shadrach; to Mishael, Meshach; and to Azariah, Abednego.

The name Daniel means *"Elohim* is my judge." *Elohim* is one of the Hebrew names for God. The name Belteshazzar means "May Bel protect his life." Bel is one of the gods of Babylon. Hananiah means, *"Yahweh* is gracious." *Yahweh* is the personal name of the God of the Bible. Shadrach means, "Aku is exalted." Mishael means, "Who is what *Elohim* is?" while Meshach means, "Who is what Aku is?" Azariah means, *"Yahweh* is my helper," and Abednego means "The servant of Nebo," another Babylonian god.

As the March 26, 1976 issue of *Christianity Today* stated, "Albania has joined the list of countries taking away one of the most personal and private possessions of its citizens: their names. After all, someone named Abraham or Ruth or Mark might someday wonder where his name came from! That could lead to a time-consuming search for a Bible or other religious literature. In the process, the unfortunately named Albanian might absorb some of the teachings of the outlawed book. That result, in the view of the government, would be very bad."[5] The Babylonians changed the Hebrew teens' names in an attempt to make them forget the true God and change their worship, but it appears throughout the entire book that Daniel never did forget the name he was given, which honored the true God. Even the king (in chapter 6), when Daniel was in the lions' den, came to him the next morning and used his Jewish name saying, "Daniel, servant of the living God . . ."

The Babylonians removed God's name from the Jewish young men then, and today in America secularists are removing God from our schools and from public life. For example, evolution is taught as a scientific fact, and the truth of God being the Creator is either repressed or openly attacked.

In a sermon entitled "Why I Believe in Creation," D. James Kennedy of Coral Ridge Presbyterian Church gave this interesting example of those who want to suppress the truth.

An article in *Time Magazine* said, "Last week, after years of study and calculation, two respected California astronomers, Allan Sandage and

James Gunn made the following announcement: "The universe will continue to expand forever."

Sandage said about his finding: "It was a terrible surprise, because we have held that the universe is eternal. If it continues to expand forever, then it shows there was a beginning." Dr. Gunn added that people will passionately hold to the idea that the universe is oscillating contrary to the evidence, because if they give it up, you have a beginning of the universe. If you have a beginning of the universe, then you have a Creator, a God, to whom you must answer.

Many want to dismiss God as the Creator of the universe, because a God that powerful would be worthy of our worship and our obedience. Some would put pressure on our children to change their views of the origin of the universe in order to change their heart and worship. Christian, though the pressure is great, take heart, stand firm, and dare to be a Daniel.

There is pressure to change our way of living (1:5, 8).

The king assigned them a daily amount of food and wine from the king's table. They were to be trained for three years, and after that they were to enter the king's service. . . . But Daniel resolved not to defile himself with the royal food and wine, and he asked the chief official for permission not to defile himself this way.

Up to this point Daniel and his three friends had shown no outward resistance to their assimilation into Babylonian culture. They didn't skip their Babylonian literature classes, and they answered to their Babylonian names. That is what makes this encounter so striking. Why did Daniel draw the line here? Why did he suddenly say, "No compromise"? What is wrong with eating the royal food and drinking wine? It was not that Daniel was a vegetarian or one who abstained from wine, because later (in Daniel 10) he refrained from meat and wine for a period of three weeks of mourning (vv. 2, 3). That implies that he normally ate meat and drank wine.

There were two problems with the royal food the king offered. First, some of the meat was unclean according to the Mosaic Law. The verb "defile" (*ga'al*) used in verse 8 denotes religious defilement. Daniel and his three friends were not willing to compromise by disobeying God's commands in eating "unclean food."

Second, all the meat served at the king's table was offered to idols before it was eaten. In his book *Ancient Mesopotamia: Portrait of a Dead Civilization,* A. Leo Oppenheim tells us about the care and feeding of the gods of Babylon. We learn in his book that sumptuous food would be offered to the gods, and after the meal, whatever was left would be brought to the king's table as the royal food.[6] Daniel would not compromise by eating meat offered to idols.

Revelation 2:14 says, "Nevertheless, I have a few things against you: You have people there who hold to the teaching of Balaam, who taught Balak to entice the Israelites to sin *by eating food sacrificed to idols.*" In Daniel's day, eating food sacrificed to idols was a sin against God. Daniel was willing to be holy regardless of the cost, but he was not willing to compromise his holiness. Are you willing to take the risks that sometimes come with holiness?

These risks are very real. Karen did refuse to sign the clearance forms for the contaminated syringes. She lost her job because of her no-compromise decision. She was not willing to disobey God's command to be honest in all things.[7]

Here is another example that was closer to home for me. My youngest daughter, Bekah, loves to play soccer. One spring she tried out for a select team and made it. She was so excited. Then we found out that most of the games were on the Lord's Day. We called the coach and told him that Bekah would not be able to play in any of the Sunday games. He said that if she would not play on Sunday, she could not be on the team. (It is interesting to note that 2 Chronicles 36:21 says that ignoring the Sabbath was a primary reason for the seventy-year captivity that took Daniel and others to Babylon.)

This was a great disappointment, but Bekah chose to remain undefiled. She dared to be a Daniel and stood firm for the Lord. To some it seemed like such a small thing. For Daniel, not eating the meat was a small thing, but it prepared him for much bigger challenges later in his life, as we will see in later chapters. Remember, he who is faithful in small things will be faithful in greater things.

Whenever we pretend that walking in holiness is easy, we fail to prepare those who must take a stand in this world. The time will come for every believer when such a stand must be made. Look with me at Daniel and his preparation to pursue holiness.

THE PREPARATION TO PURSUE HOLINESS (1:1, 6, 9, 10)

Three young teenagers living far away from home — how could they be so strong? How could they stand so firm against the pressures of the Babylonian culture? There had to be some serious preparation. Just as a soldier who goes into battle is prepared before he goes to the front lines, so we as Christians must take seriously our preparation to pursue holiness. Daniel experienced three influences.

There was the influence of the church (1:1).

"In the third year of the reign of Jehoiakim king of Judah, Nebuchadnezzar king of Babylon came to Jerusalem and besieged it."

If Daniel was sixteen years old in the third year of the reign of King Jehoiakim (606 B.C.), that means he was born in 622 B.C. Do you know what incredible event took place that year? Josiah, who became king of Israel when he was eight years old, opened the doors of the Temple of the Lord that had been sealed shut by his grandfather Manasseh. Josiah did that when he was eighteen years old.

Inside the temple, the priests rediscovered the Word of God that had been lost. The priests began to teach the people God's Word, and a great revival began in Israel. Daniel grew up in a living, vibrant church devoted to the Word of God — a church that did not compromise the teaching of Scripture.

My wife and I have been so thankful for the faithful teaching of God's Word in our church congregation. From the preaching ministry through Sunday school, from our Christian school through the youth ministry, our three girls have learned the Word of God through faithful teachers who taught the whole counsel of God and did not compromise. Our children and young people have been prepared to apply God's Word to the difficult situations of our world. They have been challenged not to compromise their holiness. Today there seem to be very few churches that teach the Word without compromise.

There is the influence of parents (1:6).

"Among these were some from Judah: Daniel, Hananiah, Mishael and Azariah."

We don't really know anything about Daniel's parents except that they named him "God is my judge." That gives us a small glimpse as to the high view of God they had, which they passed on to their son Daniel. It was as if his parents said, "You will not always have to give an account to us. But one day you will give an account to our great God who made the heavens and the earth, the sea and all that is in them. He is watching over you always. He knows what you think, and he sees all you do. He is alone is your judge; so watch your life and doctrine closely."

The psalmist likens our children to "arrows in the hand of a warrior" (Psalm 127:4). We have about eighteen to twenty years of strong influence in the lives of our children to shape them and sharpen them as we would an arrow. The psalmist says that we need to "tell the next generation the praise-worthy deeds of the LORD, his power, and the wonders he has done" (Psalm 78:4). We must first introduce them to the mighty, personal God who loves them and has blessed them.

Then the psalmist says we are ready to teach the commands of God. The next three verses say:

He decreed statutes for Jacob and established the law in Israel, which he commanded our forefathers to teach their children, so the next generation would know them, even the children yet to be born, and they in turn would tell their children. Then they would put their trust in God and would not forget his deeds but would keep his commands.

Through the teaching of God's Word in the home, and as a result of consistently living it in our homes, our children will come to know God personally and will be ready to walk in holiness. We will shoot the arrows out of our nest and into the world, and "They will not be put to shame when they contend with their enemies in the gate" (v. 5).

The godly influence of his parents along with the support and influence of the Church of Israel prepared Daniel for a life of holiness with no compromise. But there was one more very important influence. This was the most important influence of all.

There is the influence of the Lord (1:9, 10).

Now God had caused the official to show favor and sympathy to Daniel, but the official told Daniel, "I am afraid of my lord the king, who has assigned your food and drink. Why should he see you looking worse than the other young men your age? The king would then have my head because of you."

When Daniel asked Ashpenaz for permission to avoid eating the food sacrificed to idols, Ashpenaz was afraid. But God was at work in the heart of that man. Daniel 1:9 says, "God had caused the official to show favor and sympathy to Daniel." If God was moving the heart of a pagan official, how much more does he work in the heart of one who believes in him. According to verse 17, it was God who gave knowledge and understanding to Daniel and his friends.

To these four young men God gave knowledge and understanding of all kinds of literature and learning. And Daniel could understand visions and dreams of all kinds.

Apart from God's work in our heart, we cannot walk in holiness. Jesus said:

Remain in me, and I will remain in you. No branch can bear fruit by itself; it must remain in the vine. Neither can you bear fruit unless you remain in me. I am the vine; you are the branches. If a man remains in me and I in him, he will bear much fruit; apart from me you can do nothing. (John 15:4, 5)

To remain or abide in Christ you must first have received him as your personal Lord and Savior. The abiding in Christ continues as you listen to him through the reading and studying of God's Word and speak to him through prayer, asking for the grace to apply his Word to your life. As you develop these disciplines, you will bear the fruit of holiness.

In order to overcome the pressure to compromise our holiness, we need to have an adequate preparation to pursue holiness. We need to be bathed in the teaching of God's Word through our parents and the church. We also need a life of abiding in the vine, Jesus Christ, for apart from him we can do nothing and will compromise. But when we dare to be a Daniel in a world full of compromise, we will discover the power of personal holiness.

THE POWER OF PERSONAL HOLINESS (1:11-14)

Daniel then spoke to a guard appointed by Ashpenaz, because that official was too afraid of the king. This is what Daniel said:

Please test your servants for ten days: Give us nothing but vegetables to eat and water to drink. Then compare our appearance with that of the young men who eat the royal food, and treat your servants in accordance with what you see.

Daniel did not want the credit for their appearance to go to the king and his training process. He wanted God to receive the glory.

His personal choice of holiness had a powerful influence on three areas of his person (1:15-17, 20).

At the end of the ten days they looked healthier and better nourished than any of the young men who ate the royal food. So the guard took away their choice food and the wine they were to drink and gave them vegetables instead. To these four young men God gave knowledge and understanding of all kinds of literature and learning. And Daniel could understand visions and dreams of all kinds.

First, Daniel's *body* "looked healthier and better nourished than any of the young men who ate the royal food" (v. 15). Second, his *spirit* was in tune with God, who gave him a special ability to understand visions and interpret dreams of all kinds (v. 17). Third, his *mind* was sharp. "In every matter of wisdom and understanding about which the king questioned them, he found them ten times better than all the magicians and enchanters in his whole kingdom" (v. 20). They were only teenagers beginning their career, and already they were head and shoulders above grown men. God does bless his people in a unique way in body, mind, and spirit when they dare to be Daniels, walking in holiness and refusing to compromise.

Remember Karen, forced to leave her job at the pharmaceutical company? God did bless her. Because she would not sign the clearance forms for the contaminated syringes, the order was not delivered to the customer on time. Officials of that company investigated the delay and discovered how Karen had protected them from the contaminated syringes, even at the cost of her own job. The customer then hired Karen and increased her pay.[8]

Paul writes in 1 Timothy 4:8, "Physical training is of some value, but godliness has value for all things, holding promise for both the present life and the life to come."

His personal holiness had an influence on three influential kings of Babylon (1:18-21).

At the end of the time set by the king to bring them in, the chief official presented them to Nebuchadnezzar. The king talked with them, and he found none equal to Daniel, Hananiah, Mishael and Azariah; so they entered the king's service. In every matter of wisdom and understanding about which the king questioned them, he found them ten times better than all the magicians and enchanters in his whole kingdom. And Daniel remained there until the first year of King Cyrus.

According to verse 21, Daniel remained in the palace until the first year of Cyrus, King of Persia. He and his friends had an influence on Nebuchadnezzar II (606-560 B.C.) in the first three chapters of Daniel. He had an influence on Nebuchadnezzar III (555-539 B.C.), also called Nabonidus, whose pride was broken and who surrendered to the Lord in Daniel 4. Then he influenced Belshazzar (553-539 B.C.), who saw the handwriting on the wall in Daniel 5. Daniel was there to interpret the writing and give the message to the king. Daniel had a powerful influence on these three Babylonian kings, even though the kings were in authority over him.

When my daughter, Bekah, told the coach that she would not play on the Lord's Day, the coach told her that he was sorry, but the league would not allow a team or an individual to play unless they played on Sunday. She was told that this could not be changed. She was very disappointed.

I do not know the details of what happened, but about an hour later the coach called and said that they could play all their games on Saturday if they would be willing to play two games on Sundays. He agreed to do that, and so did the other girls. There is a powerful influence of personal holiness that sometimes is missed in our quickness to compromise.

I do not want to give the impression that everything always works out perfectly according to this world's standards when we practice holiness. The world may readily praise idealism, but it rarely tolerates ideals. The world did not, could not, and would not understand Jesus. Why, then, should we expect the world to understand us if we stand up for him and his Word? The Holy One suffered at the hands of sinful men and was crucified by them. Should we expect to be treated any differently? Paul writes in

2 Timothy 3:12, "In fact, everyone who wants to live a godly life in Christ Jesus will be persecuted."
His personal holiness had an influence on his three friends (1:7, 8).

The chief official gave them new names: to Daniel, the name Belteshazzar; to Hananiah, Shadrach; to Mishael, Meshach; and to Azariah, Abednego. But Daniel resolved not to defile himself with the royal food and wine, and he asked the chief official for permission not to defile himself this way.

All four young men were given new names, but it was Daniel who first resolved not to defile himself with the royal food and wine. And Daniel's three friends followed his lead. Not only that, but two chapters later in this book we will see these three young men standing all by themselves in front of a fiery furnace facing death. Daniel is nowhere to be seen. Remembering the resolve that Daniel had alone and how he brought them into the test, they then stood firm without compromise before a powerful king in a test bigger than the first.

Shadrach, Meshach and Abednego replied to the king, "O Nebuchadnezzar, we do not need to defend ourselves before you in this matter. If we are thrown into the blazing furnace, the God we serve is able to save us from it, and he will rescue us from your hand, O king. But even if he does not, we want you to know, O king, that we will not serve your gods or worship the image of gold you have set up." (3:16-18)

All of God's people face pressure to compromise their holiness. We all need to have adequate preparation to pursue holiness with the realization that personal holiness is a powerful influence on ourselves and on those around us, preparing us for future challenges.

My friend Bryan Chapell worked for a major road construction crew in western Tennessee one summer while he was in college. It was a great paying job, and since jobs were hard to come by, it was important that he keep this one.

One morning his supervisor told him he was doing such a good job that he was going to get a special privilege. The man owned a hunting lodge nearby, and he wanted Bryan to spend a day or two at the lodge enjoying the outdoors. Bryan thanked him for the privilege but explained that he really needed the money. The boss told him that was no problem because he would keep him on the payroll.

He was off like a shot to the lake. That evening Bryan was at the lodge eating catfish when the phone rang. It was his father. When he had gotten home from work, his mother explained where Bryan was and under what arrangements. The voice on the other end of the line asked, "What are you doing collecting company pay without doing the work?"

Bryan had not thought of it that way. He didn't want to think of it that way. He argued, "Dad, I can't go back to my boss and tell him what he asked me to do is not ethical. He will be offended and fire me. How am I going to get through college if I do not have this job?"

His father answered, "I know you need this job to prepare for what you want to do. I also know what you need to prepare for life . . . and this is not it."[9] What would you do? Bryan went home. God prepared him for life. Today he is president of Covenant Theological Seminary.

2

The Wisdom and Power of God

DANIEL 2:1-23

It happened to me again. I woke up in a cold sweat, my heart pounding and my mind racing. I'd had a dream, the same dream I have had over and over for the last twenty years. The dream usually occurs on Saturday nights. In the dream I am sitting in the pulpit chair on the platform of our sanctuary with my Bible open on my lap. Everyone in the church is singing, everyone except me. I am feverishly looking through my Bible for my sermon notes. As I come to the realization they are not there, I feel increasingly powerless. My legs are getting weaker, and my arms are feeling limp. I realize that I have no idea what I am going to say. In my dream the singing stops, and I get up weak and powerless, my mind empty. I begin to speak, but the people are obviously not interested in what I am saying. One by one they begin to leave. I look at my wife, and she is frowning. Finally, when everyone else has gone, my wife gets up to leave. At that moment I awake in a cold sweat, thankful that it was all just a dream.

Dreams like that are usually the result of worry and an overactive imagination. They are not a divine revelation of the future — I hope! But there are times when God has come to weak and powerless people who lack wisdom and understanding and revealed things about the future that only he would know. He knows because wisdom and power are his.

God came to a weak and powerless king who lacked wisdom and understanding. Now, by this world's standards Nebuchadnezzar was considered both wise and powerful. But Paul reminds us that "The foolishness of God is wiser than man's wisdom, and the weakness of God is stronger than man's strength" (1 Corinthians 1:25). God chose to demonstrate his almighty power and his unfathomable wisdom to a man who was inebriated with his own lust for power and wisdom in order to show just how weak and foolish that man really was. Since God is the source of all wisdom and power, we must turn to him. As we study the first part of Daniel 2 we will discover the problem, the prayer, and the praise.

THE PROBLEM (2:1-16)

One night God sent Nebuchadnezzar dreams that he could not interpret, and the king woke up in a cold sweat. "His mind was troubled and he could not sleep" (v. 1). The most powerful man came face to face with his weakness. Immediately he called for the wisest men in his kingdom — the magicians, enchanters, sorcerers, and astrologers. Using dark magic, mysterious incantations, and the position of the stars, these men had been trained to interpret dreams and give the meaning to the dreamer. Nebuchadnezzar said to them, "I have had a dream that troubles me and I want to know what it means" (v. 3).

The astrologers were the first to speak. They asked the king to tell them the dream first, so they could give the interpretation. The problem arose when King Nebuchadnezzar for some reason doubted the wisdom and integrity of his sages:

> The king replied to the astrologers, "This is what I have firmly decided: If you do not tell me what my dream was and interpret it, I will have you cut into pieces and your houses turned into piles of rubble. But if you tell me the dream and explain it, you will receive from me gifts and rewards and great honor. So tell me the dream and interpret it for me." (vv. 5, 6)

The astrologers again asked the king to first tell them the dream, but the king stood firm in his decision not to tell the dream. Then the astrologers said, "There is not a man on earth who can do what the king asks!" (v. 10). How right they were. No human being has the wisdom and power to tell a man his thoughts as well as to interpret those thoughts. As Paul asks, "Who among men knows the thoughts of a man except the man's spirit within him?" (1 Corinthians 2:11).

The astrologers continued to whine:

> No king, however great and mighty, has ever asked such a thing of any magician or enchanter or astrologer. What the king asks is too difficult. No one can reveal it to the king except the gods, and they do not live among men. (2:10, 11)

They were half-right this time. It was true that God alone could reveal the mystery, but what the sages did not know is that his Spirit does live among men. As Paul added in 1 Corinthians 2:11b, 12:

> *In the same way no one knows the thoughts of God except the Spirit of God. We have not received the spirit of the world but the Spirit who is from God, that we may understand what God has freely given us.*

But the wise men of Babylon did not have the Spirit of God living in them; so they could not know the dream or the interpretation. They were weak and powerless to do what only God can do.

This made the king so angry that he ordered the execution of all the wise men of Babylon. That included Daniel and his three friends who were in the service of the king. Arioch, the commander of the king's guard, went out to put the wise men to death when he came upon Daniel. When Daniel was told he would be executed, he did not respond with defensiveness and anger but spoke to the commander with wisdom and tact. With discretion and good taste in conversation, you can make even your enemies be at peace with you.

The pro-life ministry at the church I pastor is involved with sidewalk counseling every Saturday outside an abortion mill where babies are murdered for money. We are careful to obey all the laws, and we season our conversation with salt as we speak. The driveway into the clinic is narrow; so when a car stops to pick up literature about unborn babies, they may block the driveway for at most two minutes. The escorts at the clinic, who with smiles wave young, fearful women into the parking lot, use this as an occasion to call the police, even though we are not blocking the driveway for long. We are careful to encourage the driver to pull forward when someone pulls up.

One Saturday morning a woman was taking some literature and speaking with Pam, one of the women in our church, when a second car drove up. Pam finished the conversation quickly, but the police were called anyway by the escorts from the clinic. When the officer arrived, he immediately approached Pam who has been legally involved in sidewalk counseling for twelve years. Pam is a soft-spoken mother of three. The officer asked for her I.D. and told her that she would be arrested. She asked why, and he said that he would tell her later. People from our church responded with wisdom and tact, asking permission to videotape the arrest. Permission was granted.

They handcuffed her, even though she had broken no laws, and pushed her into the police car to take her to jail. She was not defensive at this injustice. She did not angrily demand her rights. When the captain arrived to verify the arrest, the people from our church responded with wisdom and tact. They asked permission to pray with Pam before they took her to jail. Permission was granted.

At the jail, Pam was fingerprinted and photographed. One officer came by and asked why she had been arrested. Pam told him that she was accused of "demonstrating on the street," a charge usually made against prostitutes. She asked him why the police had charged her with that crime. The officer shook his head and told her not to worry because she would not be held more than fifteen minutes.

Daniel also spoke with his potential executioner. "Why did the king issue such a harsh decree?" (2:15). When the commander told the story to Daniel, Daniel asked for more time so that he might interpret the dream.

THE PRAYER (2:17-19a)

Then Daniel returned to his house and explained the matter to his friends Hananiah, Mishael and Azariah. He urged them to plead for mercy from the God of heaven concerning this mystery, so that he and his friends might not be executed with the rest of the wise men of Babylon. During the night the mystery was revealed to Daniel in a vision.

Daniel knew immediately what he had to do, but he wasn't going to do it alone. He returned to his house where his three friends were staying. He explained to them that they would all be executed the next day if God did not reveal to them Nebuchadnezzar's dream and its interpretation. Those four men were on their knees in fervent prayer all through the night. They felt the urgency, they felt their helplessness, and they knew that only God was great enough to perform such a miracle. I think the reason that we do not pray more faithfully and fervently is because we don't feel the urgency; we tend to be self-sufficient, and we do not see our God as big enough. So there are times when God brings things like this into our lives and into the lives of our friends to bring us to our knees.

After signing the contract for this book, doctors discovered that I had cholangiocarcinoma, a rare and serious form of bile duct liver cancer. When I first heard from the doctor that I had cancer, I felt the sentence of death, just like Daniel and his three friends were faced with a sentence of death. The elders wanted to gather in our worship service to lay their hands on me and pray for healing through the surgery and follow-up treatments. On the day of my surgery a group of people gathered in a circle to pray for me in the hospital lounge, and another large group of people gathered in the sanctuary at church to engage in fervent prayer for six hours. People in our congregation felt an urgency and helplessness that many had not experienced before. They pleaded for mercy from the God of heaven.

I felt so unworthy to be the focus of such concerted prayer over the next three months, but what a delight to be used by God in this way to stimulate people to prayer. This illness brought our church closer together as a family and closer to the Lord in our dependence upon his wisdom and power.

"During the night the mystery was revealed to Daniel in a vision" (Daniel 2:19). We have a great God who hears and answers prayer. I experienced that truth. Surgery was performed, and they found that it had not invaded the bile ducts. That was the first good news. They were able to remove the entire tumor, and it had not yet spread to other vital organs. Then came an aggressive six-week treatment of chemotherapy and radiation. The chemotherapy was on a twenty-four-hour continuous pump, and radiation was five days a week. There were warnings of many physical side effects that many people experience with such an aggressive treatment. Through the prayers of God's people I not only was delivered from most of the side effects, but I was able to keep preaching and working the whole time.

Daniel and I had both felt the sentence of death. So did the Apostle Paul, for he writes in 2 Corinthians 1:9-11:

> Indeed, in our hearts we felt the sentence of death. But this happened that we might not rely on ourselves but on God, who raises the dead. He has delivered us from such a deadly peril, and he will deliver us. On him we have set our hope that he will continue to deliver us, as you help us by your prayers. Then many will give thanks on our behalf for the gracious favor granted us in answer to the prayers of many.

God's answer to the prayers of the young Israelites made them burst into thanksgiving and praise.

THE PRAISE (2:19b-23)

> Then Daniel praised the God of heaven and said: "Praise be to the name of God for ever and ever; wisdom and power are his. He changes times and seasons; he sets up kings and deposes them. He gives wisdom to the wise and knowledge to the discerning. He reveals deep and hidden things; he knows what lies in darkness, and light dwells with him."

Daniel praised the God of heaven for his power, wisdom, and revelation. Many rulers and leaders in the world have power but lack wisdom. They can be very dangerous because their power is not kept in line through wisdom. And many people in the world are wise, but they are not in positions of power; so their wisdom may be useless in bringing good to many people. But God is both powerful and wise. He governs the world with wisdom; so we need not fear his power. But what Daniel discovered that is most amazing is that God is willing to share some of that wisdom and power with simple and helpless people to bring glory to his name. Daniel prayed, "I thank and praise you, O God of my fathers: You have given me wisdom and power" (Daniel 2:23).

The Power of our God (2:21)

He changes times and seasons; he sets up kings and deposes them.

Daniel learned this from the content of the dream the Lord revealed to him. In the dream he saw a succession of four kings rise to power only to be overthrown in time. Daniel knew from Isaiah 40:22-25, written a hundred years before his birth, that God alone has the power to raise up kings and depose them.

He sits enthroned above the circle of the earth, and its people are like grasshoppers. He stretches out the heavens like a canopy, and spreads them out like a tent to live in. He brings princes to naught and reduces the rulers of this world to nothing. No sooner are they planted, no sooner are they sown, no sooner do they take root in the ground, than he blows on them and they wither, and a whirlwind sweeps them away like chaff.

Christians need to remember the power of God over the rulers of the world at times of national elections. Many Christians seem to become so frustrated if a leader is elected who leads contrary to Christian principles. Though that can be a disappointment, we must remember that the Lord tells us in Romans 13:1, "There is no authority except that which God has established. The authorities that exist have been established by God." Let us stop wringing our hands over national elections and get on our knees praying for those in leadership as we are instructed to do in 1 Timothy 2:1-2:

I urge, then, first of all, that requests, prayers, intercession and thanksgiving be made for everyone — for kings and all those in authority, that we may live peaceful and quiet lives in all godliness and holiness.

God is powerful, and "The king's heart is in the hand of the LORD; he directs it like a watercourse wherever he pleases" (Proverbs 21:1).

The Wisdom of our God (2:22)

He reveals deep and hidden things; he knows what lies in darkness, and light dwells with him.

Daniel first praised the Lord for being omnipotent — all-powerful. Now he praises him for being omniscient — all-knowing. Daniel praises God because he knows "hidden things," such as the thoughts of a man, which can be kept from other men. Nebuchadnezzar kept his dream a secret from his wise men, but he could not keep it a secret from the all-wise God because:

> *You, O LORD, have searched me and you know me. You know when I sit and when I rise; you perceive my thoughts from afar. You discern my going out and my lying down; you are familiar with all my ways. Before a word is on my tongue you know it completely, O LORD. . . . Such knowledge is too wonderful for me, too lofty for me to attain. (Psalm 139:1-4, 6)*

To know there is a God who knows all our thoughts is both humbling and gratifying. It is humbling when we realize that those sinful thoughts we thought were secret do not go unnoticed by God. As we are humbled by that, may we also therefore be challenged to "take captive every thought to make it obedient to Christ" (2 Corinthians 10:5). Knowing there is a God who knows all our sinful thoughts is also gratifying, because he still loves us. There are few things more gratifying than being known completely, warts and all, and still being loved. The Christian who is covered by the blood of Christ need not fear being fully known.

The Lord also "knows what lies in darkness." The Hebrew word translated "darkness" comes from a root word that means "concealed" *(Strong's Hebrew Lexicon*, entry 2816*)*. God knows those things that are concealed from all men, such as the future of the kingdoms of this world. Again we can take heart as we look to the future, which is all unknown to us. Though we do not know what the future holds, we know who holds the future, and we can trust him. This God who knows our future and holds our future says, "I know the plans I have for you . . . plans to prosper you and not to harm you, plans to give you hope and a future" (Jeremiah 29:11).

The Revelation of our God (2:23b)

> *You have made known to me what we asked of you, you have made known to us the dream of the king.*

Revelation is God making his thoughts known to men. Paul writes, "No one knows the thoughts of God except the Spirit of God" (1 Corinthians 2:11b). The Holy Spirit is the vehicle of revelation, as Peter makes clear in his letter.

> *Above all, you must understand that no prophecy of Scripture came about by the prophet's own interpretation. For prophecy never had its origin in the will of man, but men spoke from God as they were carried along by the Holy Spirit. (2 Peter 1:20, 21)*

The prophets of the Old Testament wrote the thoughts of God. Jesus put it this way to the apostles in the Upper Room when he authorized them to write the New Testament:

I have much more to say to you, more than you can now bear. But when he, the Spirit of truth, comes, he will guide you into all truth. . . . He will bring glory to me by taking from what is mine and making it known to you. (John 16:12-14)

The apostles of the New Testament wrote the very thoughts of Christ. If this is all true, then it says something very important as to how we approach the Bible. These are not the fallible thoughts of sinful men about God. Rather they are the infallible thoughts of God revealed to sinful men so we can know all we need to know about God, his salvation, and the future of the world. If we really believe this, we will want to know the Bible well. If we do not believe this, we will ignore what it says. This is exactly what happened when Christ was born.

We are told that in the days of Herod the King, Magi came from the east asking, "Where is the one who has been born king of the Jews? We saw his star in the east and have come to worship him" (Matthew 2:1, 2). The name "Magi" is a shortened form of the word "magician." These were among the descendants of the magicians and astrologers of Daniel's day. Daniel was the chief of the magicians. "Belteshazzar [Daniel], chief of the magicians, I know that the spirit of the holy gods is in you" (Daniel 4:9).

Though this pagan king did not fully understand, he was right in saying that Daniel had the Spirit of God in him. I am sure that Daniel, his writings, and the writings of the Old Testament that he honored were held in high esteem for generations by the Magi. The Magi studied the prophecies of Daniel about the coming of a Ruler, the Anointed One (Daniel 9:25). They knew the prophecies of the Old Testament like Numbers 24:17: "I see him, but not now; I behold him, but not near. A star will come out of Jacob; a scepter will rise out of Israel." When they saw the star in Babylon, they put the prophecies together and went in faith to see the King who was born in fulfillment of these prophecies.

When they arrived in Jerusalem, they went to the palace of King Herod because they figured that is where a future king would be born. They asked Herod where the baby was, not if such a baby existed. That is how confident they were of their interpretation of this revelation of God that Daniel had taught them.

Herod "called together all the people's chief priests and teachers of the law" and "asked them where the Christ was to be born" (Matthew 2:3). What is fascinating about that is the use of the word *Christ* or *Messiah*, the Anointed One. In the Hebrew, that word is found only twice in the

Old Testament — in Daniel 9 and Psalm 2. The Magi were looking for Daniel's Messiah.

The teachers of the law knew the answer to the Magi's question. He was to be born in Bethlehem in Judea, and they quoted Micah 5:2. The teachers of the law knew what the Bible said, but they did not take it seriously, for when the Magi went to Bethlehem, the teachers of the law did not follow. They ignored what the Bible said.

Are you like the Magi or like the teachers of the law when it comes to God's revelation? Do you read it, study it, and believe it? Or do you read it, study it, and ignore it? Those who are truly wise are those who know God's Word and put it into practice. Jesus said:

Therefore everyone who hears these words of mine and puts them into practice is like a wise man who built his house on the rock. The rain came down, the streams rose, and the winds blew and beat against that house; yet it did not fall, because it had its foundation on the rock. But everyone who hears these words of mine and does not put them into practice is like a foolish man who built his house on sand. The rain came down, the streams rose, and the winds blew and beat against that house, and it fell with a great crash. (Matthew 7:24-27)

3

Revealer of Mysteries

DANIEL 2:24-49

My oldest daughter, Katie, was grading papers at Starbucks when she noticed a woman sitting next to her. The woman had apparently convinced another young woman that she could reveal the mysteries of her future by using Tarot cards. She would flip over a card and tell this young woman about herself and her future. The young woman kept nodding in amazement as the older woman spoke of these mysteries. Soon the young woman, quite impressed with this woman's ability to reveal mysteries, thanked the psychic and left.

The psychic then turned to my daughter, fluttered her eyes, and said, "I can tell you are a schoolteacher."

"What a surprise," my daughter said as she picked up her grade book and looked at the graded papers lying all over her table.

The woman's eyes began to flutter again. She closed her eyes as she mysteriously announced, "And you are married."

"How observant," my daughter replied as she held up her diamond engagement ring and wedding band that had been in full view of the woman. "Am I supposed to be impressed?"

The woman's eyes began to flutter again. She closed her eyes and mysteriously said, "Your husband is a very neat person and doesn't like to have dishes piled up in the sink."

"Wrong," my daughter interrupted. "That is not my husband. He has dishes piled up in the sink all the time. You should have seen his house before we got married."

The woman's eyes began to flutter again. She closed her eyes and mysteriously said, "You are pregnant, and you are going to have a baby."

"Wrong," said my daughter. "I am not pregnant, and we are not even trying!" My daughter smiled and said, "Ma'am, you have been wrong two out of four times telling me about myself, my husband, and my future. And the two times you were right were obvious to anyone. I don't mean to hurt your feelings, but I am not very impressed. But would you mind if I told you something about your future? If you like, I can share with you how you could know for certain that you will spend your eternal future in heaven." The woman looked at my daughter, frowned, and walked away.

As an interesting sideline to this story, my daughter found out two weeks after she talked to this woman that she was indeed almost two months pregnant. Was this woman a revealer of mysteries? Her guesses were good, but not completely accurate. Even Satan does have limited powers to predict the future. But the true Revealer of Mysteries is accurate 100 percent of the time. Moses makes it clear in Deuteronomy 18:20-22 that anyone who is not accurate all the time is to be ignored.

Daniel had a personal relationship with the Revealer of Mysteries, the God of Israel; so he was able to predict amazing things about the future of the world. The most striking thing was that Daniel was 100 percent accurate — not one mistake.

As the historical account opens, Daniel went to Arioch, the commander of the king's guard, and said, "Do not execute the wise men of Babylon. Take me to the king, and I will interpret the dream for him" (Daniel 2:24).

As we saw earlier, the king was wary of the false interpretations of his wise men. So to be sure that they really had the miraculous ability to interpret his dream, he forced them to tell him the dream first. That would prove they had miraculous powers, because who knows the thoughts of a man but the man himself?

So when Arioch introduced Daniel to Nebuchadnezzar, the king immediately asked, "Are you able to tell me what I saw in my dream *and* interpret it?" (Daniel 2:26, emphasis added).

Daniel picked up on his words "Are you able" as he began to answer the king. "No wise man, enchanter, magician or diviner can explain to the king the mystery he has asked about" (2:27). I can see the king look sternly at Arioch as if to say, "Why are you wasting my time with yet another feeble, excuse-making 'wise man!'"

Perhaps Arioch shrugged his shoulders and muttered, "That's not what he told *me*. He told me he could interpret the dream. I don't get it."

As this exchange was taking place, Daniel made his point. ". . . but there is a God in heaven who reveals mysteries. He has shown King Nebuchadnezzar what will happen in days to come. Your dream and the visions that passed through your mind as you lay on the bed are these . . ." (v. 28).

Because God is the Revealer of Mysteries, Daniel was able to do the impossible. He would not only interpret the dream, but he would tell the king what the dream was about. Only the Revealer of Mysteries has the power to do that. In this chapter we will see that since God is the Revealer of Mysteries, we must give him the glory as Daniel did. Daniel made it clear that he could not reveal the dream, but there is a God in heaven who could. He gave God all the glory.

WE MUST STAND IN AWE AT THE REVELATION OF THE DREAM (2:29-35)

This is the first time Daniel had ever been asked to do anything like this. He had heard how his forefather Joseph had interpreted Pharaoh's dreams in Egypt. Now the king he served had a dream; so he trusted that his father's God would reveal the dream to him also. Daniel took no credit for himself but stood in awe of the God of Israel who revealed the mystery of the dream to him. This is what he said:

> As you were lying there, O king, your mind turned to things to come, and the revealer of mysteries showed you what is going to happen. As for me, this mystery has been revealed to me, not because I have greater wisdom than other living men, but so that you, O king, may know the interpretation and that you may understand what went through your mind. (2:29, 30)

Daniel proceeded to tell the king his dream. I am sure that Nebuchadnezzar was awestruck to hear the secret thoughts of his mind revealed. No human being can do that perfectly, unless the Revealer of Mysteries tells him. And when the Revealer of Mysteries became a man and dwelt among us, he too told people their secret thoughts and actions. This was one way that Jesus proved he was the Son of God. People stood in awe of his ability. After Jesus spoke with the Samaritan woman by the well of Jacob, she said to her friends, "Come, see a man who told me everything I ever did. Could this be the Christ?" (John 4:29).

When the paralyzed boy was lowered through the roof to be healed by Jesus (Mark 2), Jesus said, "Son, your sins are forgiven." Some of the teachers of the law were standing there and heard what he said. They were "thinking to themselves, 'Why does this fellow talk like that? He's blaspheming! Who can forgive sins, but God alone?' Immediately Jesus knew in his spirit that this is what they were thinking in their hearts, and he said to them, 'Why are you thinking these things?'" (Mark 2:6-8).

I am sure they were as amazed that he knew their thoughts as they were when he healed the young man moments later. Do you stand in awe of this God, the Revealer of Mysteries? He knows your heart, he knows your thoughts, and he knows your future. Give him the glory due his name.

Now we will consider the dream that the Revealer of Mysteries revealed

to Daniel, the dream that no other wise man in all the kingdom could reveal
to King Nebuchadnezzar.

The Statue Described (2:31-33)

You looked, O king, and there before you stood a large statue — an enor-
mous, dazzling statue, awesome in appearance. The head of the statue
was made of pure gold, its chest and arms of silver, its belly and thighs of
bronze, its legs of iron, its feet partly of iron and partly of baked clay.

The Statue Destroyed (2:34, 35)

While you were watching, a rock was cut out, but not by human hands. It
struck the statue on its feet of iron and clay and smashed them. Then the
iron, the clay, the bronze, the silver and the gold were broken to pieces at
the same time and became like chaff on a threshing floor in the summer. The
wind swept them away without leaving a trace. But the rock that struck
the statue became a huge mountain and filled the whole earth.

The magicians, enchanters, sorcerers, and astrologers would not even
take a chance on guessing the king's dream (2:10, 11), because
Nebuchadnezzar would kill them if they got it wrong. But when Daniel
revealed the dream to him, he was amazed, because every detail was accurate. Nebuchadnezzar did not object to one thing that Daniel described. Let
us stand in awe of the revelation of this dream.

WE MUST SIT AND PONDER THE INTERPRETATION OF
THE DREAM (2:36-45)

"This was the dream, and now we will interpret it to the king."
    Daniel was still claiming no credit for himself. He said, "we" will inter-
pret it. Once Nebuchadnezzar had heard his dream described, he was ready
to hear and believe the interpretation of the dream. If anyone could tell him
his secret thoughts, then that man's interpretation could be trusted as well.
Daniel put it this way: "The great God has shown the king what will take
place in the future. The dream is true and the interpretation is trustworthy"
(2:45). Not only was the interpretation correct, but the events predicted
would happen! We will now examine the interpretation of the dream.

The Explanation of the Statue That Looked Like a Man (2:36-43)

The four parts of the statue represented four consecutive kingdoms, beginning with the kingdom of Babylon, over which King Nebuchadnezzar was

ruler. The Revealer of Mysteries spoke most about the first and last of these four kingdoms. The head of gold represented King Nebuchadnezzar.

> *You, O king, are the king of kings. The God of heaven has given you domin-*
> *ion and power and might and glory; in your hands he has placed mankind*
> *and the beasts of the field and the birds of the air. Wherever they live, he has*
> *made you ruler over them all. You are that head of gold. (2:37, 38)*

Even here Daniel gave glory to God as he pondered the interpretation. It was God who gave King Nebuchadnezzar "dominion and power and might and glory." As the Apostle Paul wrote, "There is no authority except that which God has established. The authorities that exist have been established by God" (Romans 13:1b). That realization by anyone in power will keep him humble in his leadership. His power will not go to his head.

The Revealer of Mysteries mentions in one verse the next two coming kingdoms, Persia and Greece: "After you, another kingdom will rise, inferior to yours. Next, a third kingdom, one of bronze, will rule over the whole earth" (Daniel 2:39). Then he reveals in more detail the description of the fourth and final kingdom:

> *Finally, there will be a fourth kingdom, strong as iron — for iron breaks and*
> *smashes everything — and as iron breaks things to pieces, so it will crush*
> *and break all the others. Just as you saw that the feet and toes were partly*
> *of baked clay and partly of iron, so this will be a divided kingdom; yet it will*
> *have some of the strength of iron in it, even as you saw iron mixed with clay.*
> *As the toes were partly iron and partly clay, so this kingdom will be partly*
> *strong and partly brittle. And just as you saw the iron mixed with baked*
> *clay, so the people will be a mixture and will not remain united, any more*
> *than iron mixes with clay. (2:40-43)*

Rome was captured and burned by the Gauls under the leadership of the chieftain Brennus in 390 B.C., but the effect was only temporary. Soon the Roman army began a series of military campaigns that would eventually establish it as a world empire. Truly it was like "iron [that] breaks and smashes everything" (v. 40).

In a series of three wars extending from 343 to 290 B.C. the Romans gained control of central Italy. Then came the Punic Wars with Carthage. In the first Punic War they conquered the Carthaginian part of Sicily. In the second Punic War, when Hannibal crossed the Alps to attack Rome, he was defeated by the Romans in a series of battles that gave Rome control of the Western Mediterranean Sea.

Fifty years after becoming the foremost power in the West by defeating the Carthaginians at Zama, Rome became the mightiest state in the east by

conquering Hannibal's ally Philip V, the king of Macedonia, in the Second
Macedonian War (200-197 B.C.). From there Rome proceeded against
Antiochus III, King of Syria, who was defeated by the Romans at Magnesia
in 190 B.C. and was obliged to surrender his possessions in Europe and Asia
Minor.

The end of the Third (and final) Macedonian War in 168 B.C. gave
Western Greece to the Romans. Macedonia was made a Roman province in
146 B.C., the year that marked the end of the Third Punic War, which brought
an end to the Carthaginian Empire and gave North Africa completely to
Rome.[1]

Rome had conquered the world, but it could not control itself. It was,
as Daniel prophesied, "a divided kingdom . . . partly strong and partly brittle" (vv. 41, 42). The seeds were planted in the beginning when the aristocratic ruling class became selfish, arrogant, and addicted to luxury. The
class of peasant farmers soon became extinct, which "led to a city rabble
incapable of elevated political sentiment."[2] Conflicts between the aristocratic
party and the popular party were inevitable.

Then there was the problem of the slaves in the Roman Empire, who
made up almost half the population. Between the extreme wealth and
extreme poverty, it was a kingdom "partly strong and partly brittle."

In the latter years of the Empire, the invading peoples kept their customs and languages and did not blend into the Roman culture, which helped
to hurry the decline, because as Daniel had prophesied, "the people will be
a mixture and will not remain united" (v. 43). After the death of Constantine
in A.D. 337 the Roman Empire divided between East and West, and civil wars
continued for years.[3]

With such clear fulfillment of this prophecy by these four kingdoms, it
amazes me that some scholars still claim that we cannot say for sure that
Daniel predicts that the Messiah would be born during the rule of the Roman
Empire. Predictive prophecy thus becomes meaningless for predicting the
future. For example, Tremper Longman wrote:

> In light of this interpretive confusion, we must entertain seriously the idea
> that the vision of Daniel 2 does not intend to be precise as it writes its his-
> tory before it occurs. In other words, though it starts in the concrete pres-
> ent, it is a wrong strategy to proceed through history and associate the
> different stages of the statue with particular empires. The vision intends
> to communicate something more general, but also more grand: God is
> sovereign; He is in control despite present conditions.[4]

If the message is merely that God is sovereign, Daniel could have said
that in a sentence rather than interpreting a meaningless dream that spoke
of four nonexistent kingdoms. Dr. Longman suggests such a vague inter-

pretation "in light of this interpretive confusion." If we back away from clear interpretation when evangelicals disagree, then we will not be able to hold any position on baptism, predestination, or the Lord's Supper either. We must use basic principles of interpretation beginning with the fact that words have meaning, and we must stop reducing prophecy to vague, meaningless generalities.

The Explanation of the Rock That Was Not Made by Man (2:44, 45)

In the time of those kings, the God of heaven will set up a kingdom that will never be destroyed, nor will it be left to another people. It will crush all those kingdoms and bring them to an end, but it will itself endure forever. This is the meaning of the vision of the rock cut out of a mountain, but not by human hands — a rock that broke the iron, the bronze, the clay, the silver and the gold to pieces.

"The rock cut out of a mountain, but not by human hands" is the kingdom of God. The Revealer of Mysteries tells Daniel, Nebuchadnezzar, and all who would read the words of this book when the kingdom of God would come to earth. The Revealer of Mysteries said that the kingdom of God would come when the fourth kingdom, the kingdom of iron and clay, would be ruling the whole earth. "In the time of those kings" — the kings of Rome — "the God of heaven will set up a kingdom that will never be destroyed."

God wanted his people to follow this prophecy one generation after another as they awaited the long-expected Messiah. Those living during the rule of the Persians would know that the Messiah could not come in their day. Those living during the rule of the Greek Empire would know from this prophecy that the Messiah would not come in their day. But imagine those living in the days when they saw the new, rising kingdom from the West defeat the Greeks in Corinth in the year 146 B.C. Some astute scholars of the Old Testament would have been saying, "The time of the coming of the Messiah must be very close, for he will come to earth during the reign of these kings of Rome."

God's timetable is not always ours, for it would be another one hundred and forty years until the Messiah actually came. And God's ways are not our ways, for when the Messiah came, he came quietly as a baby born in Bethlehem, and few knew he had arrived.

When Jesus, the Messiah, did finally start preaching thirty years after his birth, the first words out of his mouth were these: "The time has come. The kingdom of God is near. Repent and believe the good news" (Mark 1:15). Later he said, "If I drive out demons by the Spirit of God, then the kingdom of God has come upon you" (Matthew 12:27). This is speaking of the entrance of the kingdom of God into the world, not the kingdom of God in all its fullness that will come when Jesus returns in power and glory (see chapters 8 and 9 of this book).

Daniel implies that this "rock" will start small when he says: "But the rock that struck the statue *became* a huge mountain and filled the whole earth" (Daniel 2:35, emphasis added). The object that struck the statue was a rock, not a huge mountain. It became a huge mountain and filled the earth. In the same way, Jesus established his kingdom in a small way during the days of the rule of the Roman emperors, and it has been growing worldwide ever since. Then one day in the future the kingdom will fill the whole earth when Jesus reigns upon the earth as King.

Zechariah 14:4, 5 tells of the Second Coming of Christ: "On that day his feet will stand on the Mount of Olives, east of Jerusalem, and the Mount of Olives will be split in two from east to west. . . . Then the LORD my God will come, and all the holy ones with him." Then Zechariah prophesies that after his return, "The LORD will be king over the whole earth. On that day there will be one LORD, and his name the only name" (v. 9).

One student of prophecy who lived in Jesus' day was Joseph of Arimathea. I call him a student of prophecy because Mark says he was "a prominent member of the Council, who was himself waiting for the kingdom of God" (Mark 15:43). He must have studied the prophecies of Daniel and put the pieces together, concluding that this Jesus was the promised Messiah. For when the disciples had fled from Jesus as he hung on the cross, Joseph of Arimathea and Nicodemus were the only men who laid him in the tomb. Could it be that Joseph knew the Messiah would have to die (Daniel 9:26) and that he would be buried with the rich (Isaiah 53:9)? Joseph was waiting for the kingdom of God to come, and he was among the few who recognized it when the kingdom came.

This should send an important message to those of us who have the prophecies of the Second Coming of Christ to study. Later chapters of Daniel will give us just as many clues to the coming of the kingdom of God in all its fullness at Christ's return as Joseph of Arimathea had for the initial coming of the kingdom. Will we take advantage of the opportunity to study them in order to know the pieces of the puzzle that will fit together before he comes? Joseph was waiting for the kingdom of God. Are you?

There is one more thing that the Revealer of Mysteries makes clear in the New Testament about this rock, this kingdom of God on earth. This is how Jesus explained the initial coming of the kingdom of God:

Once, having been asked by the Pharisees when the kingdom of God would come, Jesus replied, "The kingdom of God does not come with your careful observation, nor will people say, 'Here it is,' or 'There it is,' because the kingdom of God is within you." (Luke 17:20, 21)

The Pharisees were looking for an earthly kingdom that would overthrow and replace the Roman Empire. Jesus revealed a mystery: "The kingdom of God is within you." The Apostle Paul speaks of this mystery in Colossians 1:25-27:

> *I have become its servant by the commission God gave me to present to*
> *you the word of God in its fullness — the mystery that has been kept*
> *hidden for ages and generations, but is now disclosed to the saints. To*
> *them God has chosen to make known among the Gentiles the glorious*
> *riches of* this mystery, which is Christ in you, *the hope of glory. (empha-*
> *sis added)*

The kingdom of God now is the rule of Christ in our hearts. It is the mystery and miracle of Christianity that the Spirit of Christ actually comes to dwell in his people. Christianity is not an ethic whereby if we keep the Ten Commandments, we are good Christians. Christianity is not a philosophy whereby if we think a certain way, we are good Christians. Christianity is not a religion whereby if we do certain religious rituals, we are good Christians. No. Christianity is the miracle of a changed heart and a personal relationship with the living God.

If you don't have that personal relationship with Christ, or if you cannot say for sure that you know Christ lives in you, then know that God is making his appeal to you through me to receive Christ as Savior and Lord today. Jesus says, "Here I am! I stand at the door and knock. If anyone hears my voice and opens the door, *I will come in* and eat with him, and he with me" (Revelation 3:20, emphasis added). If you hear his voice today, don't harden your heart (cf. Psalm 95:7, 8), but humble yourself before him. Ask Christ to come and establish his kingdom within you. The hope of eternal glory will then be yours.

WE MUST BOW AND REJOICE AT THE RESPONSE TO THE DREAM (2:46-49)

> *Then King Nebuchadnezzar fell prostrate before Daniel and paid him*
> *honor and ordered that an offering and incense be presented to him.*
> *(v. 46)*

The king bowed before Daniel and treated him as a god. He even ordered that a burnt offering and incense be presented to him. I think that something occurred between verses 46 and 47 that isn't recorded, because the king's words turned from looking at Daniel as a god to speaking of Daniel's God.

Daniel's God Exalted (2:47)

The king said to Daniel, "Surely your God is the God of gods and the Lord of kings and a revealer of mysteries, for you were able to reveal this mystery."

We should rejoice that Nebuchadnezzar acknowledged and exalted Daniel's God to be the God of gods in the presence of all of those in his court. He obviously was moved by what he saw that day, but I don't think that he ever bowed his knee before Daniel's God as the Lord of kings. He bowed before Daniel, but I don't think he bowed before God because of the worship he demands for himself in the very next chapter. He had a head knowledge of God, but not a heart knowledge.

Like some professing Christians today, he knew the right words to say, but he did not bow his knee to the King of kings. A young man in one of the churches I served professed faith in Christ in about tenth grade. He became a leader among the other young people in our youth group. He discipled other younger students. He was involved in leading worship with the youth and in the worship services of our church. He publicly professed Christ as he was received into membership and shared the gospel with many of his friends.

This young man chose a Christian college to attend, writing a beautiful profession of faith as part of his application. While at that college, he led worship and was faithful in attending church for three years. But in his senior year he tired of "playing the game" and renounced his faith. He met with some of the elders of the church, explaining to them that he just did not believe in the God of the Bible anymore. He did not believe in heaven or hell and could not acknowledge that Jesus was God.

This is a situation that many Christian parents fear for their children. Children of believers grow up learning the language of heaven; so we sometimes wrongly assume that they truly know the Lord. Pray with and for your children. Pray that God will keep his covenant promises and cause your children to be born again. Talk to your children about Christ as the Lord of their lives and the need to make the Christianity of their parents their own. There are no magic formulas; we need to entrust our children to the care of our Sovereign Lord.

What a heartbreaking night that was for the elders and the parents of this young man, but a profession with the mouth without bowing the knee is not genuine and will only last a short time. Nebuchadnezzar's profession did not last long.

Daniel's Friends Promoted (2:48, 49)

Then the king placed Daniel in a high position and lavished many gifts on him. He made him ruler over the entire province of Babylon and placed him in charge of all its wise men. Moreover, at Daniel's request the king appointed Shadrach, Meshach and Abednego administrators over the province of Babylon, while Daniel himself remained at the royal court.

We can rejoice because Daniel and his friends were promoted in the government, and he was given many lavish gifts. But most importantly we should rejoice because Daniel was made chief of the wise men. These magicians, sorcerers, enchanters, and astrologers were interested in solving mysteries. They devoted their lives to it. Imagine how impressed they must have been with Daniel's ability to reveal Nebuchadnezzar's dream. I think these men were ready to sit at his feet and learn.

Where do you think Daniel would have directed these men to find the revelation of the mysteries of life? He would have turned them to the Scriptures that were written by the Revealer of Mysteries. I am sure he had them pore over the ancient prophecies. We know that he had the scroll of Jeremiah (Daniel 9:2). He probably showed them how the Revealer of Mysteries had predicted the Babylonian captivity. He showed them the prophecies in Jeremiah that predicted the fall of Babylon as well. Some of the magi, along with Daniel, lived to witness that fulfillment.

Imagine how shocked these men would have been to learn that the name of the king who conquered Babylon was Cyrus, for this man was predicted by name in the prophecy of Isaiah two hundred years before it happened (Isaiah 45:1). Cyrus was not even born yet when the prophecy was written.

I think these wise men would have passed on the prophecies of Daniel's God, this Revealer of Mysteries, from one generation to the next. Daniel did what "not a man on earth can do" (Daniel 2:10). We should not be surprised then, but rejoice that the descendants of these wise men and magi were the ones to come to Bethlehem when the Rock of the kingdom of God secretly slipped into the kingdom of Rome.

When they saw the star, they were overjoyed. *On coming to the house, they saw the child with his mother Mary, and they* bowed down *and* worshiped *him. Then they opened their treasures and presented him with gifts of gold and of incense and of myrrh. (Matthew 2:10, 11, emphasis added)*

The Revealer of Mysteries has come. Let us rejoice, bow down, and worship him.

4

Faith Standing
Before the Fire

DANIEL 3:1-30

In his book *Where is God When it Hurts?* Philip Yancey tells of Brian Sternberg. A nationally acclaimed track star, he held several records in pole vault competition. The 1963 season, when Brian was nineteen years old, held unbelievable success. He made sports headlines every week. He remained undefeated in outdoor competition, and he set his first world record. Excitement and thrills embellished the spring and summer for the Sternbergs.

Then, three weeks after Brian had set his last world record, everything changed. On July 2, 1963, while working out on the trampoline in preparation for the U.S. track team's tour of Russia, Brian landed on his neck. There was a crack; then all feeling and movement in his arms and legs were gone.

Brian Sternberg was a Christian, and his faith was put to the test. He faced a crisis that threatened to leave him a quadriplegic the rest of his life, confined to a wheelchair. Brian had faith that God could and would heal his paralysis. Now, years later, he is still paralyzed. Did his faith fail? Did he not have enough faith? Did God make a mistake? Did God forsake his child?

Less than a year after the accident, Brian was asked to write an article for *Look* magazine. He ended with these powerful words that describe a Biblical view of faith: "Having faith is a necessary step toward one of two things. Being healed is one of them. Peace of mind, if healing does not come, is the other. Either one will suffice."[1]

Philip Yancey went to visit Brian ten years after the accident. Things had changed. He had been convinced by well-meaning Christians that since

God loved him, God wanted him to walk again. They convinced him that if he would just have enough faith, he could stand up and walk away from his wheelchair. In Brian's mind, faith now meant that there remained not two options for God, but only one, and that was complete healing. Only complete healing would suffice. He was putting his faith in faith.

Some were amazed at the great faith of this young man who still said God would heal him. Others said he lacked faith or he would already be healed. Yet the fact remained that when Philip Yancey left the house of Brian Sternberg, he sensed the mood of "an uncompleted, uncomfortable struggle mixed with tough, undying faith." As Brian struggled to find enough *human* faith, he forgot that God is sovereign, and he lost his peace of mind.[2]

Daniel 3 teaches us that since God is sovereign, we must put our faith in him as we stand before the fire. This historical narrative gives us a glimpse of the faith of Shadrach, Meshach, and Abednego, illustrating two strands of Biblical faith. First, faith is obedience to God's sovereign commands; and second, faith is trust in God's sovereign will. Biblical faith will always enable us to stand firm when we stand before the fiery trials of life.

As chapter 3 opens, King Nebuchadnezzar is dedicating his new nine-story idol of gold. Now there are a couple of possibilities as to why he built this golden idol. One could have been his dream in Daniel 2. Read again the interpretation by Daniel.

> *This was the dream, and now we will interpret it to the king. You, O king, are the king of kings. The God of heaven has given you dominion and power and might and glory; in your hands he has placed mankind and the beasts of the field and the birds of the air. Wherever they live, he has made you ruler over them all. You are that head of gold. After you, another kingdom will rise, inferior to yours. (2:36-39a)*

He was the king represented by gold, and he was the greatest of all these kings in the dream.

There is another more sinister possibility. In Daniel 6 a group of Persian leaders became jealous of Daniel's high rank since he was a Jew, a foreigner, and they tried to get him in trouble. The only thing they could do was to have the king make up a law that defied one of God's laws. Now, according to Daniel 2:49, these three Jewish exiles climbed the ladder of power in Babylon by Daniel's appointment very quickly. They passed many other Babylonians who had served long and hard to get their position. Maybe jealousy caused them to encourage the king to build the statue and to pass a decree that anyone who did not bow down before the statue would be incinerated. Daniel 3:12 does record the angry words of other magicians: "There are some Jews whom you have set over the affairs of the province of Babylon — Shadrach, Meshach and Abednego — who pay no attention to you, O king." Interesting that they knew them by name. Did they have their eye on them?

Whatever the case, the king made the image of gold and set it up on the plain of Dura a few miles south of Babylon. He summoned the satraps, advisers, treasurers, judges, magistrates, and all the other provincial officials to come to the dedication of the image he had set up. Then the king's herald issued this proclamation in a loud voice:

> This is what you are commanded to do, O peoples, nations and men of every language: As soon as you hear the sound of the horn, flute, zither, lyre, harp, pipes and all kinds of music, you must fall down and worship the image of gold that King Nebuchadnezzar has set up. Whoever does not fall down and worship will immediately be thrown into a blazing furnace. (3:4-6)

Can you envision this tremendous sight? Thousands of people gathered on this desert plain and stood before a nine-story golden statue. The throne of King Nebuchadnezzar with its royal guard was on the right. To the left there was a raging furnace to remind everyone of the severity of the command. There was absolute silence as the crowd of thousands waited for the music to begin.

Suddenly the awesome silence was broken with sounds of many instruments. People all around went to their knees, and then this sea of humanity fell like a wave on their faces before the image and the throne. But in the middle of this sea of bowing humanity, three figures stood firmly, quietly, not bending a knee! Their names were Shadrach, Meshach, and Abednego.

OBEYING HIS SOVEREIGN COMMANDS (3:8-12)

These three young men were noticed. Some of the astrologers came to the king, denouncing them. They said, "There are some Jews whom you have set over the affairs of the province of Babylon — Shadrach, Meshach and Abednego — who pay no attention to you, O king. They neither serve your gods nor worship the image of gold you have set up" (3:12). Three young men stood in utter defiance of the powerful king's decree because it was in conflict with an even more firm decree of the Sovereign Lord. God had said:

> You shall not make for yourself an idol in the form of anything in heaven above or on the earth beneath or in the waters below. You shall not bow down to them or worship them; for I, the LORD your God, am a jealous God. (Exodus 20:4, 5)

Standing with the heat of a blazing fire in their face, I can see how they would have been tempted to rationalize and convince themselves that it would be all right to bow down just this once, ignoring the commands of the Sovereign Lord. Some might make a case for situation ethics. In this situation it would be all right to bow down because they would get killed if they did not. Certainly God would not want these three young men to die, would he?

Others would argue in terms of culture. "The Babylonians are not going to understand the laws of our God. We don't want to offend our culture and ruin our witness. We will bow now so they will listen to us later. Anyway, nobody that we know will see us."

Still others would argue forgiveness. "We have a loving God who is slow to anger and quick to forgive. We will bow just this one time and then ask forgiveness. God is more understanding and forgiving than these Babylonians." It is true that God does forgive the sins of his people. Jesus died to pay the penalty for all of our sins. But we misunderstand the grace of God when we base our disobedience on his gracious forgiveness. That reveals a deeper problem of the heart. Hebrews 12:15 says, "See to it that no one misses the grace of God."

Some would make a silent protest. "We will kneel on the outside, but we will be standing and worshiping the true God on the inside, in our hearts. God will understand."

The three Hebrews could have come up with many excuses to justify their disobedience to the Law of God. We do. We compromise under pressure even though the pressure we face is nothing compared to that of facing death if we obey. The three friends of Daniel considered the first two commandments. Let us consider some of the others.

The fourth commandment says to keep the Sabbath Day holy, but we compromise under the pressure of a society that totally ignores this commandment. We are drawn into activities from sports to shopping so easily and without a thought. We rationalize and justify our activities.

The sixth commandment says we should not murder, yet even among Christians there are those who murder their unborn babies because of the pressure of embarrassment or the pressure of "unwanted" children.

The seventh commandment says that we should not commit adultery, which includes all kinds of sexual immorality, but again many Christians have fallen into sin because of the pressures of our society and have used all the excuses mentioned above.

Biblical faith does not compromise God's sovereign laws, because faith is obedience. The writer of Hebrews defines faith in 11:8: "By faith Abraham, when called to go to a place he would later receive as an inheritance, obeyed and went." Faith is obedience to all God's sovereign commands even when we are standing before the heat of a blazing fire.

We need faith to obey his commands. In Luke 17:4, Jesus tells his disciples to forgive the same person even if he sins against you seven times in one day. The disciples respond in verse 5 saying, "Increase our faith!" They recognized that it takes faith to obey a difficult command like forgiving those who hurt you.

At the end of this historical account in Daniel, even King Nebuchadnezzar recognized the depth of the Hebrews' faith in the Lord and honored them. Nebuchadnezzar said:

> *"Praise be to the God of Shadrach, Meshach and Abednego, who has sent his angel and rescued his servants. They trusted him and defied the king's command and were willing to give up their lives rather than serve or worship any god except their own God. Therefore I decree that the people of any nation or language who say anything against the God of Shadrach, Meshach and Abednego be cut into pieces and their houses be turned into piles of rubble, for no other god can save in this way." Then the king promoted Shadrach, Meshach and Abednego in the province of Babylon. (Daniel 3:28-30)*

Now back to the plain of Dura where the instruments were blaring and the fire was blazing.

When the king found out about these three young men, he was furious. In a moment Shadrach, Meshach, and Abednego found themselves standing before this powerful king, and they felt the heat of the furnace on their right side. It was always before them. The king looked at these three young, promising lads whom he had recently promoted to a high place in government (2:49) and smiled. "Boys, surely there must be some misunderstanding, so I will give you a second chance." He said:

> *Now when you hear the sound of the horn, flute, zither, lyre, harp, pipes and all kinds of music, if you are ready to fall down and worship the image I made, very good. But if you do not worship it, you will be thrown immediately into a blazing furnace. Then what god will be able to rescue you from my hand? (3:15)*

These three young men, influenced by the godly character of Daniel who in chapter 1 dared to be holy, stood before the furious king and the fury of the fire and answered the king with one of the most beautiful expressions of Biblical faith.

TRUSTING HIS SOVEREIGN WILL (3:16-18)

> *They replied, "O Nebuchadnezzar, we do not need to defend ourselves before you in this matter. If we are thrown into the blazing furnace, the*

God we serve is able to save us from it, and he will rescue us from your
hand, O king. But even if he does not, we want you to know, O king, that
we will not serve your gods or worship the image of gold you have set
up." (3:16-18)

Biblical faith has the assurance to say, "I know my God is able to deliver
me." It has the confidence to say, "I believe that my God will deliver me." But
it also has the submission to say, "But even if he does not, I will still trust
him." As Job said, "Though he slay me, yet will I hope in him" (Job 13:15).

Every Christian agrees with the first statement. We know our God is able
to do all things. I commend those Christians who truly do have the confidence to believe that their God will deliver them. Our charismatic brothers
and sisters have something to teach many of us in this second step. Many
Christians are sometimes afraid to believe that God will deliver them,
because of the disappointment they will experience if he does not. Others
then point to that lack of faith as the reason they were not healed or delivered.

But it seems that very few Christians can have this firm belief that he can
and will deliver us while maintaining a submissive attitude to his sovereign
will if it differs from our request. We need to understand that faith is not a
rabbit's foot, and God is not a genie who is bound to do for us whatever we
want.

Such confidence and submission are powerfully captured in the words of
Samuel Rodigast written in 1675:

> *What e'er my God ordains is right:*
> *His holy will abideth;*
> *I will be still whate'er he doth,*
> *And follow where he guideth.*
> *He is my God; though dark my road,*
> *He holds me that I shall not fall:*
> *Wherefore to him I leave it all.*[3]

Some Christians seem to live saying, "Wherefore to faith I leave it all."
To some, faith is a power that controls God's will. After all Jesus does say,
"Have faith in God. I tell you the truth, if anyone says to this mountain, 'Go
throw yourself into the sea,' and does not doubt in his heart but believes that
what he says will happen, it will be done for him" (Mark 11:22, 23).

But in reality, God's will found in his Word should control our faith.
Jesus said, "If you remain in me and my words remain in you, then ask
whatever you wish, and it will be given you" (John 15:7).

Even Jesus realized that God's will is not always in line with our will. He
cried out in the Garden of Gethsemane, "Father, if you are willing, take this
cup from me; yet not my will, but yours be done" (Luke 22:42). Faith is

submitting to the Father's will when it is different from ours. That faith will fill you with great peace.

Several years ago I had surgery to resect a portion of my colon. The surgery went fine, but three days later I began to feel terrible. I went in for emergency surgery because a stitch had come undone and my colon was leaking. The poison of peritonitis was filling my body. The doctor performed the second operation, but he had to put in a temporary colostomy because of the damage done.

The day before I left the hospital, I was asking the doctor about the surgery that would be done in three months to reverse my temporary colostomy. He said, "That surgery should go well."

I asked, "What do you mean 'should'?"

He said, "Well, nothing has gone normally for you. You had the blood clot in your lung in addition to the stitch coming undone." He hung his head and said, "I have lost sleep over this. I have gone over this surgery in my mind step by step. I have talked to colleagues about it. I just don't get it. I have done over a thousand of these surgeries, and this has only happened twice."

I said, "It is really helpful to believe in a sovereign God who is in control of all things. He makes no mistakes. With the loving family God has given me and the loving church he has blessed me with, if it had to happen to two people, as painful as this was, I am glad I was one of them." Knowing that God is sovereign gave me the greatest peace through this entire ordeal. Did that make it easy? No. Those six weeks were very difficult. But I agree with Samuel Rodigast:

> What e'er my God ordains is right:
> Though now this cup, in drinking,
> May bitter seem to my faint heart,
> I take it, all unshrinking.
> My God is true; each morn anew
> Sweet comfort yet shall fill my heart,
> And pain and sorrow shall depart.[4]

People from our church asked me about the effectiveness of prayer. How could this have happened to me when so many people came to the hospital to pray with me before the surgery? It was quite a sight. Liz and I arrived about twenty minutes late at the hospital on the morning of the surgery. When we walked in, there were people from Twin Oaks Presbyterian Church standing everywhere. We gathered for a huge prayer meeting in the lobby of the hospital. No, those numbers of people all praying in great faith did not guarantee a flawless surgery. Rather I think God had so many people come out to pray because his plan was to take me through suffering I had never experienced before. Prayer is not a vending machine where if we put in enough faith we will always get what we want.

In the providence of God, the three Hebrew men — Shadrach, Meshach, and Abednego — were miraculously delivered. And Nebuchadnezzar was so furious that he had the furnace heated seven times hotter than usual. "[He] commanded some of the strongest soldiers in his army to tie up Shadrach, Meshach and Abednego and throw them into the blazing furnace. . . . The king's command was so urgent and the furnace so hot that the flames of fire killed the soldiers" (3:20, 22).

Nebuchadnezzar was such a hard man that he took delight in seeing these young men burn to death (or so he thought). But as he watched, his face became ashen, his eyes grew wide, and (v. 24), he "leaped to his feet in amazement and asked his advisers, 'Weren't there three men that we tied up and threw into the fire?'" When that was confirmed he said, "Look! I see four men walking around in the fire, unbound and unharmed, and the fourth looks like a son of the gods" (v. 25).

From the evening of my first surgery, every nurse who came into my room asked me the same question: "On a scale of 1 to 10 with 10 being the greatest, what is your pain?" I am sure they all tired of my response. "My wife has had a baby and has passed two kidney stones. She knows what 10 is. I have never experienced 10. So how can I describe my pain for you on a scale of 1 to 10? It is impossible." Sunday night after my surgery I experienced 10.

I had been feeling worse all day Sunday without a clue as to the problem. Of course, it was the weekend, so the doctor was not available. Liz went to church to lead the children's choir; so our friends Polly Long and Charlie Johnson stayed with me. The pain became even more intense at six o'clock. I remember just crying out in anguish. I kept looking at the clock, and it did not seem to move. It stayed six o'clock for what seemed like an eternity. Polly and Charlie were both trying to calm and comfort me. The next morning they would discover that, as I shared earlier, one stitch had come undone, and my body was filling with peritonitis. I was a very sick man, and I was in more pain than I had ever experienced.

Later I found out that at that very time, six o'clock, the time of our Sunday evening worship, the assistant pastor had called for an evening of prayer for the pastor. God sent an angel or Jesus himself into the fire with the Hebrew men and delivered them. When our church prayed, God sent his angels to sustain me, to preserve my life, to strengthen Liz so she could endure one of our most difficult nights.

Faith standing before the fire knows that God will not always bring a miraculous deliverance for his people. That is not his plan. But he will always be there to give his grace to his people in their time of need. As the psalmist says, "Even though I walk through the valley of the shadow of death, I will fear no evil, for you are with me" (Psalm 23:4). Paul writes in 2 Timothy 4:17, "But the Lord stood at my side and gave me strength, so that through me the message might be fully proclaimed and all the Gentiles might hear it."

> *Whate'er my God ordains is right:*
> *Here shall my stand be taken;*
> *Though sorrow, need, or death be mine,*
> *Yet am I not forsaken.*
> *My Father's care is round me there;*
> *He holds me that I shall not fall:*
> *And so to him I leave it all.*[5]

Our hearts rejoice at God's mighty deliverance of these three Hebrews who were thrown alive into a raging fire. And a miraculous deliverance it was.

> *Nebuchadnezzar then approached the opening of the blazing furnace and shouted, "Shadrach, Meshach and Abednego, servants of the Most High God, come out! Come here!" So Shadrach, Meshach and Abednego came out of the fire, and the satraps, prefects, governors and royal advisers crowded around them. They saw that the fire had not harmed their bodies, nor was a hair of their heads singed; their robes were not scorched, and there was no smell of fire on them. (3:26, 27)*

But what about those who are not miraculously delivered? What about those like Brian Sternberg or Joni Eareckson Tada? What about those like my dear friend Ruth Gerstung Sinnard who at age thirty-three, just two and a half weeks before her fourth wedding anniversary, died of cancer after months of prayers by many people for her healing? What about those who experience the phrase, "But even if he does not"? Does that mean they did not have enough faith? No!

Hebrews 11 is a chapter of the Bible devoted entirely to the subject of faith. In verse 32 the writer begins to bring his thoughts on the subject to a conclusion. He starts with a summary of magnificent deliverances that some of God's people had experienced through faith. This is what he says:

> *And what more shall I say? I do not have time to tell about Gideon, Barak, Samson, Jephthah, David, Samuel and the prophets, who through faith con-quered kingdoms, administered justice, and gained what was promised; who shut the mouths of lions, quenched the fury of the flames, and escaped the edge of the sword; whose weakness was turned to strength; and who became powerful in battle and routed foreign armies. Women received back their dead, raised to life again. (vv. 32-35a, emphasis added)*

What a list of miraculous deliverances through faith. But that is only half the picture.

Others were tortured and refused to be released, so that they might gain a better resurrection. Some faced jeers and flogging, while still others were chained and put in prison. They were stoned; they were sawed in two; they were put to death by the sword. They went about in sheepskins and goatskins, destitute [the word means financially poor], persecuted, and mistreated — the world was not worthy of them. (vv. 35b-38)

That last sentence says of these men and women who by faith believed in God's love and care even though they were not delivered miraculously, "The world was not worthy of them." These are the special people in God's Hall of Fame. We make stars out of those with seemingly miraculous cures. They are the ones we interview. Theirs are the books we read. They are the ones sought out as special speakers at conferences. They are the ones we put in our Hall of Fame. But the Lord's Hall of Fame is made up of those special people who maintain a trust in God's sovereign plan through the darkest times and the deepest valleys. They are the ones who are not delivered except by death. "These were all commended for their faith, yet none of them received what had been promised" (Hebrews 11:39).

That is the kind of faith that Ruth and Mark Sinnard demonstrated during Ruth's battle with cancer. They knew that God was able, and they truly believed he would heal her. But as it became apparent that God was not going to intervene, they were able to live with confidence and Biblical faith. "But even if he doesn't, we will trust him to the very end."

That trust in God's sovereign plan showered them with peace through those last months of fighting cancer. They taught a fifth and sixth grade Sunday school class and talked about issues of life and death. They witnessed to the doctor and invited people into their home to carry on a sense of normalcy.

In her last letter, Ruth included this poem, which was also a part of her funeral. The author is unknown. The poem is entitled, "He Maketh No Mistake."

My Father's way may twist and turn,
My heart may throb and ache,
But in my soul I'm glad to know,
He maketh no mistake.

My cherished plans may go astray,
My hopes may fade away,
But still I'll trust my Lord to lead
For He doth know the way.

Tho' night be dark, and it may seem
That day will never break,
I'll pin my faith, my all in Him,
He maketh no mistake.

There's so much now I cannot see,
My eyesight's far too dim;
But come what may, I'll simply trust
And leave it all to Him.

For by and by the mist will lift
And plain it all He'll make,
Through all the way, tho' dark to me,
He made not one mistake.[6]

Some question the love of a God who would put his people in a position of having to make difficult choices of obeying his sovereign commands while standing before the fire or making them trust his sovereign will while standing in the fire.

Bryan Chapell tells the story of a Christian miner who was injured at a young age and became an invalid who spent his time watching through a window from his bed as life passed him by. He watched as men his own age prospered, raised families, and had grandchildren. As he watched, his body withered, his house crumbled, and his life wasted away.

One day when the bedridden miner was quite old, a younger man came to visit him. "I hear that you believe in God and claim that he loves you. How can you believe such things after all that has happened to you? Don't you sometimes doubt God's love?"

The old man hesitated and then smiled. "Yes, it is true. Sometimes Satan comes calling on me in this fallen-down house of mine. He sits right there by my bed where you are sitting now. He points out my window to the men I once worked with who are still strong and active, and he asks, 'Does Jesus love you?' Then Satan casts a jeering glance around my tattered room as he points to the fine homes of my friends across the street and asks again, 'Does Jesus love you?' Then, at last, Satan points to the grandchild of a friend of mine — a man who has everything I do not — and Satan waits for the tear in my eye before he whispers in my ear, 'Does Jesus really love you?'"

"And what do you say when Satan speaks to you that way?" asked the young man.

The old miner said, "I take Satan by the hand. I lead him in my mind to a hill far away called Calvary. There I point to the thorn-tortured brow, to the nail-pierced hands and feet and to the spear-wounded side. Then I say, 'Satan, you tell me . . . doesn't Jesus love me!'"[7]

Calvary is the measure of the Savior's love for us. The cross is the warrant for confidence in God's love despite lifelong heartache. When our focus remains on the cross, our faith will not waver though troubles and challenges come and human answers fail.

Whate'er my god ordains is right:
He never will deceive me;
He leads me by the proper path;
I know he will not leave me.
I take content, what he hath sent;
His hand can turn my griefs away,
And patiently I wait his day.[8]

5

Pride Comes Before
the Fall

DANIEL 4:1-37

In his book *Mere Christianity,* C. S. Lewis called it "the great sin." "There is one vice of which no man in the world is free; which everyone in the world loathes when they see it in others; and of which hardly any people, except some Christians, ever imagine that they are guilty themselves. There is no fault which we are more unconscious of in ourselves; and the more we have it in ourselves, the more we dislike it in others."[1]

This vice is the sin of pride. Lewis called it "the great sin" because of the enmity it created not only between man and man, but between man and God. Jesus told the story of two men who lived in Jerusalem. One was a humble, poor beggar who loved the God of Abraham, Isaac, and Jacob. The other was a proud, wealthy man who looked down upon the poor beggar and never took the time to look up to the living and true God.

They died about the same time. Since Lazarus, the poor beggar, was trusting in Jesus Christ alone for his salvation, he immediately went to Heaven. The wealthy man died and found himself in the torment of Hell. Now he looked up and saw Abraham far away with Lazarus at his side. He begged and pleaded that Abraham would send Lazarus to him for just a moment so he could dip his finger in water and cool his tongue because he was in such agony.

Abraham answered, "No." He said, "There is a great chasm fixed so that no one in Heaven can cross over into Hell and no one in Hell can ever cross over into Heaven."

Then the proud, wealthy man begged and pleaded with Abraham to send

Lazarus back from the dead to his five brothers to tell them about this place of torment so they would not end up there. The wealthy man now understood how his pride and prosperity had kept his heart away from the Lord, and he was desperate to get his message out so his family would not end up in the same torment.

He said, "I beg you, father, send Lazarus to my father's house, for I have five brothers. Let him warn them, so that they will not also come to this place of torment" (Luke 16:27, 28). Can you feel the urgency and the passion of this proud, wealthy man to get this message out? Ah, but it was too late; there was now nothing he could do.

Nebuchadnezzar had this same sense of urgency and passion to get the same message out to those whose hearts were so filled with pride and whose lives were so filled with prosperity that they had no room for the true and living God. The lesson he learned is recorded in the last sentence of his testimony: "Those who walk in pride [God] is able to humble" (Daniel 4:37). The lesson Nebuchadnezzar learned came from the worst experience of his life, but today from Heaven he would tell you it was the best thing that ever happened to him.

This historical account of Nebuchadnezzar (Daniel 4) is broken up into four parts:

> The introduction and the dream (vv. 4-18);
> The interpretation of the dream (vv. 19-27);
> The humiliation of the dreamer (vv. 28-33);
> The exaltation of the dreamer (vv. 34-37).

THE INTRODUCTION AND THE DREAM (4:4-18)

In the introduction and the dream, we see the man and the verdict.

The Man of the Dream

First, take a look at the man. He was content and prosperous. "I, Nebuchadnezzar, was at home in my palace, contented and prosperous" (4:4).

This man had enjoyed the good life. He had grown up in and now was king of the greatest empire in the world at the time, Babylon. He was at peace with his enemies because everyone was afraid to attack him. He had hundreds of thousands of Jews in his kingdom who were virtually slaves, doing all the work the Babylonian people did not want to do. He had them under his thumb.

Nebuchadnezzar was content. His wife had given him a son, a wonderful boy who would be heir to his throne. He was getting older, nearing retirement, and was considering giving his son co-regency. Nebuchadnezzar was prosperous. He had just completed a new palace and built a new capital in southern Babylon, a place called Tema, later renamed Babylon. Life just does not get any better than this.

Now Nebuchadnezzar was not what you would call a religious man. He would bow his knee to no one — no human and no deity. He would not worship Yahweh, the God of the Jews, and he refused to worship Marduk, the God of the Babylonians. The man was content and prosperous and proud. In his pride he concluded that he did not need God. This is why Jesus said, "I tell you the truth, it is hard for a rich man to enter the kingdom of heaven" (Matthew 19:23).

This king was Nabonidus, Nebuchadnezzar III. This really gets me excited, because for years there have been proud people who tried to under-mine the Scriptures and said this story of Nebuchadnezzar going into the desert for seven years was a mistake in the Bible. Their reason was that nowhere in Babylonian written history did Nebuchadnezzar ever leave his throne for seven years. There was no mention of that or of another king tak-ing his place. Some Christians hung their heads in shame over this. Don't join them, because there is a very clear explanation for what Daniel has recorded here. The man referred to as Nebuchadnezzar in Daniel chapters 1 — 3 is a different person from the Nebuchadnezzar of Daniel 4. There were three Nebuchadnezzars in Babylonian history — well, actually four.

The first king of Babylon was Nebuchadnezzar I who reigned from 625-605 B.C. His name was also Nabopolassar. His son was Nebuchadnezzar II, and he reigned from 605-562 B.C. He is the Nebuchadnezzar of Daniel chapters 1 — 3. He had a couple of sons and relatives who reigned after him: Evil-Merodach (561-560 B.C.), Neriglisar (559-556 B.C.), and Labashi-Marduk (556 B.C.).[2]

Then a new man entered the scene. He was not a descendant of Nebuchadnezzar II. His name was Nabonidus, and he overthrew King Labashi-Marduk. According to Babylonian historical documents, he ruled from 555-539 B.C. as the last king of Babylon and was reigning when his kingdom fell to King Darius the Mede, also known by his Persian name, Cyrus.

But why would Nabonidus call himself Nebuchadnezzar? It is because he was a usurper, taking the throne away from the family of Nebuchadnezzar. If he wanted the respect of the Babylonian people, he would have to iden-tify himself with their greatest king; so he called himself Nebuchadnezzar III or just Nebuchadnezzar.

The fourth Nebuchadnezzar is still alive as of the writing of this book. His name is Saddam Hussein, former leader of Iraq, modern-day Babylon. When the allied nations of the world fought against him after he invaded Kuwait in 1990, he referred to himself as Nebuchadnezzar the Second. He used the name of the great king of Babylon. He just did not know history well enough to know he was actually the fourth man to call himself Nebuchadnezzar, not the second. At the time of the printing of this book, his whereabouts is unknown, a result of Operation Iraqi Freedom.

Let me show you some Biblical support for the assertion that this Nebuchadnezzar in Daniel 4 is different from the king mentioned in the first three chapters of Daniel. When he had the dream, verse 6 says that he commanded all the wise men of Babylon to come to the palace. According to verse 7, he told his dream to the magicians, enchanters, astrologers, and diviners, but they could not interpret it. If this was the same Nebuchadnezzar as in Daniel 2, don't you think he would have ignored the wise men and asked Daniel first? In addition, he told Daniel the dream (v. 8). Nebuchadnezzar II knew that Daniel could tell him the dream as well as the interpretation. It seems to be a different person in Daniel 4.

A second important piece of this puzzle comes from Babylonian historical documents. According to those sources, Belshazzar (Daniel 5) was the son of Nabonidus. He was not a descendant of Nebuchadnezzar II. Yet the NIV translation says, "While Belshazzar was drinking his wine, he gave orders to bring in the gold and silver goblets that Nebuchadnezzar *his father* had taken from the temple in Jerusalem" (v. 2). The Hebrew word translated "father" could also be translated "predecessor."[3] Clearly the king who took the goblets from the temple was Nebuchadnezzar II, but he was a predecessor, not an ancestor.

There is one more problem that needs to be reconciled. Daniel 5:30, 31 shows Belshazzar as king when Darius the Mede conquered Babylon. How can this be when ancient Babylonian documents show Nabonidus, Nebuchadnezzar III, as the last king of Babylon?

Here again ancient history is helpful. After Nabonidus became king, he immediately wanted to build his own palace and his own capital in the Arabian desert, in a place called Tema, later called Babylon. It was completed in his fourth year. When he left, he placed his son in the old city of Babylon as his co-regent. But the Babylonian Chronicles record something strange in the fourth year. Nabonidus was not heard from for seven years.[4] Those are the seven years Nebuchadnezzar III was insane. The Bible, once doubted by the proud, is proved to be historically accurate once again.

The Dream and the Verdict

Now that we have seen the man, let us look at the dream and its verdict. This was the dream:

> These are the visions I saw while lying in my bed: I looked, and there
> before me stood a tree in the middle of the land. Its height was enor-

mous. The tree grew large and strong and its top touched the sky; it was visible to the ends of the earth. Its leaves were beautiful, its fruit abundant, and on it was food for all. Under it the beasts of the field found shelter, and the birds of the air lived in its branches; from it every creature was fed.

In the visions I saw while lying in my bed, I looked, and there before me was a messenger, a holy one, coming down from heaven. He called in a loud voice: "Cut down the tree and trim off its branches; strip off its leaves and scatter its fruit. Let the animals flee from under it and the birds from its branches. But let the stump and its roots, bound with iron and bronze, remain in the ground, in the grass of the field.

"Let him be drenched with the dew of heaven, and let him live with the animals among the plants of the earth. Let his mind be changed from that of a man and let him be given the mind of an animal, till seven times pass by for him." (Daniel 4:10-16)

The verdict was pronounced by the messenger from Heaven in the dream. "The decision is announced by messengers, the holy ones declare the verdict, so that the living may know that the Most High is sovereign over the kingdoms of men and gives them to anyone he wishes and sets over them the lowliest of men" (v. 17).

The verdict is that God opposes the proud and gives grace to the humble, so that all people will know that God alone is sovereign over the little kingdoms of men. He delights to set the lowliest, humblest of men over them. "God opposes the proud but gives grace to the humble" (1 Peter 5:5). Such was the man, the dream, and the verdict.

THE INTERPRETATION OF THE DREAM (4:19-27)

In the interpretation of the dream, we see the prophet and his God.

Daniel the Prophet

First, take a look at the prophet. Daniel's attitude is seen in verses 19-23. "Then Daniel (also called Belteshazzar) was greatly perplexed for a time, and his thoughts terrified him. So the king said, 'Belteshazzar, do not let the dream or its meaning alarm you'" (4:19). Daniel was terrified because of the news he would have to give this powerful king who was feared by everyone.

Speaking of Nabonidus, Daniel says in Daniel 5:19:

Because of the high position he gave him, all the peoples and nations and men of every language dreaded and feared him. Those the king wanted to

*put to death, he put to death; those he wanted to spare, he spared; those
he wanted to promote, he promoted; and those he wanted to humble, he
humbled.*

Nabonidus also held the Jewish people against their will, because many
wanted to return to Jerusalem. Nevertheless, Daniel's humble attitude
demonstrated a respect for this king, because he knew that the king was
placed over him by the sovereign hand of his God (4:17). Therefore, Daniel
did not wish anything bad upon this king, only good.

"My lord, if only the dream applied to your enemies and its meaning to
your adversaries" (4:19). To this he added, "Renounce your sins by doing
what is right, and your wickedness by being kind to the oppressed. It may
be that then your prosperity will continue" (v. 27). Even though Nabonidus
was such a wicked king, Daniel did not wish him any trouble. Many of us
do not see it, but it is our ugly pride that makes us wish the leaders we do
not like would stumble and fall.

Where is the humble attitude among us that Daniel displayed? Where
is the humble attitude among us that says, "Love your enemies and pray for
those who persecute you" (Matthew 5:44)? Dare to be a Daniel, dare to be
holy, dare to humbly speak well of your leaders even if you disagree with
them, and dare to stand alone!

Daniel's God

Daniel's God and God's decree are seen in verses 24-27. God hates pride.
The decree of God found in these verses is repeated for all of us three times
in Scripture — Proverbs 3:34, James 4:6, and 1 Peter 5:5. It is repeated
three times for emphasis: "God opposes the proud but gives grace to the humble." He will smash our pride on this earth as he did with Nebuchadnezzar,
or he will smash it in eternity as he did with the proud, wealthy man of
Luke 16.

But God is also incredibly patient. He warns us of his judgment, so that
we have time to repent and turn to him. Romans 2:4 says, "Do you show contempt for the riches of his kindness, tolerance and patience, not realizing
that God's kindness leads you toward repentance?" And 1 Peter 5:6 says,
"Humble yourselves, therefore, under God's mighty hand, that he may lift
you up in due time." As pride comes before the fall, so humiliation comes
before exaltation.

THE HUMILIATION OF THE DREAMER (4:28-33)

In the humiliation of the dreamer, we see the king's pride and the king.

The King and His Pride

All this happened to King Nebuchadnezzar. Twelve months later, as the king was walking on the roof of the royal palace of Babylon, he said, "Is not this the great Babylon I have built as the royal residence, by my mighty power and for the glory of my majesty?" (4:28-30)

In his book *Mere Christianity* C. S. Lewis writes more about pride.

I have heard people admit that they are bad-tempered, or that they cannot keep their heads about girls or drink, or even that they are cowards. I do not think I have ever heard anyone who was not a Christian accuse himself of this vice [pride]. There is no fault which makes a man more unpopular, and no fault which we are more unconscious of in ourselves. And the more we have it ourselves, the more we dislike it in others. Christians are right: it is pride which has been the chief cause of misery in every nation and every family since the world began. Other vices may sometimes bring people together: you may find good fellowship and jokes and friendliness among drunken people or unchaste people. But pride always means enmity — it is enmity. And not only between man and man, but enmity to God.[5]

Pride caused Nebuchadnezzar to forget God. It can cause us to forget God too.

In Deuteronomy 8:10-18 Moses warns:

When you have eaten and are satisfied, praise the LORD your God for the good land he has given you. Be careful that you do not forget the LORD your God, failing to observe his commands, his laws and his decrees that I am giving you this day. Otherwise, when you eat and are satisfied, when you build fine houses and settle down, and when your herds and flocks grow large and your silver and gold increase and all you have is multiplied, then your heart will become proud and you will forget the LORD your God . . . you may say to yourself, "My power and the strength of my hands have produced this wealth for me." But remember the LORD your God, for it is he who gives you the ability to produce wealth, and so confirms his covenant, which he swore to your forefathers, as it is today.

Any of us can get so caught up in the world, full of pride, that we forget the Lord. I performed the marriage for a godly young couple. They were faithful in the work of the kingdom and talked much about the Lord. After they were married, they both started working in hopes of getting enough money for a home. The husband worked two jobs and became less regular at church. They soon bought their house and worked even harder to fill it with things. Soon they both drifted away from the church. I visited them, and they had grown completely cold to the things of the Lord. They weren't interested at all. In just a few short years their marriage ended too. What I saw was a sad but not infrequent progression.

First John warns, "Do not love the world or anything in the world. If anyone loves the world, the love of the Father is not in him. For everything in the world — the cravings of sinful man, the lust of his eye and the boasting of what he has and does — comes not from the Father but from the world" (2:15, 16). And remember the testimony of Nabonidus: "those who walk in pride he is able to humble."

The King's Pride Under the King of Heaven

> The words were still on his lips when a voice came from heaven, "This is what is decreed for you, King Nebuchadnezzar: Your royal authority has been taken from you. You will be driven away from people and will live with the wild animals; you will eat grass like cattle. Seven times will pass by for you until you acknowledge that the Most High is sovereign over the kingdoms of men and gives them to anyone he wishes." Immediately what had been said about Nebuchadnezzar was fulfilled. He was driven away from people and ate grass like cattle. His body was drenched with the dew of heaven until his hair grew like the feathers of an eagle and his nails like the claws of a bird. (4:31-33)

C. S. Lewis wrote:

In God you come up against something which is in every respect immeasurably superior to yourself. Unless you know God as that — and, therefore, know yourself as nothing in comparison — you do not know God at all. As long as you are proud you cannot know God. A proud man is always looking down on things and people: and, of course, as long as you are looking down, you cannot see something that is above you.[6]

For seven years Nabonidus wandered like a wild beast in the desert of Tema, the new Babylon he had built for himself. He ate grass like an ox, his hair grew like the feathers of an eagle, and his nails were like the claws of a bird. One of the greatest, most prosperous, most powerful human kings to ever live was utterly and completely humiliated by God.

Do you like getting humiliated? Chuck Colson tells how he climbed the ladder of power and prestige to become the Special Counsel to the President of the United States of America. He was filled with pride as he walked in and out of the office of the most powerful man in the world any time he wanted. That most powerful man was seeking advice from him, and Colson's heart swelled with pride.

That was when he became involved in the Watergate affair of the Nixon administration. John Dean blew the whistle in 1973, and Colson soon found himself a convicted criminal doing time in a federal penitentiary. He was so humiliated that he lifted up his eyes to the King of Heaven and gave his heart to Jesus Christ. He still admits that the worst, most humiliating experience in his life was the best thing that ever happened to him.

Nabonidus too would tell you from the gates of Heaven that those were the seven most important years of his life and that this humiliation was the best thing that ever happened to him because of what followed.

THE SALVATION OF THE DREAMER (4:34-37)

In Luke 18:14 Jesus says, "Everyone who exalts himself will be humbled, and he who humbles himself will be exalted." Nabonidus exalted himself, and he was humbled. But when he humbled himself, he was about to be exalted. He stopped looking down and started looking up! "At the end of that time, I, Nebuchadnezzar, raised my eyes toward heaven, and my sanity was restored. Then I praised the Most High; I honored and glorified him who lives forever" (Daniel 4:34).

Nabonidus came face-to-face with the Sovereign King of kings and Lord of lords. He gave this outstanding testimony to the King who gave him his salvation: "All the peoples of the earth are regarded as nothing. He does as he pleases with the powers of heaven and the peoples of the earth. No one can hold back his hand or say to him: 'What have you done?'" (4:35).

Do you know the Sovereign God of Nabonidus, or are you worshiping a God you have made in your own image? Is your God one who makes you feel comfortable? Is he one who lets you do as you please rather than the God of Nabonidus who "does as he pleases" (4:35)? Have you made a small God who must explain to you why he does what he does? Do you demand from God an explanation as to why he humbled Nabonidus and gave him another chance but later did not humble the proud, wealthy man in Jerusalem until it was too late and he was lost for eternity? Do you know the God of Nabonidus, to whom no one can say, "What have you done?" (4:35)? What pride we display when we demand an explanation from God for tragedies that happen to us or others. We do not even recognize it as pride.

Nabonidus was stripped of his pride, and he saw the true God in all his glory. He humbled himself before him, and the Lord lifted him up.

At the same time that my sanity was restored, my honor and splendor were returned to me for the glory of my kingdom. My advisers and nobles sought me out, and I was restored to my throne and became even greater than before. (4:36)

Nabonidus was lifted up in this life, but the poor beggar Lazarus was not lifted up until his death when he was lifted straight to Heaven. We cannot explain all this. But we can say with Nabonidus, "Now I, Nebuchadnezzar, praise and exalt and glorify the King of heaven, because everything he does is right and all his ways are just. And those who walk in pride he is able to humble" (4:37).

A young pastor, fresh out of seminary, went to visit a dying man in a Washington, D.C. hospital. He had never met this man before. A virulent bone cancer was quickly and painfully eating away the life of the patient, who was not a Christian. The pastor shared the gospel several times, but there was no spiritual response. Nevertheless, a friendship did form between the two. Through a number of visits the pastor learned that the patient was a remarkable self-made man. He had been raised in Spain. His father was killed by the Franco regime, and because Spain's official church supported Franco, this young man turned his back on God and religion completely. He fled his country as a teenager and came to America knowing no English. He worked and studied hard. He eventually went to college and studied psychiatry, using it to confirm his unbelief. Despite his early disadvantages in life, he became wealthy and successful. He became chairman of the psychiatry department of one of our nation's most prestigious hospitals. Then came the cancer.

In just a few months the malignancy destroyed the accomplishments of a lifetime. It devastated the man's body, once kept in top shape by miles of daily swimming. Even his mind began to deteriorate because of the advances of the disease. Finally, with his spirit broken and his body racked with pain, the man ran out of pride and became tired of his own answers, which really weren't answers at all. When the pastor next visited, the despairing psychiatrist confronted him: "I have treated depression all my life, but I have no answers for what I am going through. If your God really has some answers, please help me with the hell I am experiencing now. Give me some peace — if you can."

The young pastor said, "You have gained everything a man could gain in every avenue of life. You have wealth, respect, intelligence, and achievement. These may all have to be put aside before you gain this thing you want. You have succeeded in every sphere of life except the spiritual, and to succeed there you must not follow any of the rules you have used before. You cannot conquer the spiritual world by your own efforts. You must first admit your helplessness and inability, confessing that you have nothing to stand on. To enter God's kingdom and know his peace, you must not come as a self-sufficient man but as a helpless child."

The man stared at him but remained silent. The pastor prayed with him and soon left. A few days later the cancer had progressed to the extent that the man's leg broke spontaneously as he moved in his bed. The doctors decided to operate on him, even though he was in such a weakened condition.

On the eve of his operation, unbeknownst to his family, the patient wrote the pastor a letter. It began with the Apostle's Creed written in Spanish. Then the note continued in English with these words: "Jesus, I hate all my sins. I have not served or worshiped you. Father, I know the only way to come into your kingdom is by the precious blood of Jesus. I know you stand at the door and will answer those who knock. I now want to be your lamb, me with you."

The man who wrote those words never regained consciousness after his operation. He learned Nebuchadnezzar's lesson that those who walk in pride, God is able to humble. The Sovereign God chose to break him of his pride with a virulent case of cancer. It was the worst thing that ever happened in this man's life, but in reality it was the best. He is in Heaven now, where Jesus is saying, "I am with you forever."

6

The Handwriting on the Wall

DANIEL 5:1-31

The Herods were infamous examples of rulers who blasphemed God and persecuted his people. Herod the Great, a non-Jew, reigned over Israel from 37 B.C. to 4 B.C. Though he instigated the rebuilding of the temple, he persecuted the Jews for many years. He became best known for ordering the death of the Jewish babies in Bethlehem two years old and younger in hopes of killing the Messiah (Matthew 2:16). Within months of this evil deed, Herod the Great was dead. Was this the judgment of God?

When he died, his kingdom was divided into four regions that were ruled by three of his sons. The most famous was Herod Antipas who reigned in Galilee and Perea from 4 B.C. to A.D. 39. He also persecuted God's people and became best known for having John the Baptist beheaded (Matthew 14:1-12) and ridiculing Jesus when Pilate sent Jesus to him (Luke 23:7-12). Within six years this Herod too was dead, and his son never ascended the throne. Was this the judgment of God?

Instead, his nephew Herod Agrippa became King of Judea from A.D. 39-44. He picked up where his uncle left off in persecuting God's people, but now he had a new group called the Church to deal with. Ten years after the resurrection and ascension of Christ, the Church was growing like a wildfire, and Herod tried to think of some way to put out the fire. He arrested a large number of disciples in Jerusalem, including James, the brother of the Apostle John. James was the patriarch of Jerusalem, and Herod thought if he could silence James and other key leaders, he could quench the flames of Christianity. So he had James put to death with the sword. Since this pleased the unbelieving Jews who kept him in power, he decided to arrest Peter during the Feast of Unleavened Bread.

Much to Herod's surprise, he heard the next morning an unbelievable story. His prize prisoner, whom he was planning to present to the Jews for pubic trial at Passover, had escaped. Herod was told by one of his aides that Peter had been chained to two soldiers, with two other soldiers standing guard. Somehow he broke out of his chains and got away from those four guards. Then he passed by four more armed guards who were standing by the locked inner gate and from there passed by four additional armed guards by the locked central gate. As incredible as it seems, Peter then walked right out of the heavily guarded outer gate that led to the streets of the city of Jerusalem. To top it all off, not one guard saw a thing.

You would think by now Herod might have realized that he was dealing with a power far greater than his own. You would think that after seeing what had happened to his grandfather and uncle after they persecuted God's people, he could have seen the handwriting on the wall. But as with so many proud, cocky rulers of this world, he did not.

Shortly after killing James and trying to imprison Peter, Herod was seated on his throne addressing some of his loyal subjects. Before he finished speaking, his loyal subjects began to shout, "This is the voice of a god, not of a man." Acts 12:23 says, "Immediately, because Herod did not give praise to God, an angel of the Lord struck him down, and he was eaten by worms and died." There is no question that this was the judgment of God! Isaiah had earlier written:

> *[God] brings princes to naught and reduces the rulers of this world to nothing. No sooner are they planted, no sooner are they sown, no sooner do they take root in the ground, than he blows on them and they wither, and a whirlwind sweeps them away like chaff. (Isaiah 40:23, 24)*

God is sovereign over the kings and rulers of this world today as well as yesterday. We must be aware of that, but we cannot always say that the death of a ruler is a direct judgment of God for his evil ways.

German leader Adolf Hitler presided over the death of six million Jews and millions of "born-again" Christians. When the Germans were defeated in 1945 and Hitler committed suicide in a bunker in Berlin, was that the judgment of God? Great care and wisdom are needed to discern the hand of God, but that should not lead us to the conclusion that God does not at times intervene and judge the rulers of this world.

Daniel 5 shows an obvious example of God bringing his judgment to bear upon a wicked, godless, and arrogant young ruler in Babylon named Belshazzar. This is history with a theological and didactic purpose, which is the significance of what is called "prophetic history."[1] In this chapter we learn things about the nature of God and what our response to him should be, whether we are a prince or a pauper. Since God is a God of justice, we must humble ourselves before him.

Humility before a just God is what Nebuchadnezzar (Nabonidus) learned through his experience recorded in Daniel 4. This lesson forms his closing message in the last verse of that chapter, setting the stage for chapter 5 and giving fatherly advice to his wild son. "Now I, Nebuchadnezzar, praise and exalt and glorify the King of heaven, because *everything he does is right and all his ways are just*. And those who walk in pride *he is able to humble*" (Daniel 4:37, emphasis added).

This proposition will be unfolded as we meet the three main characters of this chapter of prophetic history. Through them the author shows us what we must do to walk humbly before our just God. From the example of King Belshazzar we learn that we must avoid profaning God's holy name. The queen modeled for us one who humbly acknowledged God's infinite wisdom. And Daniel shows us that we must accept God's righteous judgments.

WE MUST AVOID PROFANING HIS HOLY NAME (5:1-9)

Life in the magnificent city of Babylon, with its Hanging Gardens, one of the Seven Wonders of the ancient world, seemed normal on the night of October 12, 539 B.C.[2] The biggest event in town was a huge banquet thrown by King Belshazzar for a thousand of his nobles (5:1). We learn from extrabiblical sources, both cuneiform records and Greek historians Herodotus and Xenophon,[3] that the Persians were at that time poised on the plains outside of Babylon ready to take the city.

So why was King Belshazzar hosting this big banquet? There are at least three possibilities. This could have been a show of power the day before the big battle, like the banquet King Xerxes hosted in the days of Esther before he left to try to conquer the Greeks. Knowing the Persians were ready to attack, Belshazzar was perhaps bragging about his power to his nobles. There seems to be no mention of this in the text.

Or, a second possibility, maybe he knew the Persians were at his door, but he also knew he was powerless to do anything about it. The Babylonia Chronicle indicates that just a few days earlier, Cyrus the Persian had defeated Nabonidus and the Babylonian army near Sippar, which was only fifty miles from Babylon.[4] King Belshazzar was co-reigning with his father Nabonidus, and perhaps he knew they were going to lose the battle. So maybe his attitude that night was, "Eat, drink, and be merry, for tomorrow we die."

The third scenario seems most plausible. King Belshazzar was completely oblivious to the fact that Babylon the Great was about to be invaded. Darius, the King of Persia, had conquered his father in his capital city of

Tema and moved north to Babylon. In those days there was no fast communication, and King Belshazzar just did not know. He was a riotous, arrogant young man who loved his wine and loved to throw banquets. Banquets like this were celebrated on a regular basis. It just so happened this occurred on the night that Babylon would fall.

This scenario seems most plausible because history records that the Persian army conquered Babylon with a sneak attack. The city of Babylon was considered invincible. There were double walls all around the city, and the walls were too thick to destroy by ancient methods. But the Euphrates River ran right through the middle of the city, and the plan was for some men from the Persian army to go upstream and dam the river. In a few hours the water stopped flowing, and the Persian army walked into the city under the walls using the muddy riverbeds. There was no resistance by the Babylonian army, and Babylon fell that very night as a result of the judgment of God. Why didn't King Belshazzar see the handwriting on the wall? Oh, but he did.

The Arrogance of Belshazzar (5:2-4)

> While Belshazzar was drinking his wine, he gave orders to bring in the gold and silver goblets that Nebuchadnezzar his predecessor [alternate reading in the footnote of the NIV Study Bible] had taken from the temple in Jerusalem, so that the king and his nobles, his wives and his concubines might drink from them. . . . As they drank the wine, they praised the gods of gold and silver, of bronze, iron, wood and stone. (5:2-4)

His first act of arrogance in profaning the holy name of God was to bring in the gold and silver goblets that his predecessor King Nebuchadnezzar had taken from the temple in Jerusalem. This was Nebuchadnezzar II who had destroyed the temple in 586 B.C. As we saw in the last chapter, he was not the biological father or forefather of King Belshazzar. Belshazzar's father was Nabonidus, who took the name Nebuchadnezzar for political purposes, but was not blood-related to Nebuchadnezzar the Great.

These gold and silver goblets were holy unto the Lord, like the pieces of the tabernacle the Lord told Moses to make. For example, the altar of incense (Exodus 30:1-10) was "most holy to the LORD." There were special instructions on to how to treat this altar. Special poles were made to carry the altar of incense so no human hand would ever touch it. The ark of the covenant was another piece of the tabernacle that was "most holy to the LORD." It too was to be carried using poles, so no human hand would touch it.

In the days of King David when the Israelites were returning the ark to Jerusalem, they ignored the rule of treating the ark as holy by carrying it with two poles. Instead they set the ark on a new cart. As they were walking, the oxen stumbled, and the ark began to fall off. Uzzah reached out his hand to keep the ark from falling, and God struck him dead instantly "because of his irreverent act" (2 Samuel 6:7).

Many people find it difficult to understand why God would do that since Uzzah was only trying to help. Even King David was upset with God. "David was angry because the LORD's wrath had broken out against Uzzah" (v. 8). What we need to realize is that God is holy, and we are sinful. We are much more filthy than the ground upon which the ark would have fallen. We must not profane the holy things of God. If that is how God treated Uzzah who truly was trying to help, how much more was Belshazzar in trouble by using God's holy vessels for such revelry. And what about us?

We don't have the holy temple vessels anymore, but that does not mean there is not an application for us. Paul wrote about this in his letters. "Flee from sexually immorality. . . . Do you not know that your body is a temple of the Holy Spirit, who is in you, whom you have received from God? You are not your own; you were bought with a price. Therefore honor God with your body" (1 Corinthians 6:18-20). And in another place he wrote, "It is God's will that you should be sanctified: that you should avoid sexual immorality; that each of you should learn to control his own body in a way that is holy and honorable, not in passionate lust like the heathen, who do not know God; and that in this matter no one should wrong his brother or take advantage of him. The Lord will punish men for all such sins, as we have already told you and warned you" (1 Thessalonians 4:3-6). We are the holy vessels of God and should use our bodies only for holy, not profane, ends.

King Belshazzar's second act of arrogance in profaning the holy name of God was idolatry. Not only did he misuse the holy vessels — he also used them to worship his gods of gold, silver, bronze, iron, wood, and stone. The Babylonians were polytheists. King Belshazzar did not deny the existence of Yahweh, the God of Israel; rather he brought the gold and silver of Yahweh to join the gold and silver gods he worshiped. By using these golden goblets for wine to drink to the gods of the Babylonians, he was obviously making Yahweh subservient in his mind. And why not? Had not his gods given the Babylonians victory over Israel and their God?

But the God of Israel will not be made subservient to any other god. He says, "I will be exalted among the nations, I will be exalted in the earth" (Psalm 46:10). Again he says, "For great is the LORD and most worthy of praise; he is to feared above all gods. For all the gods of the nations are idols, but the LORD made the heavens" (Psalm 96:4, 5). He will not share his glory with another! To do so is idolatry.

The actions of Belshazzar are reminiscent of the actions of the Philistines when they captured the ark of the covenant. They acknowledged the existence of the God of Israel; so they did not destroy the ark. Instead they put it in the temple of their god, Dagon (1 Samuel 5). They set the ark beside

Dagon in a subservient position. The next morning when the priests came
to worship, Dagon had fallen on his face. God had made the idol look like
he was worshiping Yahweh. The Philistines did not catch the significance
of this picture. After all, these were two inanimate objects. Surely Dagon had
just fallen over. The next day when the priests entered, Dagon had fallen
again, but this time his head and his hands were broken off. Now the
Philistines got the message. "The ark of the god of Israel must not stay here
with us, because his hand is heavy upon us and upon Dagon our god" (1
Samuel 5:7). Yahweh addressed the idolatry dramatically and got their attention. They sent the ark of God back to Israel.

This subtle form of idolatry, acknowledging Yahweh as God but making him equal to or even subservient to other gods, is more prevalent than
we may think. A missionary in Taiwan once told me that it is very easy to
get a profession of faith in Jesus among the Taiwanese people. The problem
is that they put Jesus on their shelf with many other idols. The rub comes
when they are encouraged to be baptized. The genuinely born-again
Taiwanese surface at this point, because to be baptized in the name of the
Father, the Son, and the Holy Spirit is to renounce all idols. When they are
baptized, they are often forsaken by family, unable to get jobs, and rejected
by their friends.

In America it is very easy to put Jesus on the shelf with our other gods.
We worship him on Sunday, but the rest of the week we worship the god of
sports, the god of family, the god of money, or the god of pleasure. He will
get our attention. The Lord said through the prophet Isaiah, "I am the LORD;
that is my name! I will not give my glory to another or my praise to idols"
(Isaiah 42:8). Again the Lord says, "For my own sake, for my own sake, I
do this. How can I let myself be defamed? I will not yield my glory to
another" (Isaiah 48:11).

Christians, wake up before he needs to get your attention. As Yahweh got
the attention of the Philistines by knocking the god Dagon off his pedestal,
he got the attention of Belshazzar and knocked him off his pedestal too.

The Answer of God (5:5-9)

Suddenly the fingers of a human hand appeared and wrote on the plaster
of the wall, near the lampstand in the royal palace. The king watched the
hand as it wrote. His face turned pale and he was so frightened that his
knees knocked together and his legs gave way. The king called out for the
enchanters, astrologers and diviners to be brought and said to these wise
men of Babylon, "Whoever reads this writing and tells me what it means
will be clothed in purple and have a gold chain placed around his neck, and
he will be made the third highest ruler in the kingdom." Then all the king's
wise men came in, but they could not read the writing or tell the king what

*it meant. So King Belshazzar became even more terrified and his face
grew more pale. His nobles were baffled.*

God's answer was sudden and frightening. With no warning a mysterious hand appeared in midair and started writing an enigmatic message. The arrogant king turned pale, his knees knocked together, and his legs gave way. In his terror he called for his wise men, but they could not help. He turned to his nobles, but they were baffled. Yahweh answered Belshazzar's blasphemy and arrogance, knocking him off his pedestal!

God's answer shows again that the wisdom of God confounds the wisdom of men. All the wise men came in, but they could not read the writing or tell the king what it meant. The Lord said through Isaiah, "I will destroy the wisdom of the wise; the intelligence of the intelligent I will frustrate" (quoted in 1 Corinthians 1:19). He definitely frustrated these wise men. The message, as we will see, was written in their language, but it probably did not have any spaces between the words, and God used that to prevent them from reading the message, much less interpreting it. Where was their great wisdom?

*Where is the wise man? Where is the scholar? Where is the philosopher of
this age? Has not God made foolish the wisdom of the world? For since
in the wisdom of God the world through its wisdom did not know him,
God was pleased through the foolishness of what was preached to save
those who believe. (1 Corinthians 1:20, 21)*

God's answer verified the truthfulness of Scripture once again. The hand wrote the message on "the plaster of the wall." The throne room of the kings of Babylon was excavated by Koldewey in 1899.[5] Of course, the message was not found, but they did find that the walls were coated with white gypsum. Archaeology once again verified the truthfulness of Scripture, showing this message was not just a figment of someone's imagination. It appeared on a white wall, and it was written "near the lampstand" so all could see it clearly.

Further evidence of the truthfulness of Scripture is the fact that Belshazzar promised that the one who could interpret the message would "be made third highest ruler in the kingdom." The reason for "third highest" was not clear for many years until archaeology showed that Belshazzar was co-regent with his father Nabonidus at the time. Thus the highest position in the land after father and son was third in the kingdom.

God's answer confronted the arrogance, idolatry, and blasphemy of this young ruler. He would not stand by and allow his holy vessels to be profaned in front of all these people. Belshazzar saw the handwriting on the wall. Tremper Longman III writes:

We do not have to look too far to see contemporary misuses of God's Word that look eerily similar to Belshazzar's profanation of the holy vessels. Not everyone who practices a postmodern approach to the Bible is guilty of profanation . . . however, it is wrong simply to assume the validity of the culture that we happen to live in without submitting it to a biblical critique. Unfortunately, there are too many examples of the reverse, submitting the Bible to a postmodern critique.

One glaring example may be found in a recent interpretation of Psalm 24. (D. J. A. Clines, *A World Established on Water: Psalm 24*. Valley Forge, Pa: Trinity Press International, 1993, 79-90) This essay's purpose is to demonstrate an approach to the text as well as to discuss Psalm 24. The author proclaims the postmodern dictum that texts have no determinate meaning. *There is no presence, divine or authorial, to rein in our interpretation.* We, as readers, can ascribe whatever meaning we like to the text. He promotes the idea that Biblical interpreters should simply cut the cloth of the text to fit the needs of the audience who is paying for our skills. Nonetheless, with a move that seems to fit uneasily with his idea that the text itself has no meaning, he argues that Psalm 24 presents a view of God and war that he finds repulsive and argues that we must read "against the grain" of the apparent meaning of this text. Belshazzar takes the holy vessels of God and mocks God by drinking and toasting his idols; is Clines' treatment of the Bible far removed from this act?[6] (emphasis added)

WE MUST ACKNOWLEDGE HIS INFINITE WISDOM (5:10-16)

The banquet hall was in confusion. Belshazzar was shaking in sheer terror. The wise men were quaking, because they might be put to death due to their inability to interpret the handwriting on the wall (cf. Daniel 2:5). And the nobles were faking it, trying to stay cool, calm, and collected. The queen was near enough that she could hear the frightened voices of the king and the nobles. Though not in the banquet hall, she figured out that the wise men could not interpret the message. Without formal invitation, she entered the hall. "O king, live forever! Don't be alarmed! Don't look so pale!" (5:10).

The Remembrance of the Queen (5:11-12)

There is a man in your kingdom who has the spirit of the holy gods in him. In the time of your predecessor [NIV margin] he was found to have insight and intelligence and wisdom like that of the gods. King Nebuchadnezzar your predecessor [NIV margin] — your predecessor [NIV margin] the king, I say — appointed him chief of the magicians, enchanters, astrologers and diviners. This man Daniel, whom the king called

Belteshazzar, was found to have a keen mind and knowledge and under-standing, and also the ability to interpret dreams, explain riddles and solve difficult problems. Call for Daniel, and he will tell you what the writing means.

The king referred to here is King Nebuchadnezzar II. He is the one who made Daniel chief of the magi (2:48) and named him Belteshazzar (1:7). Daniel was very close to this king, and that ruler gave glory to the God of Israel: "Surely your God is the God of gods and the Lord of kings" (2:47).

We know the king who is referred to in these verses, but who is this queen? She is not the wife of Belshazzar, because his wives and concubines were in the banquet hall (5:2). "She has not been attending the party, but she enters at the moment of crisis, acting with authority and dignified confidence."[7] This would indicate that perhaps she was the queen mother, a figure of importance in most Near Eastern societies. Ever since Josephus, the queen here has been identified as the queen mother.

But whose mother was she? If she was Belshazzar's mother, the wife of Nabonidus, we do not know her name. She could not be his grandmother, the mother of Nabonidus, Adad-guppi, because she died a few years before this fateful night. She could have been Nebuchadnezzar the Great's wife, Nitocris, who was still influential two decades after her husband's death in 562 B.C.[8] This may be the most likely possibility because of her emphasized reference to her husband when she spoke to Belshazzar. "King Nebuchadnezzar your predecessor [NIV margin] — your predecessor [NIV margin] the king, I say" (5:11). In addition, Herodotus, the Greek historian, celebrates her wisdom in his writings.

Whoever she was, she knew where to go to get the answer to the puzzle that even Belshazzar's wise men could not solve. "There is a man in your kingdom who has the spirit of the holy gods in him. In the time of your predecessor [NIV margin] he was found to have insight and intelligence and wisdom" (5:11). We don't know who the queen mother was, much less anything about her faith, but she did acknowledge that Daniel's God dwelt in him and had given him superior wisdom. Even unbelievers can recognize this.

I think of the men who were involved in the founding of our nation. Not all the Founding Fathers were Christians, but there was a reverence for and acceptance of the wisdom of the Word of God. They established a government based on the Scriptures. They based the laws of the land upon the Word of God. Many acknowledged the wisdom of God in the Scriptures even though they did not believe in Jesus Christ as their personal Lord and Savior.

Even the principal of the public high school I attended in the sixties began each day reading from the "wisdom of God" as he called it, reading from the Psalms or Proverbs over the loudspeaker. He was not even a professing Christian.

As Christians, we need to publicly acknowledge the wisdom of God found in the Scriptures and encourage people to search the Scriptures for answers to this world's problems. When we do, we need to keep in mind the words that God spoke to Ezekiel:

> *The people to whom I am sending you are obstinate and stubborn. Say to them, "This is what the Sovereign LORD says." And whether they listen or fail to listen — for they are a rebellious house — they will know that a prophet has been among them. (Ezekiel 2:4, 5)*

The Response of the King (5:13-16)

> *So Daniel was brought before the king, and the king said to him, "Are you Daniel, one of the exiles my predecessor [NIV margin] the king brought from Judah? I have heard that the spirit of the gods is in you and that you have insight, intelligence and outstanding wisdom. The wise men and enchanters were brought before me to read this writing and tell me what it means, but they could not explain it. Now I have heard that you are able to give interpretations and to solve difficult problems. If you can read this writing and tell me what it means, you will be clothed in purple and have a gold chain placed around your neck, and you will be made the third highest ruler in the kingdom."*

Belshazzar seemed cynical and condescending toward Daniel, who now was an old man. He reminded Daniel from the start that he was one of the Jewish exiles. He must have known of Daniel because Daniel had been chief of the magi for at least forty years, and though he was now in his eighties, he still was highly respected. Maybe the king did not call him earlier because of his disdain for Nebuchadnezzar II or because of his disdain for Daniel's God. Another way you can see the king's low view of Daniel was in contrast to the queen. The queen mother acknowledged that Daniel had "the spirit of the holy gods in him," whereas Belshazzar simply said that he "heard" that the spirit of the gods was in him. He did not acknowledge the infinite wisdom of God. But he was desperate and was willing to let *anyone* help him.

Do you acknowledge the infinite wisdom of God and seek first his wisdom in the pages of Scripture to keep your life free from the pain of the consequences of disobedience to his commands? Or do you turn to him only as a last resort when you are desperate? So many people live as though God's wisdom is unimportant and irrelevant to daily living. They hear about it, but they don't pursue it. Then their life gets messed up by sinful choices, and they cry out to God. Like Belshazzar, they make promises to God of riches from their pocket if he will only help them this once.

A professing Christian I once knew had lived a very undisciplined, ungodly life. He was not kind to his wife. He abused alcohol and had virtually destroyed his business. He had also been unfaithful to his wife on several occasions. We tried to get him involved in Bible studies, but he was not interested. We encouraged him to be consistent in worship, but he preferred to be at the stadium. We challenged him to read his Bible on his own daily, but he said he did not have time. He had no interest in seeking the wisdom of God for his life. He wanted to pursue pleasure.

When he realized that he was about to lose everything, he cried out to the Lord and came back to the people of the church for help. One of the members took him to a program to overcome the alcohol and drug abuse. He met with me and made a promise to meet with me weekly for discipleship. He also promised to attend church regularly on the Lord's Day for both morning and evening worship. But these turned out to be vain promises just to get his family back; he really was not interested in the wisdom of God any more than Belshazzar was. The man was soon separated from his wife and back on the bottle. He just could not see the handwriting on the wall.

WE MUST ACCEPT HIS JUST JUDGMENTS (5:17-31)

Daniel waited patiently for his turn to speak. Unimpressed with the king's offer of riches and power, Daniel responded, "You may keep your gifts for yourself and give your rewards to someone else. Nevertheless, I will read the writing for the king and tell him what it means" (5:17). Daniel would first deliver a message to Belshazzar and then tell him the meaning of the inscription. In spite of the king's insolence, Daniel greeted him with respect for his office; but you can detect the prophet's annoyance and dislike for this cocky, young monarch.

The Message of Daniel (5:18-24)

O king, the Most High God gave your father Nebuchadnezzar sovereignty and greatness and glory and splendor. Because of the high position he gave him, all the peoples and nations and men of every language dreaded and feared him. Those the king wanted to put to death, he put to death; those he wanted to spare, he spared; those he wanted to promote, he promoted; and those he wanted to humble, he humbled. But when his heart became arrogant and hardened with pride, he was deposed from his royal throne and stripped of his glory. He was driven away from people and given the mind of an animal; he lived with the wild donkeys and ate grass like cattle; and his body was drenched with the dew of heaven, until he acknowledged that the Most High God is sovereign over the kingdoms of men and sets over them anyone he wishes. (5:18-21)

Daniel first reminds the king of the humbling experience of his biological father Nabonidus, also known as Nebuchadnezzar III. When the king's father's heart became arrogant and hardened with pride, the Lord humbled him by deposing him from his royal throne and stripping him of his glory. Belshazzar had seen how God dealt with his father's pride and should have learned an important lesson about pride and arrogance. He should have seen the handwriting on the wall in his own life. He also should have learned from what happened when his father repented and acknowledged that the Most High God is sovereign over the kingdoms of men and sets over them anyone he wishes. His father was graciously restored to his right mind and his royal throne. Daniel then turned his attention to the pride of Belshazzar.

> But you his son, O Belshazzar, have not humbled yourself, though you knew all this. Instead, you have set yourself up against the Lord of heaven. You had the goblets from his temple brought to you, and you and your nobles, your wives and your concubines drank wine from them. You praised the gods of silver and gold, of bronze, iron, wood and stone, which cannot see or hear or understand. But you did not honor the God who holds in his hand your life and all your ways. Therefore he sent the hand that wrote the inscription. (vv. 22-24)

Calvin wrote, "I have no doubt that he meant to speak roughly to the ungodly Belshazzar, a man beyond hope."[9] God's patience ran out with Belshazzar. Paul writes in Romans 2:4, 5, "Do you show contempt for the riches of his kindness, tolerance and patience, not realizing that God's kindness leads you toward repentance? But because of your stubbornness and your unrepentant heart, you are storing up wrath against yourself for the day of God's wrath, when his righteous judgment will be revealed."

The king foolishly honored gods of silver and gold who cannot see, hear, or understand, while dishonoring the true God who held Belshazzar's life and all his ways in his divine, cosmic scales. He had stored up wrath against himself, and now he was going to experience the humiliation of the judgment of God.

The Meaning of the Inscription (5:25-31)

"This is the inscription that was written: MENE, MENE, TEKEL, PARSIN" (5:25). Daniel was given the responsibility of reading the handwriting on the wall and delivering the bad news to the king.

> This is what these words mean: MENE: God has numbered the days of your reign and brought it to an end. TEKEL: You have been weighed on the

*scales and found wanting. PERES [singular of Parsin]: Your kingdom is
divided and given to the Medes and Persians. (5:26-28)*

Al Wolters argues that the reason the Babylonian wise men could not
read the inscription was because it was continuous script without vocaliza-
tion. They would have seen the following handwriting on the wall: *mn'tql-
prs.*[10] Typical of writing language in those days and in that part of the world,
it contained only consonants with no vowel pointings.

God gave Daniel special insight into this message. Daniel first understood that it was three words each with three letters. Then he understood
that the words could have three different meanings depending on the vowel
pointing used. This explains Daniel's interpretation of the handwriting on the
wall.

He first considered the vowel pointing for these words and interpreted
them as nouns. That is how he arrived at the three words: MENE, MENE,
TEKEL, PARSIN. Considering them as nouns, they are three kinds of
Babylonian coins: the mina, the shekel, and half a shekel.

Now when he takes the same three words and gives then verbal vowel
pointings, they are actually passive participles. MENE is related to the verb
m-n-h, "numbered." TEKEL is related to the verb *t-q-l*, "weighed." And
PARSIN is related to the verb *p-r-s*, "divided."[11] This explains why Daniel
interpreted these three words on the wall as follows. MENE: "God has numbered the days of your reign"; TEKEL: "You have been weighed on the
scales"; and PARSIN: "Your kingdom is divided."

Now there is one more level of understanding for these three words using
a third set of vowel pointings (*menah, tiqqal, paras*). These indicate the
consequences of God's judgment on Babylonia: "He has paid out, you are too
light (the pe'al of *qll*), and Persia."[12] Look at the last phrase of Daniel's
interpretation of the three words. "MENE: God has numbered the days of
your reign and brought it to an end. TEKEL: You have been weighed on the
scales and found wanting. PERES: Your kingdom is divided and given to
the Medes and Persians."

Belshazzar now saw the handwriting on the wall, and he knew his kingdom would come to an end. He ordered that Daniel be clothed in purple
with a gold chain placed around his neck. He proclaimed him the third highest ruler in the land (5:29). Though there is no evidence of repentance, the
king appeared to resign himself to the reality of God's coming judgment
upon him. He accepted the judgment of God.

"Hallelujah! Salvation and glory and power belong to our God, for true
and just are his judgments" (Revelation 19:1, 2). Daniel accepted the just
judgment of God as well and delivered the message of doom without waver-
ing. Think how risky it would be to tell a proud, rebellious king in front of
all of his nobles that his kingdom is about to end. Belshazzar could have been

so angry at the message that he would kill the messenger. If Daniel had that fear, he could have made up an interpretation of the handwriting on the wall that would have been more favorable, and no one would have ever known. He could have said, "That inscription means God loves you, and so do I." But Daniel accepted the judgment of God as true and just; so he did not hide the message.

I wish preachers today would not hide the message of God's judgment upon the sins of men. Many must not believe God's judgments are true or just, because they do not warn the people of the coming wrath of God. God's coming judgment upon this nation ought to be resounding from the pulpits of our land. What nation can exist very long whose laws call evil good and good evil?

We prohibit prayer at high school football games and demand that homosexuals be allowed in the Boy Scouts. We acquit a murderer because he is famous and kill unborn babies for money and convenience. We are a nation of idolatry and greed. We have embraced sexual immorality as a way of life and have a high rate of divorce. The list could go on and on, but we have to see the handwriting on the wall for America. If we preach the gospel and believe that God is a just God who judges nations, then we need to sound the warning boldly like Daniel and the other prophets did. God calls us to be watchmen.

> The word of the LORD came to me: "Son of man, speak to your countrymen and say to them: 'When I bring the sword against a land, and the people of the land choose one of their men and make him their watchman, and he sees the sword coming against the land and blows the trumpet to warn the people, then if anyone hears the trumpet but does not take warning and the sword comes and takes his life, his blood will be on his own head. Since he heard the sound of the trumpet but did not take warning, his blood will be on his own head. If he had taken warning, he would have saved himself. But if the watchman sees the sword coming and does not blow the trumpet to warn the people and the sword comes and takes the life of one of them, that man will be taken away because of his sin, but I will hold the watchman accountable for his blood.' Son of man, I have made you a watchman for the house of Israel; so hear the word I speak and give them warning from me. When I say to the wicked, 'O wicked man, you will surely die,' and you do not speak out to dissuade him from his ways, that wicked man will die for his sin, and I will hold you accountable for his blood. But if you do warn the wicked man to turn from his ways and he does not do so, he will die for his sin, but you will have saved yourself." (Ezekiel 33:1-9)*

Babylon had two proud kings, father and son. One was humbled and given a heart of repentance; so his life and kingdom were spared for a time.

I would not be surprised to see Nabonidus in Heaven one day. The other was humiliated in front of his wives, nobles, and concubines but did not repent of his pride. "That very night Belshazzar, king of the Babylonians was slain, and Darius the Mede took over the kingdom, at the age of sixty-two" (5:30, 31). Belshazzar was a man who had it all — a wealthy king of the once most powerful nation in the world who became a fool and lost it all. Jesus said, "What good will it be for a man if he gains the whole world, yet forfeits his soul?" (Matthew 16:26).

On the other hand, if you receive Jesus Christ as your Lord and Savior, you get it all. The story is told of a father who had one son. He was the apple of his eye. The father was a collector of art, and when his son was old enough, he took him around the world to teach him how to collect the finest paintings at the best price. Over the years this man's house became quite a museum of fine art, from Picasso to Raphael.

One day his son responded to the call of his country to go to war. The father kissed the son and proudly, though reluctantly, sent him off to the conflict. He received word a few weeks later that his son had been killed in battle saving the life of another man. Stricken with grief, the man would not leave the house.

Some weeks later a soldier appeared at his door with a large wrapped package under his arm. The soldier said, "Sir, you don't know me, but I am the soldier for whom your son gave his life. He saved many lives that day, and he was carrying me to safety when a bullet struck him in the heart, and he died instantly. He often talked about you and your love for art."

He did not know how to say thank you to the father, but he knew he loved paintings. The soldier was not a painter, but he had tried his hand at painting a picture of the beloved son. The father took the wrapping off the portrait and wept as he saw his son. It was not a good painting, but it had a good resemblance. The soldier had captured the personality of the son in the painting.

The father thanked the man for the painting and offered to pay. The soldier replied, "Oh no, sir, I could never repay what your son did for me. This is a gift."

The father placed the portrait upon the mantel and looked at it every day. As the man became older, dealers in the area began to makes plans for the day he would auction off all his paintings. Soon the day came that the man died, and the date of the auction was set.

The auctioneer began by holding up the painting of the man's son. "We will start the bidding with this picture of his son. Who will bid for this picture?" There was silence.

The buyers complained, "Forget about that amateur portrait — let's get to the good stuff. We're here for the famous paintings."

The auctioneer said that it was in the will of the father that this painting should go first. He insisted, "What am I bid for this painting of the son? One hundred dollars? Two hundred dollars?" No one offered a bid.

"We want the treasures," they complained. "Give us the treasures. We want to bid on the true works of art. Give us van Gogh and Rembrandt. Get on with the real bids."

An old man in the back of the room had been the gardener of the father and the son. So he raised his hand and bid ten dollars.

"Is there another bid?" asked the auctioneer. Hearing no one he said, "Going once, going twice, sold for ten dollars." He banged the gavel and announced that the auction was over.

All the art dealers began protesting loudly. "How can you say the auction is over when we haven't had a chance to bid on the good paintings? Let's start bidding on the treasures."

The auctioneer announced with a smile, "It was in the will of the father that he who gets the son, gets it all."

7

Family Sedans of
the Faith

DANIEL 6:1-28

M ax Lucado tells of an extraordinary pitcher who performed few extraordinary feats.

Though a veteran of 21 seasons, in only one did he win more than twenty games. He never pitched a no-hitter and only once in his career did he lead the league in any category. In 1980 he led the National League with a 2.21 earned run average. Yet on June 21, 1986, pitcher Don Sutton rubbed shoulders with the true legends of baseball pitchers when he became only the 30th pitcher in baseball to win 300 games.

His own analysis of his success is worth noting. "I am a grinder and a mechanic. I never considered myself flamboyant or exceptional. But all my life I've found a way to get the job done." And get it done he did. Through two decades, six presidential terms, four trades, he consistently did what pitchers are paid to do: win. With tunnel vision, he spent 21 seasons redefining greatness and many of you never heard of his name.

In September 1986 *Inside Sports Magazine* called him the "family sedan" of baseball's men on the mound. He certainly boasted none of the Ferrari style of the last thirty game winner, Denny McClain, who rose to stardom but faded quickly. He boasted none of the Mercedes sparkle of a Sandy Koufax, but after their types were parked in museums or junk piles, Don Sutton was still on the mound "getting the job done."[1]

The Bible has its share of "family sedans," and Daniel certainly is one of them. Rather than strive to be spectacular, he aspired to be faithful and dependable. Daniel had been faithfully serving the Lord in pagan Babylon for nearly seventy years. He was now about eighty-five years old. And what did he have to show for it? Almost nothing. The people of Babylon remained unchanged. Kingdoms had come and gone, but the rulers were still idolatrous, wicked, and cruel.

Even God's chosen people remained in captivity despite Daniel's frequent promotions to positions of power. Think of how frustrating it must have been for him year after year to be able to do nothing to set his people free as Moses had. Not only that, but the spiritual condition of the people of Israel was not much better. When the new king, Cyrus, finally did allow the people to go back to Israel, most of them stayed since they were caught up in the Babylonian lifestyle. Those who returned to Jerusalem started rebuilding the temple, but after two years they lost sight of their priorities, stopped the work, and settled down in their own paneled houses rather than finish God's house.

No revival swept through the captive nation as a result of Daniel's ministry, no national repentance in Babylon like Jonah saw in Nineveh. Few people seemed to learn anything from Daniel. For all his wisdom, integrity, and faithfulness, Daniel reaped the jealousy of peers, the hatred of the ungodly, a plot against his life, and a death sentence in a lions' den. But he was one of those "family sedans" that does not need to make a big splash but just wants to prove faithful to what he saw as a faithful God.

Since God is faithful, we too must conduct our lives faithfully. We will see in this chapter that we are called to handle our affairs faithfully and our prayers faithfully. Then we will see how God handled Daniel's attempted slayers faithfully — affairs, prayers, and slayers.

WE MUST HANDLE OUR AFFAIRS FAITHFULLY (6:1-4)

According to Daniel 5:31, Darius the Mede was sixty-two when he conquered Babylon (in 539 B.C.). This conqueror was the ruler of the Medo-Persian empire, located in modern-day Iran. The name *Iran* means "the land of the Aryans." These Aryan-speaking people settled on the highland around 1500 B.C. The two Aryan tribes that attained the greatest importance were the Medes and the Persians. The Medes dominated the Persians until Cyrus the Great conquered the Medes around 559 B.C. He gave the Medes and the Persians equal power so that foreigners spoke of either the Persians and the Medes (Esther 1:19) or "the Medes and Persians" (Daniel 5:28). We know from history that Cyrus the Great conquered Babylon in 539 B.C.[2] So who is Darius the Mede? Most likely Darius was the conqueror's name among the Medes and Cyrus his name among the Persians. We could translate Daniel 6:28, "So Daniel prospered during the reign of Darius — that is, the reign of Cyrus the Persian."[3]

Darius — Cyrus — appointed 120 satraps with three administrators over them. Daniel was one of the three administrators. At the time he was probably about eighty-five years old and not yet ready to retire. Daniel so distinguished himself above the other two administrators that King Darius planned to place him as number two over the entire kingdom. This happened because Daniel handled his affairs faithfully.

Daniel Was Not Corrupt (6:4a)

At this, the administrators and the satraps tried to find ground for charges against Daniel in his conduct of government affairs, but they were unable to do so. They could find no corruption in him.

Today there is much corruption in government. Lord Acton well said, "Power corrupts, and absolute power corrupts absolutely." Corruption is prevalent among government officials. Here is a list of the corruption found among members of the 100th U.S. Congress:[4]

29 arrested for spousal abuse;
7 convicted of fraud;
19 arrested for writing bad checks;
117 bankrupted two or more businesses;
14 arrested on drug charges;
8 arrested on shoplifting charges;
21 with lawsuits against them;
84 charged with driving while intoxicated.

But when King Darius made it known that he was going to place Daniel over the whole kingdom, "the administrators and the satraps tried to find grounds for charges against him in his conduct of government affairs, but they were unable to do so. They could find no corruption in him" (6:4a). Daniel was a government official who distinguished himself because "no corruption" was found in him.

Daniel Was Not Negligent (6:4b)

"They could find no corruption in him, because he was trustworthy and neither corrupt nor negligent."

When I was twelve, I delivered advertisement circulars for a grocery store. Several of us worked routes in different parts of our small town. We would pick up the circulars on Monday after school, and they were to be delivered by Wednesday afternoon for the advertised sales available Thursday through Saturday. We were paid one penny for each circular, and

I delivered a hundred. Several times I was rather negligent and didn't get them passed out until Thursday. One of the brothers who owned the store would reprimand me for my negligence and tell me to do better next time. Then he would give me my new crisp dollar.

Sadly, I took their graciousness for granted. One time I was so negligent, I had not delivered them by Friday night. I decided it was too late; so I threw them away. I went to collect my dollar anyway. Before he gave me the dollar, he gave me a list of people on my route who had called to complain that they had not received a circular. Then he asked me if I had delivered the product. I was caught in my corruption and negligence. I learned a painful lesson in work ethics that humiliating day — a lesson that has shaped my work practices since then. I also learned a lesson in mercy, for the owner did not fire me but gave me another chance.

When Daniel was given a job to do, the king knew it would be done thoroughly with excellence, and nothing would be left undone. The king did not have to look over his shoulder all the time or worry about whether the job would be done. Daniel was as trustworthy as a family sedan. There was no neglect, no corruption. What do people say about you on the job? By God's grace let us handle our affairs faithfully.

WE MUST HANDLE OUR PRAYERS FAITHFULLY (6:5-11)

One can almost feel the jealousy that developed among the other two vice presidents and the 120 satraps when Daniel was elevated to second in charge. Their anger burned, to put it mildly. Their anger intensified when they realized that they could not see one skeleton in his closet or find one fault in this man to accuse him of in order to have him removed from office. So they began their fiendish plot.

They knew Daniel was faithful to his God. The only way they could discredit or destroy him was to force King Darius to issue a decree that would be diametrically opposed to one of the laws of the God of Israel. "We will never find any basis for charges against this man Daniel unless it has something to do with the law of his God" (6:5). So these scheming men came before King Darius and began to play on his pride.

> O King Darius, live forever! The royal administrators, prefects, satraps, advisers and governors have all agreed that the king should issue an edict and enforce the decree that anyone who prays to any god or man during the next thirty days, except to you, O king, shall be thrown into the lions' den. Now, O king, issue the decree and put it in writing so that it cannot be altered — in accordance with the laws of the Medes and the Persians, which cannot be repealed. (6:6b-8)

They could not pray to any god or man? Who would pray to a man? I saw an article recently that said more and more physicians are beginning to believe that relaxing techniques, meditation, and prayer might help the healing process. These physicians group prayer with meditation because many do not think we really pray to an omnipotent God who can actually do anything. For all practical purposes, they would think that you might as well be praying to yourself.

We are sometimes tempted to pray to men. We are not content to let God hear and answer prayers. Instead we try to get our message to men in prayer. The story is told of a little boy who was saying his bedtime prayers. He asked Jesus to bless his mommy, daddy, and little sister. He asked Jesus to help him in school the next day. Then he closed his prayer with a loud voice, asking Jesus to get him a new bicycle. When his mother asked why he said the last part of his prayer so loudly, he answered, "I wanted to be sure Daddy heard me." Do you sometimes send messages to people in prayer? A person in one of my staff meetings corrected my staff devotional in his prayer. Our understanding of the purpose of prayer is not always much better than the administrators of the pagan Persian Empire.

By now these men had Darius in the palm of their hand. "So King Darius put the decree in writing" (6:9). Did Daniel stop praying? No, he did not. We know because he ended up in the lions' den. But did he get thrown in the lions' den because he was unaware of the king's decree? Daniel 6:10 says, "Now when Daniel learned that the decree had been published, he went home to his upstairs room where the windows opened toward Jerusalem. Three times a day he got down on his knees and prayed, giving thanks to his God, *just as he had done before*" (emphasis added).

When he learned about the decree, he headed for one of the most prominent, visible locations in the city. He opened the windows for everyone to see, got down on his knees, and prayed. For Daniel, a man faithful in prayer, the family sedan of prayer life, nothing, absolutely nothing, was able to keep him from his time of prayer — not even a death sentence attached to an irrevocable decree!

Think of the lame excuses that stop us from a faithful, consistent prayer life. We have to get our work done, we need more sleep, or we are too busy. I saw a sign over the desk of a retirement center chaplain that read, "If you are too busy to pray, then you are too busy."

There are "family sedans" of prayer in the church I pastor [Twin Oaks Presbyterian Church, St. Louis]. People who do not make a big splash but are faithful week in and week out, praying for years. A faithful group of women in our church meets every Monday afternoon to pray for the congregation and its ministries. A faithful group of about thirty people meets for an hour on the second Sunday of each month before the evening worship to pray for revival. A faithful group of men and women meets on Wednesday evenings from 6:30-7:15 to pray for the missionaries, the pastors, the ministries, the sick, and other needs of the congregation. These groups are nothing splashy, no great attractions, no big names, just the faithful "family sedans" of the church doing what Daniel did because it is the most important thing we can do.

I was convicted in my own heart of my lack of a disciplined prayer life while I was in the hospital for surgery some years ago. It is so easy to let the urgent things of life crowd the important things out of one's life. A woman in our congregation introduced me to a tool for an effective, organized prayer life, *Memos to God* by E. M. Bounds. This notebook has helped me greatly, increasing my appreciation for prayer through the daily meditations of E. M. Bounds and improving my discipline of prayer through organization. I know what my excuses have been. What are your excuses? They had better be good, because one day at the final judgment you might be standing right next to Daniel. Let us look at his prayer.

Daniel Prayed in Faith Toward Jerusalem (6:10a)

Now when Daniel learned that the decree had been published, he went home to his upstairs room where the windows opened toward Jerusalem.

Was Daniel superstitious? Was Jerusalem to the Jews what Mecca is to the Muslims? The Muslims always bow and pray toward Mecca so their prayers will be answered. Or maybe Daniel thought God was in Jerusalem? Of course not. Then why did Daniel pray toward Jerusalem?

This was not the first time Daniel prayed in this way. We find in verse 10 that he prayed "as he had done before." As you will see in Daniel 9, one of the things that he was praying for was the restoration of Jerusalem. At the end of that prayer, God gave him eyes of faith to see the future of Jerusalem when it would be restored and when a Savior would come to that city to save his people from their sins. Daniel opened the windows of prayer out of faithfulness, but it was in faith that Daniel prayed, believing that God would do an incredible work in the future.

In 1940 Vincent and Margaret Crossett were missionaries in Mainland China. They struggled against poverty and paganism in a remote village in order to tell others about Jesus. The work was very slow and difficult, but after much sacrifice a small church was established. The church was no larger than a small Bible study group. Right on the threshold of this small triumph for the kingdom of God, Satan began his work. The Communist takeover of China during the Cultural Revolution forced all missionaries to leave China.

The Crossetts hated to leave. Their fledgling flock of believers hardly seemed ready to withstand the coming onslaught. An atheistic, dictatorial government dedicated to wiping out all Christian influence was beginning its rule with ruthless power. How could the little church survive? From the world's perspective there was nothing anyone could do. The church seemed destined to die. But Vincent and Margaret did not see through the world's eyes. They saw through the eyes of faith that their God was faithful to those who honor him. The Crossetts were like faithful family sedans. They continued to do their duty. Though the missionaries were chased out, their prayers were not. For nearly forty years the Crosetts daily kept their prayer window opened toward China. They dutifully prayed in faith that God would one day triumph over Communism. The Crosetts heard nothing of their Chinese friends for forty years, but still they faithfully prayed for God to be victorious in the church they had left behind.

Finally the walls of China came down. As the political climate changed, the nation was opened to western visitors. The Crossetts returned to the village where they had left the tiny, struggling group of believers. There was no small church in the village anymore! Instead, from that Bible study had grown a church of four thousand people! This body of believers had planted dozens of other churches as well, each with a membership of at least a thousand. All the Crossetts did was pray with their prayer window open to the focus of their prayer — China. The God of Daniel is alive and well.

Daniel Prayed in Faith Toward God (6:11)

"Then these men went as a group and found Daniel praying and asking God for help."

Daniel was not meditating. He was not praying to men. He was asking God for help. Prayer includes asking God for help.

When I was diagnosed with liver cancer in the fall of 1999, our church's visitation pastor, Bud Moginot, gave me Paul's words in 2 Corinthians 1:9-11. These were powerful and encouraging words for me as we looked to the Lord for deliverance from this dreaded disease. When the doctor tells you on the phone that you have a malignant tumor growing in your liver, you feel helpless. Indeed, you feel the sentence of death. These are the words that lifted my spirit:

> *Indeed, in our hearts we felt the sentence of death. But this happened that we might not rely on ourselves but on God, who raises the dead. He has delivered us from such a deadly peril, and he will deliver us. On him we have set our hope that he will continue to deliver us, as you help us by your prayers. Then many will give thanks on our behalf for the gracious favor granted us in answer to the prayers of many.*

In answer to the prayers of God's people, I was able to recover quickly from my surgery and get back to work at the church. I was able to preach and carry on most of my other duties during the six weeks of radiation and chemotherapy. By God's grace in answer to the prayers of God's people, the side effects were minimal. Yes, God does help us through the prayers of God's people, but there are some important stipulations we need to remember.

Daniel Was Righteous Before God (6:12-22)

> So they went to the king and spoke to him about his royal decree: "Did you not publish a decree that during the next thirty days anyone who prays to any god or man except to you, O king, would be thrown into the lions' den?" The king answered, "The decree stands — in accordance with the laws of the Medes and Persians, which cannot be repealed." Then they said to the king, "Daniel, who is one of the exiles from Judah, pays no attention to you, O king, or to the decree you put in writing. He still prays three times a day." When the king heard this, he was greatly distressed; he was determined to rescue Daniel and made every effort until sundown to save him. Then the men went as a group to the king and said to him, "Remember, O king, that according to the law of the Medes and Persians no decree or edict that the king issues can be changed."
>
> So the king gave the order, and they brought Daniel and threw him into the lions' den. The king said to Daniel, "May your God, whom you serve continually, rescue you!" A stone was brought and placed over the mouth of the den, and the king sealed it with his own signet ring and with the rings of his nobles, so that Daniel's situation might not be changed. Then the king returned to his palace and spent the night without eating and without any entertainment being brought to him. And he could not sleep.
>
> At the first light of dawn, the king got up and hurried to the lions' den. When he came near the den, he called to Daniel in an anguished voice, "Daniel, servant of the living God, has your God, whom you serve continually, been able to rescue you from the lions?" Daniel answered, "O king, live forever! My God sent his angel, and he shut the mouths of the lions. They have not hurt me, because I was found innocent in his sight. Nor have I ever done any wrong before you, O king."

The Lord honored Daniel's righteous life by answering prayer. James wrote, "Therefore confess your sins to each other and pray for each other so that you may be healed. The prayer of a righteous man is powerful and effective" (James 5:16). King David wrote, "If I had cherished sin in my heart, the Lord would not have listened" (Psalm 66:18). And Peter wrote, "Husbands, in the same way be considerate as you live with your wives, and treat them with respect as the weaker partner and as heirs with you of the gracious gift of life, so that nothing will hinder your prayers" (1 Peter 3:7).

We know that our righteous acts cannot save us. We are justified through faith alone in the atoning work of Jesus Christ when the perfect righteousness of Christ is imputed to us. God then declares us righteous in his sight.

This righteousness from God comes through faith in Jesus Christ to all who believe. There is no difference, for all have sinned and fall short of the glory of God, and are justified freely by his grace through the redemption that came by Christ Jesus. (Romans 3:22-24)

Nevertheless, after we have been declared righteous in God's sight, we are called to live a righteous life in Christ. John wrote, "Dear children, do not let anyone lead you astray. He who does what is right is righteous, just as he is righteous. . . . Anyone who does not do what is right is not a child of God" (1 John 3:7, 10).

If we cherish sin in our heart, meaning that we delight in it and refuse for a time to repent of it, our prayer life will be negatively impacted. Even not respecting our wives can hinder our prayers. We need to confess our sins and repent of our sins.

And we should never get the impression that our righteous living makes God owe us anything. Righteousness is not rewarded with answered prayer. We cannot make demands on God according to our righteousness. Daniel prayed, "We do not make requests of you because we are righteous, but because of your great mercy" (Daniel 9:18). Any answer to prayer is certainly undeserved favor, but sin that is unconfessed does hinder our prayers.

Daniel Was Trusting in God (6:23)

The king was overjoyed and gave orders to lift Daniel out of the den. And when Daniel was lifted from the den, no wound was found on him, because he had trusted in his God.

Prayer unleashes the power of God to do his will, but we must believe he will do amazing things. "Now to him who is able to do immeasurably more than all we ask or imagine, according to his power that is at work within us . . ." (Ephesians 3:20). Jesus said to his disciples:

Have faith in God. I tell you the truth, if anyone says to this mountain, "Go, throw yourself into the sea," and does not doubt in his heart but believes that what he says will happen, it will be done for him. Therefore I tell you, whatever you ask for in prayer, believe that you have received it, and it will be yours. (Mark 11:22-24)

Faith is not a coin that you put into a vending machine, so that if you put in enough you will get what you want from God. Faith is the empty hand of a beggar reaching out to receive the gift of a king. Faith is a basic trust that God does hear and answer prayer.

In the same way that sin hinders our prayers, Jesus said that doubt hinders them too. So what can we do when we doubt? A father of a demon-possessed boy came to Jesus asking, "If you can do anything, take pity on us and help us." Jesus responded, "'If you can'? Everything is possible for him who believes." The boy's father exclaimed, "I do believe; help me overcome my unbelief" (Mark 9:22-24). Admitting his struggle with doubt was all God was looking for, and the man's son was delivered from the demon.

God's people who, by his grace, walk righteously before him and have a simple childlike faith are the "family sedans" of prayer. The Church needs more "family sedans" who will devote as much time and energy praying for the members and ministries of their church as they do planning and talking about them in the church business meetings.

Daniel was a "family sedan," faithful in his affairs of government and faithful in his prayers. But Daniel's success was not a result of his faithfulness to God, but God's faithfulness to him.

GOD HANDLED DANIEL'S SLAYERS FAITHFULLY (6:12-18)

Daniel was thrown into the lions' den because of unfair accusation and an unjust edict. How could God do this to such a faithful child of his? It seems so unfair. But the Lord works his plan so that the nations will glorify him. In the end he does bring justice to every situation, either in this life or the one to come.

Death for the False Accusation (6:24)

> At the king's command, the men who had falsely accused Daniel were brought in and thrown into the lions' den, along with their wives and children. And before they reached the floor of the den, the lions overpowered them and crushed all their bones.

Some are bothered by the fact that the women and children were also thrown into the lions' den to be killed. They conclude that this was done because the wicked Persians practiced such injustice. Some conclude that God would never do that. That is not true. This is what we read in 1 Samuel 15:2, 3, the Lord's command to King Saul:

> This is what the LORD Almighty says, . . . "Now go attack the Amalekites and totally destroy everything that belongs to them. Do not spare them;

put to death men and women, children and infants, cattle and sheep, camels and donkeys."

How could God justly do this? First of all, the Lord usually operates on the principle of federal headship. Adam sinned, and as a result we sinned in him and are made liable to death, even infants who did not willfully break a commandment like Adam did. Listen to what Paul writes in Romans 5:12-14:

> *Therefore, just as sin entered the world through one man, and death through sin, and in this way death came to all men, because all sinned — for before the law was given, sin was in the world. But sin is not taken into account when there is no law. Nevertheless, death reigned from the time of Adam to the time of Moses, even over those who did not sin by breaking a command, as did Adam, who was a pattern of the one to come.*

It should not then surprise us when the whole family is punished for the sins of the fathers. In addition to that, God is just because the wages of sin is death. All involved in the account of Saul or Daniel were sinners and therefore liable to the death penalty at the hand of God.

Though it will not always mean death for those who treat you wrongly, God will bring justice in his time and in his way. Jesus said in Luke 18:7, 8, "Will not God bring about justice for his chosen ones, who cry out to him day and night? Will he keep putting them off? I tell you, he will see that they get justice, and quickly."

New Life for True Affirmation (6:25-28)

> *Then King Darius wrote to all the peoples, nations and men of every language throughout the land: "May you prosper greatly! I issue a decree that in every part of my kingdom people must fear and reverence the God of Daniel. For he is the living God and he endures forever; his kingdom will not be destroyed, his dominion will never end. He rescues and he saves; he performs signs and wonders in the heavens and on the earth. He has rescued Daniel from the power of the lions." So Daniel prospered during the reign of Darius — that is, the reign of Cyrus the Persian [literal translation].*

Through the faithful testimony of Daniel, the "family sedan," and this incredible miracle, King Cyrus came to trust in the Lord and received new life in Christ. This is the man that God spoke of in Isaiah 45:1-3, 150 years before he was born.

> *This is what the LORD says to his anointed,*
>   *to Cyrus, whose right hand I take hold of*
> *to subdue nations before him*
>   *and to strip kings of their armor,*
> *to open doors before him*
>   *so that gates will not be shut:*
> *I will go before you . . .*
> *so that you may know that I am the LORD,*
>   *the God of Israel, who summons you by name.*

A life of faithfulness would be worth it, even if just one or two people came to Christ because they saw Jesus in you. No, Daniel did not make a big splash in Babylon. There was no huge revival among the Jews while they were in Babylon. There was no national repentance in Babylon like Jonah saw in Nineveh. Just two people that we know of, two kings, came to trust in the true and living God. But as Paul writes to the Thessalonians, "For what is our hope, our joy, or the crown in which we will glory in the presence of our Lord Jesus when he comes? Is it not you? Indeed, you are our glory and joy" (1 Thessalonians 2:19, 20).

God just calls us to be reliable, like a family sedan. *Liable* means to be responsible. *Re* means over and over again. Some of you are like Daniel, "family sedans" of reliability. You are models and examples for others. I want to say two things to you. First, thank you for your faithfulness in the little things as well as in the big.

Thank you, senior saints, for a generation of prayer and forest clearing. Thank you, teachers, for the countless Sunday school lessons and Bible study lectures prepared and delivered. Thank you, evangelism workers, who faithfully and quietly go out again and again and share your faith. Thank you, deacons, for your tireless efforts in worship and the care of the church. Thank you, elders, for shepherding and praying for the flock. Thank you, choir members and nursery workers, who show up Sunday after Sunday.

Thanks to all who practice on Monday what you hear on the Lord's Day. You spend selfless hours with hurting people, in meetings, on your knees, away from family. Thank you for being the "family sedans" of the kingdom. "You can be called on cold mornings and you'll deliver the goods. You can be sent over rough terrain and you'll make it on time. You can go miles without the pampering of a good polish or the luxury of a tune-up and you never complain. You get the job done."[5]

I said I had two things to say. What is the second? Keep pitching. Your Hall of Fame reward is just around the corner, and Daniel will be standing right next to you.

8

What Is the Meaning of All This?

DANIEL 7:1-16

Many people love the book of Daniel, but few venture into these last six chapters. In Sunday school we learned the stories of Daniel in the lions' den, the handwriting on the wall, as well as Shadrach, Meshach, and Abednego being thrown into the blazing furnace. But how many Sunday school classes even ventured across the line of chapter 6 into the dark mysteries of Daniel 7 — 12? I would venture to say that most Christians could not tell you what is contained in chapters 7 — 12 of the book of Daniel. I was encouraged that the community Bible study that meets in the church I pastor studied the entire book of Daniel.

Some people do not study the prophecies of Daniel 7 — 12 because they are convinced they will never be able to understand them. They have the opinion that if scholars cannot agree on the interpretation of these chapters, they will not be able to understand the true meaning.

Other people do not study these chapters because they think the prophecies are too frightening. I was reading an excerpt from a book by Kathleen Norris in *U.S. News & World Report*. In her book *Amazing Grace: A Vocabulary of Faith*, she wrote, "Preparing a sermon for a large Methodist Church on some of the Bible's more frightening apocalyptic texts like those in Daniel 7-12, I had to consider that many of the people in church that morning would find the readings hard to take."[1] Should preachers not preach on a portion of God's Word because it is hard to take or hard to understand? Listen, if these prophecies trouble you or disturb you, you are in good company. Daniel 7:15 says, "I, Daniel, was troubled in spirit, and the visions that passed through my mind disturbed me."

Some people's approach to apocalyptic literature — that is, predictive prophecy — is all too often like that of Daniel in 7:28: "I, Daniel, was deeply troubled by my thoughts, and my face turned pale, but I kept the matter to myself." Kathleen Norris continued in her article, "So I decided not to look at the prophecies, but to talk about what apocalyptic literature is and is not."[2] Like so many, she kept the matter to herself, afraid to open up the text of Daniel and let the people try to understand it.

So how does one find out the true meaning of these prophecies? First, put away your fear, and ask somebody like Daniel did. Daniel 7:16 says, "I approached one of those standing there and asked him the *true meaning of all this.* So he told me and gave me the interpretation of these things" (emphasis added). He was asking an angel, but we do not know any angels. At least I do not. So who can we ask? We need to ask the Lord himself as we meditate on his Word. In 2 Timothy 2:7 Paul says, "Reflect on what I am saying, for the Lord will give you insight into all this."

The key to uncovering "the true meaning of all this" is first to study the text, then study the context, and finally to go to the new text, which we call the New Testament. When you study the prophecies using this method, you will find that those passages that seemed like dark mysteries will begin to become very clear. In fact, they will become so clear that one begins to get very excited about studying more and more prophecies to see all that God tells us will take place. As the Apostle Peter wrote in 2 Peter 1:19, "We have the word of the prophets made more certain, and you will do well to pay attention to it, as to a light shining in a dark place, until the day dawns and the morning star rises in your hearts." If God took so many precious pages of Scripture to reveal the future to us, he must think it is very important for us to know. So why don't we? Ignorance of the future is not bliss.

TO UNDERSTAND THE TRUE MEANING OF ALL THIS, WE MUST STUDY THE TEXT

The text of Daniel 7 describes a vision that Daniel had in the first year of the reign of Belshazzar. You may remember that Belshazzar became co-regent with his father in 553 B.C., just two years before his father Nabonidus or Nebuchadnezzar III became incapacitated for seven years. We saw in Daniel 4 that God turned Nabonidus into a wild animal with hair like the feathers of an eagle and claws like those of a bird, and he ate grass like cattle.

Verses 2, 3 of Daniel 7 says, "In my vision at night I looked, and there before me were the four winds of heaven churning up the great sea. Four great beasts, each different from the others, came up out of the sea." That is what the text says, but what does it mean? The place to begin is to see if the text explains the meaning, and it does in verse 17: "The four great beasts

are four kingdoms that will rise from the earth." You can use some sanctified imagination to see the picture of the imagery of the prophecy. God in
Heaven is the one who in his sovereignty moves and stirs the peoples of the
world, raising up kingdoms from among all the people on earth. But what are
these four kingdoms, and why are they important?

TO UNDERSTAND THE TRUE MEANING OF ALL THIS, WE MUST STUDY THE CONTEXT

We will answer that question by studying the parallel of Daniel 7, which is
found in chapter 2. Remember, King Nebuchadnezzar had a dream in which
he saw a great statue made out of four different kinds of material. Each of
these four materials represented a different nation. As we review these four
kingdoms, we will compare them to their parallel in Daniel 7. You will see
that it is not the similarities but the *differences* between chapters 2 and 7
that are most important in helping us interpret this text. God reveals to
Daniel, and to all who will read his words in chapter 7, detailed predictions
of the future. Contrary to the opinion of some, that is a large part of what
predictive prophecy is. It is interesting to note that Kathleen Norris wrote,
"Apocalyptic literature *is not detailed predictions of the future*."[3] It is hard for
me to understand how people could study Daniel 2 and 7 and conclude that
prophecy is not history written in advance. Seeing how these symbolic
prophecies are fulfilled will help us know how to interpret the symbolic
prophecies of the Second Coming of Christ.

Consider the following chart that compares and contrasts Daniel 2 and
7. Note the detailed predictions as we walk through these verses. First, the
head of gold on the statue was Babylon. In Daniel 2:38 the prophet told
Nebuchadnezzar, "You are that head of gold." This parallels Daniel 7:4: "The
first was like a lion, and it had the wings of an eagle. I watched until its wings
were torn off and it was lifted from the ground so that it stood on two feet like
a man, and the heart of a man was given to it."

DANIEL 2		DANIEL 7	
Head of gold	BABYLON (626–539 B.C.)	Lion	(v. 4)
Chest of silver	MEDES/PERSIANS (539–330 B.C.)	Bear	(v. 5)
Thighs of bronze	GREECE (330–63 B.C.)	Leopard	(v. 6)
Legs of iron	ROME (63 B.C.–430 A.D.)		
	(The kingdom of God comes initially.)		
	ANTICHRIST	Terrifying Beast	(vv. 7-28)
	(The kingdom of God comes in fullness.)		

This first beast is Babylon too. In much of ancient literature, Babylon's
symbol is a lion with eagle's wings. The Ishtar Gate gave access to the city's
processional street whose walls were lined with enameled lions.[4] This

prophecy in Daniel 7 also includes a detailed prediction of what would happen to Nabonidus, the reigning king, two years after this was written. He whose hair became like the feathers of an eagle would have his wings torn off for a time, but then the Lord would stand him on his feet like a man and give the heart of a man to him.

The next kingdom in the statue of Daniel 2 was the chest and arms of silver. That stood for the Medo-Persian empire, which conquered Babylon in 539 B.C., under the reign of Cyrus. Daniel 7:5 says, "And there before me was a second beast, which looked like a bear. It was raised up on one of its sides, and it had three ribs in its mouth between its teeth. It was told, 'Get up and eat your fill of flesh!'" It is important to note the details of predictive prophecy. The bear, raised up on one of its sides, is a picture showing that the Persian Empire soon became dominant over the Medes. The three ribs the bear has in its mouth pictures the three major kingdoms conquered by the Medo-Persian empire. They were Lydia (546), Babylon (539), and Egypt (525).[5] Now, it is important to realize that when Daniel wrote these words, he would not have known why the bear was raised up on one side and why he had three ribs in his mouth. I like how 1 Peter 1:10-12 describes the Old Testament prophets' thoughts:

Concerning this salvation, the prophets, who spoke of the grace that was to come to you, searched intently and with the greatest care, trying to find out the time and circumstances to which the Spirit of Christ in them was pointing when he predicted the sufferings of Christ and the glories that would follow. It was revealed to them that they were not serving themselves, but you.

We only know because we can study history and observe how the prophecies were fulfilled.

We need to remember two important things about predictive prophecy as we study Daniel 7 — 12. First, prophecy does give us important details about the future that God says we need to know in advance, so when they occur we are ready. God wanted Israel to understand something about the Medo-Persian Empire, so the people would know for certain who was in control of human history. Persia would become stronger than the Medes and would conquer three major kingdoms.

The second thing we need to understand is that we should never speculate as to how prophecies yet future to us might be fulfilled. Can you imagine Daniel trying to speculate what the bear raised up on its side with three ribs in his mouth meant? He could never have guessed; and if he tried to speculate, he might throw people off track because they would get the speculations in their mind and miss the real fulfillment.

For example, John tells us in Revelation 13:18 that the number of the Antichrist, or the Beast, will be 666. Some have said that means the Antichrist will have three names, and each name will have six letters in each name. (I remember hearing that Ronald Wilson Reagan might fit the bill.) But the prophecy doesn't say that 666 means three names with six letters each; so we might miss the real person if we are looking for the wrong thing. We should just know what to look for, and it will be clear when it happens.

The third empire in the statue of Daniel 2 was described as the belly and thighs of bronze. That empire was Greece. Daniel 7 adds a little more detail that we can understand because it has already taken place. Daniel 7:6 says, "After that, I looked, and there before me was another beast, one that looked like a leopard. And on its back it had four wings like those of a bird. This beast had four heads, and it was given authority to rule." Note again the incredible detail. The wings on the back of the leopard point to swiftness, a perfectly accurate characterization of Alexander the Great. He overthrew the rule of Persia and conquered all the kingdoms of the known world in twelve years (336-324 B.C.). His kingdom included the entire eastern Mediterranean world in the west and extended as far as India in the east. According to Plutarch, when Alexander conquered Persia, it took ten thousand pairs of mules and five thousand camels to carry away the booty. In 324 B.C. the youthful conqueror of the world returned and visited the tomb of Cyrus the Great at Pasargadae. Alexander died a year later at the age of thirty-three trying to rebuild Babylon, which God said, through the prophet Jeremiah, would never be rebuilt.

"Before your eyes I will repay Babylon and all who live in Babylonia for all the wrong they have done in Zion," declares the LORD.

> *"I am against you, O destroying mountain,*
> *you who destroy the whole earth,"*
> *declares the LORD.*
> *"I will stretch out my hand against you,*
> *roll you off the cliffs,*
> *and make you a burned-out mountain.*
> *No rock will be taken from you for a cornerstone,*
> *nor any stone for a foundation,*
> *for you will be desolate forever,"*
> *declares the LORD. (Jeremiah 51:24-26)*

In the late 1980s, Saddam Hussein, then the dictator of Iraq, tried to rebuild Babylon. He was working on the palace when Operation Desert Storm broke out. God raised up five hundred thousand troops from the nations of the world to stop this man's invasion of Kuwait. In the bombing raids that followed, the allies destroyed everything in Babylon that he had built, and it remains desolate to this very day.

Alexander's kingdom was divided among his four generals, hence the four heads of the leopard. The generals were known as the *Diadochi* or the "successors." In Egypt, Ptolemy I ruled. In the eastern provinces, the general was Seleucus I. In Macedonia and Greece, Antipater and Cassander took power. And in Thrace and Asia Minor, Lysimachus became the general.[6]

Ultimately just two of these kingdoms remained strong, and they battled each other for almost two centuries. Some of the details of their battles were told in advance in the prophecies found in Daniel 11. In fact, the prophecy is so clear that some people think a scribe using the name of Daniel must have written it in the second century before Christ.

The fourth and final kingdom of Daniel 2 was a kingdom made of iron with feet of clay. We saw earlier in this book that the kingdom of iron and clay was Rome. Daniel spoke of Babylon, Persia, Greece, and Rome. Why weren't any more kingdoms mentioned? Why did he stop there? I think there are two reasons for this.

First, Rome was the last empire to rule the whole known world. Listen to the words of Daniel 2:39-43:

> *After you, another kingdom will rise, inferior to yours. Next, a third kingdom, one of bronze, will rule over the whole earth. Finally, there will be a fourth kingdom, strong as iron — for iron breaks and smashes everything —* and as iron breaks things to pieces, so *it* will crush and break all the others. *Just as you saw that the feet and toes were partly of baked clay and partly of iron, so this will be a divided kingdom; yet it will have some of the strength of iron in it, even as you saw iron mixed with clay. As the toes were partly iron and partly clay, so this kingdom will be partly strong and partly brittle. And just as you saw the iron mixed with baked clay, so the people will be a mixture and will not remain united, any more than iron mixes with clay. (emphasis added)*

Rome was a strong world empire, strong as iron, that smashed everything, but it had internal weaknesses, feet of clay, due to the mixtures of people that eventually spelled Rome's doom. Rome was later invaded by the barbarians and fell in A.D. 476. Never again were there nations like Babylon, Persia, Greece, and Rome that ruled the whole civilized world.

The second and more important reason that Rome was the last kingdom mentioned is because of the main point of the vision of Daniel 2. Something very unusual, very important, and completely divine was going to occur when the fourth kingdom came on the scene.

> *In the time of those kings, the God of heaven will set up a kingdom that will never be destroyed, nor will it be left to another people. It will crush all those kingdoms and bring them to an end, but it will itself endure forever.*

This is the meaning of the vision of the rock cut out of a mountain, but not by human hands — a rock that broke the iron, the bronze, the clay, the silver and the gold to pieces. (Daniel 2:44, 45)

During the rule of Rome, the kingdom of God would come to earth in the person of the Messiah, Jesus Christ. The rock smashed those four kingdoms. Not immediately, but in time God will destroy all the kingdoms of the earth, and his kingdom alone will remain. The kingdom of God would expand according to Daniel 2:35 until it became a huge mountain that would fill the whole earth. As we know, that has taken almost two thousand years, and it is still growing worldwide. Matthew 24:14 says, "This gospel of the kingdom will be preached in the whole world . . . and then the end will come." Daniel 2 introduces the time when the kingdom of God would be inaugurated on the earth.

But the fourth kingdom of Daniel 2 is the point at which the main difference between Daniel 2 and Daniel 7 must be noted. The fourth beast of Daniel 7 is not Rome. That is very important to understand. Let me explain why I say this so emphatically.

In Daniel 2, there is one statue with a continuation of four different but related materials: gold, silver, bronze, and iron. In Daniel 7 there is an important break. The first three animals are different from each other but are related as real animals. There were lions and tigers and bears — well, lions, leopards, and bears anyway. But the fourth beast is totally, utterly unique.

Daniel 7:7 says, "After that, in my vision at night I looked, and there before me was a fourth beast — terrifying and frightening and very powerful. It had large iron teeth; it crushed and devoured its victims and trampled underfoot whatever was left. It was different from all the former beasts, and it had ten horns." This was not identified with a normal animal like a lion, leopard, or bear. It was strangely, uniquely different. You will see why in a moment.

Daniel continues in verse 8, "While I was thinking about the horns, there before me was another horn, a little one, which came up among them; and three of the first horns were uprooted before it. This horn had eyes like the eyes of a man and a mouth that spoke boastfully." Daniel 7:19 adds, "Then I wanted to know the true meaning of the fourth beast, which was different from all the others and most terrifying." Daniel did not ask that about the fourth kingdom in chapter 2; it was just another one of four kingdoms in a row. But something was strikingly different about this kingdom. Daniel did not express such frightful concern about any of the other beasts or even of the fourth part of the statue in Daniel 2. The beast of Daniel 7 is not Rome. The imagery does not fit. Daniel is told that the ten horns represent ten kings. There were not ten kings of the Roman Empire — there were over sixty.

Some believe this fourth beast is the Roman Empire revived in the last days or the Roman Catholic Church. They teach this because they think that Daniel 2 and 7 must be identical. I do not see any evidence that the kingdom spoken of in Daniel 7 is going to be a revived Roman Empire in the last days. It will be a totally new kingdom. The next and last worldwide kingdom led by a king who will rule the whole world will be the kingdom of the terrifying beast of Daniel 7, the one Paul calls the Lawless One and John calls the Antichrist and the Beast.

So why does Daniel skip the kingdom of Rome in chapter 7 and go right to the end of the age? The answer lies in putting together the pictures of chapters 2, 7, and 8 of the book of Daniel. Daniel 2 speaks of Babylon, Persia, Greece, and Rome. Daniel 8 speaks only of Persia and Greece. It purposefully skips Babylon and Rome because it is focused on what was going to happen in the future of those two kingdoms. In a similar way, Daniel 7 speaks of Babylon, Persia, and Greece but skips Rome for the purpose of that chapter. What might be that purpose?

The purpose of Daniel 2 is to show the nature of the kingdom that would be dominating the world when the kingdom of God first came to earth. Daniel 2 then ends with the kingdom of God expanding until it covers the world at the end of the age. In Daniel 7, after reviewing the first three worldwide kingdoms, we pick up on what is happening with the kingdoms of men at the time that the kingdom of God is expanding all over the whole world. That worldwide kingdom in the last days will be the kingdom of the terrifying beast, the Antichrist. In the last days God will destroy the kingdom of the Beast, and the kingdom of God will finally be handed over to the saints in all its fullness.

> As I watched, this horn was waging war against the saints and defeating them, until the Ancient of Days came and pronounced judgment in favor of the saints of the Most High, and the time came when they possessed the kingdom. . . . Then the sovereignty, power and greatness of the kingdoms under the whole heaven will be handed over to the saints, the people of the Most High. His kingdom will be an everlasting kingdom, and all rulers will worship and obey him. (7:21, 22, 27)

We will study that in detail in the next chapter. So the context of Daniel 2 helps us see that the text of Daniel 7 predicts the coming of the worldwide kingdom of the Antichrist. But what will it be like?

TO UNDERSTAND THE TRUE MEANING OF ALL THIS, WE MUST STUDY THE NEW TEXT — THAT IS, THE NEW TESTAMENT

Many details of the coming kingdom of the Antichrist are revealed in Daniel 7, but they are not all very clear. The Old Testament is like walking into a room full of furniture with the lights out. All the furniture is there, and you can feel your way around, but it is sometimes hard to see. The New Testament is like turning the light on in the room. Let me show you an example of what Daniel 7 reveals and how the New Testament clarifies it. We will look at several more in the next chapter. Daniel 7:19, 20, 23-25 says:

> *Then I wanted to know the true meaning of the fourth beast, which was different from all the others and most terrifying, with its iron teeth and bronze claws — the beast that crushed and devoured its victims and trampled underfoot whatever was left. I also wanted to know about the ten horns on its head and about the other horn that came up, before which three of them fell — the horn that looked more imposing than the others and that had eyes and a mouth that spoke boastfully. . . . He gave me this explanation: "The fourth beast is a fourth kingdom that will appear on earth. It will be different from all the other kingdoms and will devour the whole earth, trampling it down and crushing it. The ten horns are ten kings who will come from this kingdom. After them another king will arise, different from the earlier ones; he will subdue three kings. He will speak against the Most High and oppress his saints and try to change the set times and the laws. The saints will be handed over to him for a time, times and half a time."*

Note four things in the text. This world leader will speak boastfully. He will speak against the Most High God. He will have ten horns. And the saints will be handed over to him for a time, times, and half a time. That is a symbolic Hebrew expression for 1 year + 2 years + ½ year, a total of 3½ years.

Now let us compare this with the new text, Revelation 13:1-6. But first let's consider Revelation 12:17, which says, "The dragon [that is, Satan] was enraged at the woman and went off to make war against the rest of her offspring — those who obey God's commandments and hold to the testimony of Jesus." The devil's final tactical maneuver against the world, after everything else has failed, is to become incarnate like God did when he came into the world in the person of Jesus Christ. Satan will enter the world in human form in the person of the Antichrist.

Revelation 13:1 says, "And the dragon stood on the shore of the sea. And I saw a beast coming out of the sea." Remember how the four kingdoms of Daniel 7 arose out of the great sea, which represented the sea of people from the nations? Revelation 17:15 reinforces that when it says, "The waters you saw, where the prostitute sits, are peoples, multitudes, nations and languages."

Verse 1 of Revelation 13 continues, "He had ten horns and seven heads, with ten crowns on his horns, and on each head a blasphemous name." We can be confident that the beast of Daniel 7 and Revelation 13 are the same because of the ten horns. But the mention of the ten horns also tells us this

Beast is Satan incarnate, because Revelation 12:3 says the red dragon also has ten horns and seven heads. He is the same being but a different person. This is an attempt on Satan's part to imitate the Trinity.

Then verse 2 says, "The beast I saw resembled a leopard, but had feet like those of a bear and a mouth like that of a lion." It is as if this kingdom of the Antichrist is a composite of the three kingdoms of Daniel 7 — the lion, the leopard, and the bear. At least the Lord expects us to make the connection to Daniel 7. Those three animals in the two chapters are not a mere coincidence. John is telling us that both he and Daniel are speaking of the same coming, frightening kingdom. The Scripture continues:

The dragon gave the beast his power and his throne and great authority. One of the heads of the beast seemed to have had a fatal wound, but the fatal wound had been healed. The whole world was astonished and followed the beast. (Revelation 13:2, 3)

The Antichrist will attempt to be just like Jesus in that he will die and come back to life. Only he is a counterfeit, because he only "seemed to have had a fatal wound." But the world will be fooled by the counterfeit. Thinking that he really did rise from the dead, "the whole world was astonished and followed the beast." (Though Revelation uses the past tense, these events are yet future.) Now, according to verses 4-6:

Men worshiped the dragon because he had given authority to the beast, and they also worshiped the beast and asked, "Who is like the beast? Who can make war against him?" The beast was given a mouth to utter proud words and blasphemies [remember the words of Daniel 7:20] and to exercise his authority for forty-two months [remember the words of Daniel 7:25, because forty-two months is three and a half years]. He opened his mouth to blaspheme God, and to slander his name and his dwelling place and those who live in heaven [remember the words of Daniel 7:25].

Daniel 7:21, 22 says, "As I watched, this horn was waging war against the saints and defeating them, until the Ancient of Days came and pronounced judgment in favor of the saints of the Most High, and the time came when they possessed the kingdom." The new text of the New Testament in Revelation 13:7-10 says:

He was given power to make war against the saints and to conquer them. And he was given authority over every tribe, people, language and nation. All inhabitants of the earth will worship the beast — all whose names have not been written in the book of life belonging to the Lamb that was slain from the creation of the world. He who has an ear, let him hear. If any-

*one is to go into captivity, into captivity he will go. If anyone is to be killed
with the sword, with the sword he will be killed. This calls for patient
endurance and faithfulness on the part of the saints.*

Here is why we need to know the prophecies. *Christians will be on earth
during the reign of the Antichrist.* His reign is known as the Great Tribulation,
and it will last forty-two months or three and a half years. This Tribulation
period will precede the Rapture. Paul says in 2 Thessalonians 2:1-5:

Concerning the coming [the parousia*] of our Lord Jesus Christ and our
being gathered to him [the Rapture], we ask you, brothers, not to become
easily unsettled or alarmed by some prophecy, report or letter supposed
to have come from us, saying that the day of the Lord [the day of the Lord
is used interchangeably with* parousia *and rapture] has already come.
Don't let anyone deceive you in any way, for that day [the* parousia, *the
Rapture, and the day of the Lord] will not come* until *the rebellion occurs*
and *the man of lawlessness is revealed, the man doomed to destruction.
He will oppose and will exalt himself over everything that is called God
or is worshiped, so that he sets himself up in God's temple, proclaiming
himself to be God. (emphasis added)*

The Lawless One, the Beast, will be revealed when a world leader
appears to rise from the dead. Then the persecution of Christians will begin
in earnest worldwide. John says, "He who has an ear, let him hear. If anyone is to go into captivity, into captivity he will go. If anyone is to be killed
with the sword, with the sword he will be killed. This calls for patient
endurance and faithfulness on the part of the saints." If we are going to be
in Heaven, missing all of this, why this call for "patient endurance and
faithfulness on the part of the saints"?

In his book *No Fear of the Storm*, Tim LaHaye teaches that the church
will not be on earth during this time of the Great Tribulation. The reason he
gives is that the word *church*, which appears in Revelation 1 — 3, does not
appear again until the eternal state is described in Revelation 22. The word
church (ecclesia), which means "the called-out ones," may not appear in
those chapters, but the word "*saints*" ('agios), which means "the holy ones,"
does appear. In the New Testament, Christians are sometimes called "the
church," and sometimes they are called "the saints." Paul writes to "the
churches in Galatia" (Galatians 1:2) and to "the saints in Ephesus"
(Ephesians 1:1). The words *church* and *saints* are used interchangeably in the
New Testament.

There is no such thing in Scripture as "the Tribulation saints" (that is,
people saved during the Tribulation though the church has been raptured).
That is a man-made invention. John says that Christians will be on earth

during the three-and-a-half-year tribulation of the Antichrist. This might happen in your lifetime; so you need to begin to prepare your heart now, so that you do not become confused and lose heart in the Tribulation like John, the baptizer of Jesus, did when Christ came the first time.

John was related to Jesus. Their mothers were cousins. He baptized Jesus in the Jordan and saw the Spirit come down from heaven as a dove and remain on him. He called himself the forerunner of Christ. But when he found himself in prison after opposing King Herod's immoral marriage, he sent a message to Jesus saying, "Are you the one who was to come [i.e., the Messiah], or should we expect someone else?" (Matthew 11:3).

John felt that since he was so close to the Messiah, since he was the forerunner of Christ, and since he was a blood relative of the Lord, surely he would be delivered from prison by the man who healed the sick and raised the dead. When he was *not* released from prison, he became confused. If John was confused, how do you think Christians who are expecting to be raptured before the Tribulation will respond when they find themselves undergoing intense, unexpected persecution? Even some Christian men and women will be confused and will follow the Beast for a time, because the Antichrist will be so believable. But eventually they will come to their senses and return to the Lord. Jesus said in Matthew 24:21-25:

> For then there will be great distress, unequaled from the beginning of the world until now — and never to be equaled again. If those days had not been cut short, no one would survive, but for the sake of the elect those days will be shortened. At that time if anyone says to you, "Look, here is the Christ!" or, "There he is!" do not believe it. For false christs and false prophets will appear and perform great signs and miracles to deceive even the elect — if that were possible. See, I have told you ahead of time.

The words of 2 Peter 1:19 ring true: "And we have the word of the prophets made more certain, and you will do well to pay attention to it, as to a light shining in a dark place, until the day dawns and the morning star rises in your hearts."

9

Thy Kingdom Come

DANIEL 7:17-28

Shortly before his death, Charles Haddon Spurgeon preached a sermon on the Second Coming of Christ. He said, "Brethren, no truth ought to be more frequently proclaimed, next to the first coming of the Lord, than His Second Coming; you cannot thoroughly set forth all the ends and bearings of the first advent if you forget the second."[1] Toward the end of his ministry he preached much on the Second Coming and the millennial reign of Christ, but it was not always that way.

Early in his ministry he wrote, "I scarcely think it would be justifiable for me to spend my time upon prophetic studies for which I have not the necessary *talent*, nor is it the *vocation* to which my Master has ordained me."[2] I think many people have that attitude these days when they approach the study of prophecy. But why does anyone need to have a special talent to study the prophetic portions of Scripture? No special talent was needed by the Jewish people to understand the prophecies of the first coming. The prophecies were veiled in imagery, but it took no particular skill to study and understand them. It just takes the Holy Spirit. Paul wrote:

> We have not received the spirit of the world but the Spirit who is from God, that we may understand what God has freely given us. . . . The man without the Spirit does not accept the things that come from the Spirit of God, for they are foolishness to him, and he cannot understand them, because they are spiritually discerned. (1 Corinthians 2:12, 14)

Granted, many Jewish people made the same mistakes with the Old Testament prophecies of Christ's first coming that some do today in studying the prophecies of his return. Some Jews did not believe that the prophecies were to be taken literally. Isaiah said, "The virgin will be with child and will give birth to a son" (Isaiah 7:14), but most Jews did not think that would be fulfilled literally. Zechariah wrote, "See, your king comes to you, righteous and having salvation, gentle and riding on a donkey, on a colt, the foal of a donkey" (Zechariah 9:9), but few Jews believed that would be fulfilled literally. Most Jews did not believe Gentile soldiers would literally pierce the hands and feet of the Messiah and cast lots for his clothing, in spite of the prophecies of Psalm 22:16, 18: "Dogs have surrounded me; a band of evil men has encircled me, they have pierced my hands and my feet. . . . They divide my garments among them and cast lots for my clothing." They did not believe Jesus was the Messiah. Either they did not take the prophecies about him literally, or even worse, they did not know the content of the prophecies at all. Many Christians make the latter mistake too.

Young Spurgeon added that he did not think it was his "vocation," his calling, to study prophecy.[3] But the call to every preacher is to preach the whole counsel of God, as stated by the Apostle Paul in Acts 20:27: "I have not hesitated to proclaim to you the whole will of God." What if men would not feel called to preach on worship or spiritual gifts or justification or sanctification? Who are we to determine which passages of Scripture are to be preached and which are to be avoided? Second Timothy 3:16 says, "All Scripture is God-breathed and is useful for teaching, rebuking, correcting and training in righteousness."

Fortunately, Charles Spurgeon changed his thinking about prophecy, partially through the influence of Puritan writers. He said in a later sermon:

I find that the most earnest of the Puritanic preachers did not hesitate to dwell upon this mysterious subject. I turn to Charnock, who did not hesitate to speak of the conflagration of the world and of the millennial reign of Christ on earth. I turn to Richard Baxter and I find him making a barbed arrow out of the doctrine of the coming of the Lord, and thrusting this great truth into the very heart and conscience of unbelievers, as though it were heaven's own sword. I do not think therefore I need tremble very much if the charge should be brought against me of bringing before you an unprofitable subject. It shall profit if God shall bless the Word; and if it be God's Word we may expect His blessing if we preach it all. But He will withdraw His blessing if we refrain from teaching any part of His counsel because in our pretended wisdom, we fancy that it would not have practical effect."[4]

Understanding the timing of the coming of the kingdom of God on earth in the millennial reign of Christ is not an unprofitable study. Understanding the timing of the Millennium takes no special talent, but it takes careful exegesis of the appropriate texts with the help of the Holy Spirit.

In this chapter I will set forth why I believe Christ will rapture his saints after the Tribulation and then establish his kingdom on earth, reigning with them for a thousand years.

This view is known as Historic or Reformed Premillennialism. It is called historic because it is the oldest view held by the Church. The list of proponents includes names of such second-century church fathers as Papias, Irenaeus, and Justin Martyr. Papias was a contemporary of Polycarp, who was discipled by John, the author of Revelation. Papias asserted, "The Apostles state that there will be a certain period of a thousand years after the resurrection from the dead when the kingdom of Christ must be set up in a material order on this earth."

This view is called Reformed to distinguish it from Dispensational Premillennialism. Dispensationalism claims that the Church will be raptured before the Tribulation so that God can begin working with Israel once again. It teaches that the Tribulation will be seven years long, with the Antichrist being kind to the Jews for three and a half years and then turning against them the last three and a half years. I will address that false teaching in chapter 11 of this book. Also in contrast to Reformed Premillennialism, dispensationalists use a "wooden" literal interpretation of every detail of prophecy and distinguish between the Church and Israel.

My view of the millennial reign of Christ is also called Reformed because of the many great Reformed scholars and pastors who have held this position, including Charles Haddon Spurgeon. Called the last of the Puritans, Spurgeon wrote in his confessional statement, "Our hope is in the personal, premillennial return of Christ in glory."[5] He saw the historic premillennial view as an eschatology of victory, affirming that the gospel will succeed as the church of Jesus Christ grows larger and stronger in the last days. In January 1860 he said to his congregation, "Brethren, where we have seen one converted, we may yet see hundreds; where the word of God has been powerful to scores, it shall be blessed to thousands; and where hundreds in past years have seen it, nations shall be converted to Christ."

The other two views of the millennial reign of Christ are called Postmillennialism and Amillennialism. The Postmillennial view teaches that Christ will come back after the Millennium, after the Church through the power of the Spirit "Christianizes" the world. In this view, the kingdom of God not only spreads all over the world, as the historic premillennialist believes, but it actually takes over the control of all governments and all nations.

The Amillennial view or Realized-millennialism says that Christ is reigning in Heaven right now. When Christians die, we go to Heaven and reign with him. In this view there is no millennial reign of Christ on earth; so when he returns there will be a general resurrection of the dead, the judgment, and then the new heavens and new earth will begin.

Daniel 7 is a chapter that needs to be understood before anyone arrives at a position on the millennial reign of Christ. We will see as we study this chapter and several related texts that the kingdom of God will be ushered in during the reign of the Antichrist on the earth; that the kingdom of God will come when Christ comes with the clouds of Heaven; and that when the kingdom of God comes, Christ will reign on earth for a thousand years.

THE KINGDOM OF GOD WILL COME DURING THE REIGN OF THE ANTICHRIST ON THE EARTH (7:7, 19-25)

After that, in my vision at night I looked, and there before me was a fourth beast — terrifying and frightening and very powerful. It had large iron teeth; it crushed and devoured its victims and trampled underfoot whatever was left. It was different from all the former beasts, and it had ten horns. . . . Then I wanted to know the true meaning of the fourth beast, which was different from all the others and most terrifying, with its iron teeth and bronze claws — the beast that crushed and devoured its victims and trampled underfoot whatever was left. I also wanted to know about the ten horns on its head and about the other horn that came up, before which three of them fell — the horn that looked more imposing than the others and that had eyes and a mouth the spoke boastfully. As I watched, this horn was waging war against the saints and defeating them, until the Ancient of Days came and pronounced judgment in favor of the saints of the Most High, and the time came when they possessed the kingdom. (Daniel 7:7, 19-22)

After seeing this disturbing vision, in verse 19 Daniel asked for the true meaning of this fourth beast that was different from all the others. He wanted to know about the ten horns on its head and about the other horn that came up, before which three of them fell. Fortunately for us, the angel gives Daniel an explanation in verses 23-25a:

He gave me this explanation: "The fourth beast is a fourth kingdom that will appear on earth. It will be different from all the other kingdoms and will devour the whole earth, trampling it down and crushing it. The ten horns are ten kings who will come from this kingdom. After them another king will arise, different from the earlier ones; he will subdue three kings. He will speak against the Most High and oppress his saints."

The ten horns are ten kings who will come from this last worldwide kingdom. One of those kings will be the Antichrist who speaks against the Most High and oppresses the saints. We will know who he is when a world leader subdues three kings. It would be foolish to try to speculate now who those ten kings and three kings are. If we get a picture in our mind of how it might happen and what countries these kings might represent, we might miss the fulfillment because we are looking for the wrong thing.

Let me give you an illustration. We do evangelistic visitation on Tuesday evenings at the church I pastor. We follow up on those who visit our church. Bud Moginot, our visitation pastor, prepares the maps because in most cases he has already dropped some material by the house on Sunday. If he had trouble finding a place, he will often add helpful hints to the map.

My team had one of his maps one night when we were visiting far out in the country. His helpful hint said, "Turn right at the sign high and into the intersection." We did not have a clue as to what that meant because we had never heard of a "sign high and into the intersection." We could not even picture it in our mind. We kept driving and looking up. As we rounded a curve, we saw a street sign twenty feet in the air hanging on a limb of a tree that reached into the intersection. When we saw it, we had no question what Bud meant. We turned there and soon found the house.

That is the way it is with some of the prophecies regarding the Second Coming of Christ. We may have no idea now what they mean, but if we will just keep these prophecies tucked away in our mind, then if we are alive when they occur, we will know what is happening. That is what the early church fathers did. Take the words of Irenaeus, Bishop of Lyons in the late second century, as an example.

> In a still clearer light has John, in the Apocalypse, indicated to the Lord's disciples what shall happen in the last times, and concerning the ten kings who shall arise, among whom the empire that now rules the earth shall be partitioned. He teaches us what the ten horns shall be which are seen by Daniel, telling us that thus it had been said to him (Revelation 17:12-14). It is manifest, therefore, that of these potentates, he who is to come shall slay three, and subject the remainder to his power, and that he shall be himself the eighth among them. And they shall lay "Babylon" to waste, and burn her with fire, and shall give their kingdom to the beast, and put the Church to flight. After that they shall be destroyed by the coming of our Lord.

This beast or world leader, who was so different from all the other beasts, is the Antichrist, the counterfeit Christ, Satan incarnate. Daniel says that he will wage war against the saints and defeat them (v. 21). John repeats this in Revelation 13:7, 10: "He was given power to make war against the saints and to conquer them. . . . If anyone is to go into captivity, into captivity he will go. If anyone is to be killed with the sword, with the sword he will be killed."

Daniel also says that "He will speak against the Most High and oppress his saints and try to change the set times and the laws. The saints will be handed over to him for a time, times and half a time" (7:25b). In Revelation

John writes, "The beast was given a mouth to utter proud words and blasphemies and to exercise his authority for forty-two months" (13:5).

Both prophets, using different terminology, indicate that the persecution of Christians under the Antichrist will last three and a half years. The three and a half years will begin when the Antichrist appears to receive a fatal wound, then come back to life (Revelation 13:3). Those Christians living on the earth at that time will know that the return of Christ is near. They will be able to count down those three and a half years. That is why Paul, writing to the Thessalonians about the Rapture, said:

> *About the times and dates [of Christ's return] we do not need to write to you, for you know the day of the Lord will come like a thief in the night. While people are saying, "Peace and safety," destruction will come on them suddenly, as labor pains on a pregnant woman, and they will not escape. But you, brothers, are not in darkness so that this day should surprise you like a thief. (1 Thessalonians 5:1-4)*

Paul did not need to write to them because he had already taught them about those times and dates when he was with them. In 2 Thessalonians 2:5, after explaining that the Antichrist had to appear before the return of Christ, he writes, "Don't you remember that when I was with you I used to tell you these things?" They did not need to hear about the times and dates again, not because it is impossible to know such details, but because they already knew them. Since they knew God's time frame, Jesus' coming would not surprise them like a thief.

Some people object to this because of Jesus' words in Matthew 24:36 — "No one knows about that day or hour, not even the angels in heaven, nor the Son, but only the Father." It is true that no one knows the exact day or the exact hour, but that still does not mean we cannot know when his return is within three and a half years. Both Jesus and Paul likened Christ's return to the experience of a pregnant woman. A pregnant woman knows she is in the ninth month and will deliver any day, but she does not know "the day or the hour" of her child's birth. So it will be in the last days. Christians who know the prophecies will know approximately when Christ will return, even though they do not know the exact day or hour.

So the kingdom of God will come during the reign of the Antichrist. Daniel says, "As I watched, this horn was waging war against the saints and defeating them, until the Ancient of Days came and pronounced judgment in favor of the saints of the Most High, and the time came when they possessed the kingdom" (Daniel 7:21, 22). At the end of the forty-two months of worldwide persecution, the Ancient of Days will come, destroy the Antichrist, and allow the saints to possess the kingdom. How exactly will that happen?

THE KINGDOM OF GOD WILL COME WHEN CHRIST
RETURNS ON THE CLOUDS OF HEAVEN (7:13, 14)

In my vision at night I looked, and there before me was one like a son of man, coming with the clouds of heaven. He approached the Ancient of Days and was led into his presence. He was given authority, glory and sovereign power; all peoples, nations and men of every language worshiped him. His dominion is an everlasting dominion that will not pass away, and his kingdom is one that will never be destroyed.

Daniel 7:22 indicated that the Ancient of Days would come and pronounce judgment in favor of the saints. Now in these verses we get a picture of what that means. Daniel says that "one like a son of man" would come with the clouds of heaven. Jesus picked up on this name while he was here on earth. The name Jesus used for himself more than any other was the Son of Man. He took it from this text to remind the people who he really was. Reminiscent of John 1:1, he was with the Ancient of Days, and he was the Ancient of Days. Jesus quoted part of Daniel 7:13, 14 in Matthew 24 so we could understand what Daniel was seeing.

Immediately after the distress of those days [the Great Tribulation], "the sun will be darkened, and the moon will not give its light; the stars will fall from the sky, and the heavenly bodies will be shaken." At that time the sign of the Son of Man will appear in the sky, and all the nations of the earth will mourn. They will see the Son of Man coming on the clouds of the sky, with power and great glory. And he will send his angels with a loud trumpet call, and they will gather his elect from the four winds, from one end of the heavens to the other. (vv. 29-31)

This describes the rapture of all believers, whether dead or alive, Jew or Gentile, Old Testament saint or New Testament saint. The English Bible does not use the word *rapture*. But the word translated "gather," *episunago*, is the Greek word that is used to describe the rapture of God's people that will, according to Jesus, occur after, not before, the Great Tribulation.

Paul says virtually the same thing as Jesus, using the terminology of Daniel: "For the Lord himself will come down from heaven, with a loud command, with the voice of the archangel and with the trumpet call of God, and the dead in Christ will rise first. After that, we who are still alive and are left will be caught up together with them in the clouds to meet the Lord in the air" (1 Thessalonians 4:16, 17).

When Christ comes with the clouds of heaven, the Ancient of Days gives to him the kingdom. "He approached the Ancient of Days and was led into his presence. He was given authority, glory and sovereign power; all peoples, nations and men of every language worshiped him. His dominion is an everlasting dominion that will not pass away, and his kingdom is one that will never be destroyed" (Daniel 7:13, 14).

John says in Revelation 11:15, "The seventh angel sounded his trumpet, and there were loud voices in heaven, which said: 'The kingdom of the world [one united kingdom under the Antichrist] has become the kingdom of our Lord and of his Christ, and he will reign forever and ever.'" The seventh trumpet of Revelation is the last trumpet. This is what Paul tells us will occur at the last trumpet.

I declare to you, brothers, that flesh and blood cannot inherit the kingdom of God, nor does the perishable inherit the imperishable. Listen, I tell you a mystery: We will not all sleep, but we will all be changed — in a flash, in the twinkling of an eye, at the last trumpet. For the trumpet will sound, the dead will be raised imperishable, and we will be changed. (1 Corinthians 15:50-52)

Paul also says that flesh and blood cannot inherit the kingdom of God. Christians will not experience the kingdom of God in their mortal bodies. "Nor does the perishable inherit the imperishable." Those who hold to a postmillennial view need to answer this exegetical problem.

We also learn from Daniel that when Christ returns, he will destroy the Beast and cast him into the lake of fire. "Then I continued to watch because of the boastful words the horn was speaking. I kept looking until the beast was slain and its body destroyed and thrown into the blazing fire" (Daniel 7:11). Again, John confirms this in the book of Revelation.

Then I saw the beast and the kings of the earth and their armies gathered together to make war against the rider on the horse and his army. But the beast was captured, and with him the false prophet who had performed the miraculous signs on his behalf. With these signs he had deluded those who had received the mark of the beast and worshiped his image. The two of them were thrown alive into the fiery lake of burning sulfur. (19:19, 20)

Irenaeus understood John the same way. He made clear that when this Antichrist shall have devastated all things in this world, the Lord will come from heaven in the clouds, in the glory of the Father, sending this man into the lake of fire, but bringing in for the righteous the times of the kingdom.

Paul wrote to the Thessalonians and described the scene this way: "The lawless one will be revealed, whom the Lord Jesus will overthrow with the breath of his mouth and destroy by the splendor of his coming" (2 Thessalonians 2:8).

THE KINGDOM OF GOD WILL COME, AND WE WILL REIGN WITH HIM FOR A THOUSAND YEARS (7:12)

Notice what happens immediately after the Beast is thrown alive into the fiery lake of burning sulfur. According to Daniel 7:12, "The other beasts [that is, the other kingdoms of men] had been stripped of their authority, but were allowed to live for a period of time." How long were they allowed to live? That question is answered in the verses that follow Revelation 19:19, 20.

Revelation 20:1 begins with the words, "And I saw." That phrase is used eight times between Revelation 19:11 and Revelation 21:1, which shows that this entire section of Scripture is an unfolding sequence — one event after the other. Daniel confirms at least that Revelation 20:1 follows in sequence Revelation 19:19, 20 because he says that the other beasts' living for a period of time follow the beast that was different from all the others being cast into the lake of fire.

Revelation 20 teaches us three things about this period of time in which the other beasts are allowed to live.

Satan Will Be Bound for a Thousand Years

And I saw an angel coming down out of heaven, having the key to the Abyss and holding in his hand a great chain. He seized the dragon, that ancient serpent, who is the devil, or Satan, and bound him for a thousand years. He threw him into the Abyss, and locked and sealed it over him, to keep him from deceiving the nations anymore until the thousand years were ended. After that, he must be set free for a short time. (vv. 1-3)

Some people say that we are in this thousand-year (millennial) reign of Christ right now because Satan was bound by Christ two thousand years ago. When accused of being Beelzebub, the prince of demons, Jesus said, "How can Satan drive out Satan? . . . if Satan opposes himself and is divided, he cannot stand; his end has come. In fact, no one can enter a strong man's house and carry off his possessions unless he first ties up the strong man. Then he can rob his house" (Mark 3:23, 26, 27). The idea is that since Jesus was able to cast out demons, he must have already bound Satan.

The problem with that interpretation is that it does not do justice to the words of the text of Revelation 20. In verse 3 John writes that Satan will be bound for a thousand years to "keep him from deceiving the nations *anymore*." I ask you, is Satan still deceiving the nations? Of course he is. Satan is making war against the saints, and his main tactical maneuver is to deceive us, luring us away from our sincere and pure devotion to Jesus Christ. Paul wrote:

But I am afraid that just as Eve was deceived by the serpent's cunning, your minds may somehow be led astray from your sincere and pure devotion to Christ. For if someone comes to you and preaches a Jesus other than the Jesus we preached, or if you receive a different spirit from the one you received, or a different gospel from the one you accepted, you put up with it easily enough. (2 Corinthians 11:3, 4)

Put on the full armor of God so that you can take your stand against the devil's schemes. For our struggle is not against flesh and blood, but against the rulers, against the authorities, against the powers of this dark world and against the spiritual forces of evil in the heavenly realms. Therefore put on the full armor of God, so that when the day of evil comes, you may be able to stand your ground, and after you have done everything, to stand. (Ephesians 6:11-13)

Satan is also still deceiving the world. Paul wrote, "The god of this age has blinded the minds of unbelievers, so that they cannot see the light of the gospel of the glory of Christ" (2 Corinthians 4:4). In 2 Thessalonians 2:9, 10 Paul warns, "The coming of the lawless one will be in accordance with the work of Satan displayed in all kinds of counterfeit miracles, signs and wonders, and in every sort of evil that deceives those who are perishing."

After Christ returns, the Beast will be cast into the lake of fire. Then Christ will bind Satan for a thousand years so that he cannot deceive the nations. That is the kingdom of God on earth when Christ reigns as king over all the earth.

The Nations Will Be Allowed to Live for a Thousand Years

I find the way Daniel 7:12 puts it very interesting: "The other beasts [nations of the world] had been stripped of their authority, but were allowed to live for a period of time." There will be unbelievers from the nations, stripped of their authority, living with us during the thousand-year, earthly reign of Christ. That is why Revelation 12:5 says that Jesus will rule the nations with an iron scepter. You do not need an iron scepter if you are ruling perfect people. How will it come about that some unbelievers from the nations are left here? Zechariah the prophet answers that question. Read this description of the return of Christ when the nations are gathered against Jerusalem to fight against it.

I will gather all the nations to Jerusalem to fight against it; the city will be captured, the houses ransacked, and the women raped. Half of the city will go into exile, but the rest of the people will not be taken from the city. Then the LORD will go out and fight against those nations, as he fights in the day of battle. On that day his feet will stand on the Mount of Olives, east of Jerusalem, and the Mount of Olives will be split in two from east to west, forming a great valley, with half of the mountain moving north and half moving south. You will flee by my mountain valley, for it will extend to Azel. You will flee as you fled from the earthquake in the days of Uzziah king of Judah. Then the LORD my God will come, and all the holy ones with him. (Zechariah 14:2-5)

This is a description of the return of Jesus to the Mount of Olives, just as the angels had said when Jesus ascended into heaven in A.D. 30 (Acts 1:11). When he returns, all the nations will be gathered against Jerusalem under the leadership of the Antichrist, whom Jesus will destroy by the splendor of his coming. When the Lord comes to the Mount of Olives, he will have all the holy ones with him, just as Paul wrote in 1 Thessalonians 3:13: "May he strengthen your hearts so that you will be blameless and holy in the presence of our God and Father when our Lord Jesus comes with all his holy ones."

How are we going to be brought to the earth if Paul says that we will meet the Lord in the air? Paul writes, "We who are still alive and are left will be caught up together with them in the clouds to meet the Lord in the air. And so we will be with the Lord forever" (1 Thessalonians 4:17). The late author and theologian William Hendricksen explains that the Greek word translated "to meet" is a technical military term. The word was used to describe the events that occurred when the emperor returned victoriously from battle. As he approached the city gates, the people of the city would go out "to meet" him and escort him back home. So the word not only means to meet someone, but to meet and escort them back.

Some of you may not know Greek and may question this historical use. This Greek word is only used three times in the New Testament. This interpretation of this word is confirmed in both of the other passages. First, consider Acts 28:15, 16, which describes Paul coming to Rome for the first time: "The brothers there had heard that we were coming, and they traveled as far as the Forum of Appius and the Three Taverns to meet us. When we got to Rome, Paul was allowed to live by himself." The other use of this word is found in Matthew 25:6, which describes the bridesmaids going out to meet the bridegroom when he returns at the sound of the trumpet. They go out to meet him in order to escort him back to the banquet hall for the wedding feast.

The Bible says that all believers will be caught up to meet the Lord in the air, and we will escort him back to earth. We will be taken out of this world for a brief time so that the bowls of wrath may be poured out upon all the unbelievers who remain. Nowhere does the Bible tell us how long that will last. The description of the seven bowls of wrath that God will pour out on the godless people of the world is found in Revelation 16:1-21. When you read those verses, you will see that there will be total devastation of this world. For example:

The first angel went and poured out his bowl on the land, and ugly and painful sores broke out on the people who had the mark of the beast and worshiped his image. The second angel poured out his bowl on the sea, and it turned into blood like that of a dead man, and every living thing in the sea died. The third angel poured out his bowl on the rivers and springs of water, and they became blood. (vv. 2-4)

Peter said, "The day of the Lord will come like a thief. The heavens will disappear with a roar; the elements will be destroyed by fire, and the earth and everything in it will be laid bare" (2 Peter 3:10). Here is the description of what will happen to the people on earth during the bowls of wrath:

This is the plague with which the LORD will strike all the nations that fought against Jerusalem: Their flesh will rot while they are still standing on their feet, their eyes will rot in their sockets, and their tongues will rot in their mouths. On that day men will be stricken by the LORD with great panic. Each man will seize the hand of another, and they will attack each other. . . . Then the survivors from all the nations that have attacked Jerusalem will go up year after year to worship the King, the LORD Almighty, and to celebrate the Feast of Tabernacles. If any of the peoples of the earth do not go up to Jerusalem to worship the King, the LORD Almighty, they will have no rain. (Zechariah 14:12, 13, 16, 17)

There will be "survivors" of this wrath. Recently a seminary student sat down with me to ask questions about my view of the Second Coming of Christ. One question he asked was, "How could anyone survive such destruction?" My first answer was that I did not know, but the Bible says that some will survive. But secondly, when Hiroshima was bombed, the city and all the people were completely destroyed in a matter of seconds. But amazingly, some did survive. Some jumped into the rivers and lived. Others were blocked by rubble. Whatever the case, seeing how some people survived that mass destruction helps me understand how some could survive the bowls of wrath.

The survivors are the unbelieving people who will be on the newly created earth during the one thousand-year reign of Christ. We know that the earth will be re-created because Paul says:

The creation waits in eager expectation for the sons of God to be revealed. For the creation was subjected to frustration, not by its own choice, but by

the will of the one who subjected it, in hope that the creation itself will be
liberated from its bondage to decay and brought into the glorious free-
dom of the children of God. (Romans 8:19-21)

And Isaiah says, "Behold, I will create new heavens and a new earth. The
former things will not be remembered, nor will they come to mind" (Isaiah
65:17). But we also know this is talking about the temporary kingdom of
which Daniel speaks and not the eternal state of believers, because Isaiah
says there will be death on the new earth. "Never again will there be in it an
infant who lives but a few days, or an old man who does not live out his years;
he who dies at a hundred will be thought a mere youth; he who fails to reach
a hundred will be considered accursed" (Isaiah 65:20). How can there be
death at the time of the new heavens and new earth? There is only one explanation. The first one thousand years of the new heavens and new earth are the
millennial reign of Christ when he will rule with a rod of iron. If the peoples of the earth do not go up to worship him, the Lord Almighty will judge
them by sending no rain.

This is what Daniel was speaking of when he wrote:

But the court will sit, and his [the Beast's] power will be taken away and
completely destroyed forever. Then the sovereignty, power and greatness
of the kingdoms under the whole heaven will be handed over to the saints,
the people of the Most High. His kingdom will be an everlasting kingdom,
and all rulers will worship and obey him. (7:26, 27)

Unbelieving nations will be here on earth for the thousand-year reign
of the Lord Jesus. Many people are quick to ask, "Why would God do it
this way? Why not just end everything when Christ returns?" I think the
reason for the thousand-year reign of Christ on earth is that Jesus Christ
wants to show the world what righteous rule is all about. Every time there
is an election, every time a new dictator comes to power, everyone hopes he
will bring justice, equality, and prosperity. But no human government has
ever brought about a righteous government, and none ever will. But in the
kingdom of God on earth Jesus will rule even unbelievers in perfect righteousness. As Zechariah wrote:

On that day there will be no light, no cold or frost. It will be a unique
day, without daytime or nighttime — a day known to the LORD. When
evening comes, there will be light. On that day living water will flow out
from Jerusalem, half to the eastern sea and half to the western sea, in
summer and in winter. The LORD will be king over the whole earth. On
that day there will be one LORD, and his name the only name.
(Zechariah 14:6-9)

The Saints Will Possess the Kingdom for a Thousand Years

*I saw thrones on which were seated those who had been given authority
to judge [1 Corinthians 6:2 says that is all believers]. And I saw the souls
of those who had been beheaded because of their testimony for Jesus and
because of the word of God. They had not worshiped the beast or his
image and had not received his mark on their foreheads or their hands.
They [all believers who will judge the world] came to life and reigned
with Christ a thousand years. (The rest of the dead [the unbelievers] did not
come to life until the thousand years were ended.) This is the first resurrection. (Revelation 20:4, 5)*

Irenaeus again made it clear that the resurrection of the just will take
place after the coming of the Antichrist and the destruction of all nations
under his rule; in the time of that resurrection, the righteous shall reign on the
earth, becoming stronger when they see the Lord.

This is what Daniel referred to when he wrote, "As I watched, this horn
was waging war against the saints and defeating them, until the Ancient of
Days came and pronounced judgment in favor of the saints of the Most High,
and the time came when they possessed the kingdom" (7:21, 22). And in
Daniel 7:17, 18 we read, "The four great beasts are four kingdoms that will
rise from the earth. But the saints of the Most High will receive the kingdom and will possess it forever — yes, for ever and ever."

Notice that we will *receive* the kingdom — we do not bring in the kingdom ourselves through an ever-expanding Church. But why does it say this
kingdom will be "forever and ever" rather than a thousand years? Let me
explain. When Jesus comes back to earth, this world, destroyed by God's
wrath, will be re-created with no more thorns, thistles, or curse. It will be perfect like the Garden of Eden before the Fall. All the believers will be in resur-
rected bodies. For us there will be no more pain, no more sorrow, and no more
sin. We will spend eternity on this new earth. We will live here forever and
ever. The first thousand years of this new earth will be different in that it will
include the unbelieving survivors of the nations who will go up to Jerusalem
to worship every year. That is why John says in Revelation 20:7-15:

*When the thousand years are over, Satan will be released from his prison
and will go out to deceive the nations in the four corners of the earth — Gog
and Magog — to gather them for battle. In number they are like the sand on
the seashore. They marched across the breadth of the earth and surrounded
the camp of God's people, the city he loves. But fire came down from heaven
and devoured them. And the devil, who deceived them, was thrown into
the lake of burning sulfur, where the beast and the false prophet had been
thrown. They will be tormented day and night forever and ever.*

After the thousand-year reign of Christ, the devil and his followers will be thrown into the lake of fire where the Beast and the prophet had been since before the Millennium. There is no indication that any of these unbelievers ever came to trust in Christ during the Millennium. The eternal destiny of all people is sealed when Christ returns. After that final rebellion comes the final judgment.

> *Then I saw a great white throne and him who was seated on it. Earth and sky fled from his presence, and there was no place for them. And I saw the dead, great and small, standing before the throne, and books were opened. Another book was opened, which is the book of life. The dead were judged according to what they had done as recorded in the books. The sea gave up the dead that were in it, and death and Hades gave up the dead that were in them, and each person was judged according to what he had done. Then death and Hades were thrown into the lake of fire. The lake of fire is the second death. If anyone's name was not found written in the book of life, he was thrown into the lake of fire. (Revelation 20:11-15)*

Is your name written in the book of life? If it is not, let this be the day of your salvation. Acknowledge that you are a sinner in need of a Savior. Believe that Jesus is God and that he died on the cross suffering God's wrath in your place. Then commit your life to Jesus Christ by asking him to come into your life as Lord. Bow your knee before Jesus, and trust in him alone for your salvation — today. Don't delay.

If you know the Savior, then fervently pray, *May your kingdom come and your will be done on earth as it is in heaven.* Take heed these words of Charles Spurgeon:

> If we believe that the Lord Jesus has come the first time, we believe also that He will come the second time; but are these equally assured truths to us? Have we with equal firmness grasped the thought that He comes again? Do we say to each other, as we meet in happy fellowship, "Yes, our Lord cometh"? It should be to us not only a prophecy assuredly believed among us, but a scene pictured in our souls, and anticipated in our hearts. My imagination has often set forth that dread scene: but better still, my faith has realized it. I have heard the chariot-wheels of the Lord's approach, and I have endeavored to set my house in order for His reception. I have felt the shadow of that great cloud which shall attend Him, damping the ardor of my worldliness. I hear even now in spirit the sound of the last trumpet, whose tremendous blast startles my soul to serious action, and puts force into my life. Would God that I lived more completely under the influence of that august event![6]

10

A Stern-faced Man of Intrigue

DANIEL 8:1-27

Judith Viorst tells of a little boy, Alexander, who had a terrible day.

I went to sleep with gum in my mouth and now there is gum in my hair when I got up this morning. I tripped on the skateboard and dropped my sweater in the sink when the water was running, and I could tell it was going to be a horrible, terrible, no-good, very bad day.

In the carpool, Mr. Gibson let Becky have the seat by the window and Audrey and Elliot got seats by the window too. I said I was scrunched. I said I was smushed. I said, "If I don't get a seat by the window I am going to get carsick." Nobody even answered me. I could tell it was going to be a terrible, horrible, no-good, very bad day.

There were two cupcakes in Phillip Barker's lunch bag and Howard got a Hershey bar with almonds, and Paul's mother gave him a jelly roll-up that had little coconut sprinkles in the top, and guess whose mother forgot to put dessert in his lunch. It was a terrible, horrible, no-good, very bad day.

There were lima beans for dinner. I hate lima beans. There was kissing on TV. I hate kissing. My bath was too hot, I got soap in my eyes, my marble went down the drain, and I had to wear my railroad pajamas. I hate my railroad pajamas. And when I went to bed, Nick took back the pillow he said I could keep, and my Mickey Mouse night-light burned out and I bit my tongue. The cat wants to sleep with Anthony and not me. It has been a terrible, horrible, no-good, very bad day.[1]

Now I am sure you have had terrible, horrible, no-good, very bad days from time to time. We all experience them. Daniel 8 encourages us, through an amazing prophesy, to trust God when times get difficult because he is in control of all things. No matter how hard life gets, no matter how long the tough times last, the Lord God is sovereign, he is in control, and he will bring deliverance in his time. He will turn those difficulties into a blessing. That is the kind of God that we have; so we need to trust him.

Daniel learned this lesson as he watched this vision in the third year of King Belshazzar (8:1). The previous vision recorded in chapter 7 had occurred in the first year of the reign of Belshazzar. The year was now 548/547 B.C. With this chapter, the writer reverts to Hebrew (Aramaic was used in chapters 2 — 7).[2]

In his vision, Daniel saw himself standing in the citadel of Susa in the province of Elam. There is no reason to believe that Daniel actually went to the province of Elam, which was hundreds of miles east of Babylon in modern-day Iran. Susa was the leading city of Elam.[3] Later Susa became the winter residence of the Persian kings. The significance of the location is that it was outside Babylon and in the center of the new future power.

In the vision Daniel was standing beside the Ulai Canal (8:2). This was a man-made canal that was called the Eulaeus in later classical writings.[4] In this vision Daniel saw the coming of a terrible, horrible, no-good, very bad day for the people of God. But in the vision God also revealed that he is a sovereign King and a wonderful Savior who can turn a curse into a blessing.

In this chapter Daniel saw a vision of a ram with two horns, a goat with a prominent horn, and a man with a stern face. The chapter can be divided into two main sections. First is the vision in 8:1-14 and then the interpretation in 8:15-27. The vision can then be further divided into three parts: the powerful ram, the shaggy goat, and the man of intrigue. The interpretation has the corresponding three parts. In this book we will study each part of the vision separately with an immediate look at the interpretation. You will see how the vision and the interpretation can be an encouragement to us when we have a terrible, horrible, no-good, very bad day.

A RAM WITH TWO HORNS (8:3)

I looked up, and there before me was a ram with two horns, standing beside the canal, and the horns were long. One of the horns was longer than the other but grew up later.

The Vision (8:4)

Daniel saw a ram with two horns. The vision is described in verse 4: "I watched the ram as he charged toward the west and the north and the south.

No animal could stand against him, and none could rescue from his power. He did as he pleased and he became great."

Now this sounds similar to 7:5. In the prophecy in that chapter, the prophet saw four beasts. Daniel wrote, "There before me was a second beast, which looked like a bear. It was raised up on one of its sides." This is similar to the picture of the two horns because one was growing bigger than the other. The second beast of Daniel 7, a bear, was the Medo-Persian Empire that would replace the kingdom of Babylon. That empire was raised up on one of its sides (Daniel 7) and had one horn that later grew longer than the other (Daniel 8), because the Persian Empire in time overshadowed the Medes who were much weaker.

So here in Daniel 8 we actually have the third time that the Medo-Persian Empire, with Persia growing stronger than the Medes, is prophesied. The first was Daniel 2 where the Medo-Persian Empire was portrayed as the chest and arms of silver.

In Daniel 8, unlike the visions of Daniel 2 and 7, there is no prophecy of Babylon, because the ruler at the time of the vision, Belshazzar, is the last ruler of Babylon. The Babylonian Kingdom was virtually finished. Therefore Daniel 8 begins with the second empire, the Medes and the Persians.

The Interpretation (8:15, 16)

Now if there is any question as to what this vision means or if there is any doubt about what I am telling you, consider the interpretation found in verses 15, 16: "While I, Daniel, was watching the vision and trying to understand it, there before me stood one who looked like a man. And I heard a man's voice from the Ulai, calling 'Gabriel, tell this man the meaning of the vision.'" Whenever I read words like this in a book of prophecy, I get excited because I know that I will not have to figure out the prophecy on my own. The Lord will explain it, and that is precisely what he does — through Gabriel, which means "God's hero."

The End of the Wrath (8:17-19)

First of all, we need to understand that the vision represents the end of the wrath. In other words, this vision is good news, not bad news. It is the coming of the end of a terrible day that was to come upon the Jewish people before the birth of Christ. "As he came near the place where I was standing, I was terrified and fell prostrate. 'Son of man,' he said to me, 'understand that the vision concerns the time of the end'" (vv. 17-19).

End of what? Verses 18, 19 explain, "While he was speaking to me, I was in a deep sleep, with my face on the ground. Then he touched me and raised me to my feet. He said: 'I'm going to tell you what will happen later in the time of wrath, because the vision concerns the appointed time of the end.'" Another translation of the Hebrew could be, "It concerns the end and will be at the appointed time."

Now when some people read the words, "time of the end," they assume immediately that Daniel has to be speaking about the last days or the Second Coming of Jesus Christ. But that does not have to be the case. When Peter quoted Joel 2:28 to describe the events of Pentecost, he said, "In the last days, God says, I will pour out my Spirit on all people." The last days there referred to the day of Pentecost in the first century, not the return of Christ.

In the words of Keil, "'Time of the end' is the general prophetic expression for the time which, as the period of fulfillment, lies at the end of the existing prophetic horizon — which in this case is the time of Antiochus."[5] If we force the interpretation of Daniel 8 to refer to events yet future, we will not only miss the main event predicted here, but we will also bring more confusion to the study of the return of Christ.

Jerome stated in the fifth century that not until his day did anybody ever interpret Daniel 8 as having anything to do with the Second Coming. That was in Jerome's day, and then just a handful of people began to say that this was a "type" of the Antichrist and not the Antichrist himself. But there is nothing in this text to indicate that this is a "type." Rather, this is prophecy, history written in advance. The prophecy revealed to Israel that a crisis would occur that would create a horrible day.

In verse 19 Daniel says, "I am going to tell you what will happen later in the time of wrath" (or in some translations, "indignation"). In other words, a difficult time was coming upon the Jewish people (within 350 years), and he was warning them about this terrible day.

But the end — here is the good news — the end spoken of is not the end of the world, but the end of the time of anger, the end of the time of indignation, the end of the time of wrath that was going to come upon the Jewish people. Daniel was saying, "Be encouraged!" Yes, the time of indignation was coming for the Jews, but they should take heart because it was going to last only a short time; its end would come at the appointed time. It would be a short-lived, terrible, horrible, no-good, very bad day. The vision represents the end of the time of this future wrath that would occur, as we will see, in the second century.

The Ram Represents the Kings of Media and Persia (8:20)

Again, if there is any question about this, look at verse 20. This understanding of the text cannot be doubted. "The two-horned ram that you saw represents the kings of Media and Persia." There is no question. He tells them this so they can watch history unfold year by year, decade by decade, and know approximately when this future time of indignation, this horrible day, would come upon God's people.

A GOAT WITH A PROMINENT HORN (8:5)

As I was thinking about this, suddenly a goat with a prominent horn between his eyes came from the west, crossing the whole earth without touching the ground.

The Vision (8:6-8)

He came toward the two-horned ram I had seen standing beside the canal and charged him in great rage. I saw him attack the ram furiously, striking the ram and shattering his two horns. The ram was powerless to stand against him; the goat knocked him to the ground and trampled on him, and none could rescue the ram from his power. The goat became very great, but at the height of his power his large horn was broken off, and in its place four prominent horns grew up toward the four winds of heaven.

Again, this is parallel to Daniel 7, particularly verse 6, where Daniel wrote: "After that, I looked, and there before me was another beast, one that looked like a leopard. And on its back it had four wings like those of a bird." These verses show the swiftness of this coming king in the same way that Daniel 8:5 does with the words, "crossing the whole earth without touching the ground."

Daniel continues in 7:6, "This beast had four heads," like the four prominent horns that replaced the one prominent horn. Again we see the parallel between chapters 2, 7, and 8. We saw in chapter 7 that this was the kingdom of Greece, and the prominent horn was Alexander the Great, who died at the height of his power and was replaced by four kings and four kingdoms. If there is any question about that, look at the interpretation.

The Interpretation (8:21, 22)

"The shaggy goat is the king of Greece." God says that. "The large horn between his eyes is the first king." That large horn represents Alexander the Great, the first major king of Greece who conquered the world. "The four horns that replaced the one that was broken off represent four kingdoms that will emerge from his nation but will not have the same power." God explains the meaning for us.

Alexander the Great achieved unprecedented domination of the world — from Italy to India. He died suddenly at age thirty-three in 323 B.C., leaving behind two young sons, Alexander and Herakles. These boys were ultimately murdered, and the world was carved up between Alexander's powerful generals, the Diadochi.

There is no question now as to what Daniel 7 — 8 are talking about. Those four horns represent four kingdoms. Two of those kingdoms are taught in detail in most high school Western Civilization courses. They are the Selucids and the Ptolemies. Do you remember studying these? We are going to hear more about them when we get to chapter 11, but just keep them in mind for a moment.

It is important to understand that Alexander's rise to power was two centuries after Daniel made this prophecy — two hundred years! These four kingdoms could not have been imagined by any normal human mind. There would be no way a human could predict this. In fact, these prophecies are so accurate that liberal scholars, those who do not believe that the Bible is God's holy and inerrant Word, suggest that Daniel must have written this book in the first century before Christ. For them that is the only explanation for the accuracy of Daniel. They do not believe this is prophecy. They think it is recorded history, because it is so accurate.

We know why this prophecy is so accurate. It is because God wrote the book of Daniel, through the prophet. God not only knows the future, but he also controls, holds, and plans the future. He is the "wonderful" Savior (Isaiah 9:6). The word "wonderful" means "miraculous." He is an incredible Savior. He is not just somebody who died on the cross for our sins. He is the Lamb upon the throne. He planned all the events of history. He is the sovereign Lord who controls all the events of history.

He is a wonderful Savior, Jesus our Lord. If you can say along with King David, "The LORD is my shepherd," then know for certain that he wants the very best for you. He promises that he will work all things together for the good of those who love him, even a terrible, horrible, no-good, very bad day. This Shepherd does not always tell his sheep why they must go through such days, but he asks them to trust him.

Elisabeth Elliot Leitch tells the story of a shepherd she met in Scotland. Insects would often infest the skin of his animals; so he would have to give them a special treatment. This treatment involved dipping them in a barrel of antiseptic.

The shepherd would take his staff and run it under the horns of the ram. He then would turn the ram upside down and push his head and body under the healing water. The ram would kick and flail, trying to get away from the shepherd, but he was not strong enough. The shepherd would push him under for thirty seconds and then bring him up. The ram would be frightened, gasping for breath, still trying to get away.

Then the shepherd would take his staff and push him under the healing water a second time. He wanted so desperately to be able to tell this poor little ram that everything was all right and that this was being done for his good, but such knowledge was "too wonderful" for him, past finding out (Psalm 139:6). For the ram it was just a bad day. For the shepherd it was just part of his plan to give his little ram the best.

Now these two animals in Daniel's vision, images of two future nations, the goat and the ram, were reintroduced here for one reason. The loving shepherd of Israel graciously gave his sheep a time line so the people of God would know approximately when the time of the indignation would come upon them. This time of indignation is explained in the third and final part of the vision.

A MAN WITH A STERN FACE (8:23)

In the latter part of their reign, when the rebels have become completely wicked, a stern-faced king, a master of intrigue, will arise.

This "stern-faced . . . master of intrigue" would arise in the latter part of "their reign." The pronoun "their" refers to the reign of the four horns or kings. Daniel predicted that this "stern-faced man" would arise in the latter part of the reign of the Selucids and Ptolemies. Greece came to power over the Persians around 330 B.C. They stayed in power until Rome replaced Greece as a world power around 146 B.C. Just as Daniel predicted, a "stern-faced . . . master of intrigue" came to power around 175 B.C., the latter part of the rule of the four kings of Greece. If you take the plain reading of this prophecy, there is no way that this could refer to the Antichrist, who will appear before Jesus comes back for his saints.

In the prologue to his commentary on Daniel, Jerome wrote:

And because Porphyry saw that all these things had been fulfilled and could not deny that they had taken place, he overcame this evidence of historical accuracy by taking refuge in this evasion, contending that whatever is foretold concerning Antichrist at the end of the world was actually fulfilled in the reign of Antiochus Epiphanes, because of certain similarities to things which took place at his time. But this very attack testifies to Daniel's accuracy. For so striking was the reliability of what the prophet foretold, that he could not appear to unbelievers as a predicter of the future, but rather a narrator of things already past.

The Vision (8:9-14)

Out of one of them [that is, one of the four horns or kings of Greece that appeared after Alexander the Great died, v. 8] came another horn, which started small but grew in power to the south and to the east and toward the Beautiful Land [that is, Israel]. It grew until it reached the host of the

heavens, and it threw some of the starry host down to the earth and tram-
pled on them. It set itself up to be as great as the Prince of the host; it
took away the daily sacrifice from him, and the place of his sanctuary was
brought low. Because of the rebellion, the host of the saints and the daily
sacrifice were given over to it. It prospered in everything it did, and truth
was thrown to the ground. Then I heard a holy one speaking [an angel], and
another holy one said to him, "How long . . . ?" (vv. 9-13)

Is that not the question we always ask in the midst of a terrible, horrible, no-good, very bad day? How long do I have to stay in this job? How long
do I have to remain in this horrible marriage? How long do I have to wait
for a job since I have been out of work so long? How long until I know the
outcome of this disease? How long?

Usually God does not tell us how long, but in this case he did. He told
the people of God how long it would be so that they would trust him during
this terrible day. He could tell us how long our difficulties will last if he
wanted us to know. Instead, he wants us to learn from Daniel that he has
things under control, and he is working them out in his time for our good.
So in the meantime we must trust him in quiet submission.

The prophecy tells us how long it would take for the vision to be
fulfilled:

Then I heard a holy one speaking, and another holy one said to him, "How
long will it take for the vision to be fulfilled — the vision concerning the
daily sacrifice, the rebellion that causes desolation, and the surrender of
the sanctuary and of the host that will be trampled underfoot?" He said
to me, "It will take 2,300 evenings and mornings; then the sanctuary will
be reconsecrated." (8:13, 14)

Daniel says that in 2,300 evenings and mornings the sanctuary or the
temple would be reconsecrated. What sanctuary? Remember, Daniel and
his people are in exile in Babylon, and the sanctuary had been destroyed in
586 B.C. This is the first indication to Daniel that there will again be a sanctuary in Jerusalem. He had patiently waited twelve years (551-539 B.C.) for
this to happen, and this may explain why Daniel finally asked the Lord to
rebuild the sanctuary in his prayer found in Daniel 9.

The sanctuary he is speaking of here is the one that was rebuilt in 516
B.C. under the leadership of Zerrubbabel. It was still there in Jesus' day.
Daniel's first glimpse of the new temple was a little tarnished when he
learned that a man would persecute God's people, shutting down the sanctuary in one horrible, very bad day. That was the bad news. The good news
was that after 2,300 evenings it would be reconsecrated! But what did all
this mean? The Lord does not leave us without an interpretation.

The Interpretation (8:23-27)

"In the latter part of their reign, when rebels have become completely wicked, a stern-faced king, a master of intrigue, will arise. He will become very strong, but not by his own power. He will cause astounding devastation and will succeed in whatever he does. He will destroy the mighty men and the holy people. He will cause deceit to prosper, and he will consider himself superior. When they [the Jewish people] feel secure, he will destroy many and take his stand against the Prince of princes [the Son of God, the Lord in heaven]. Yet he will be destroyed, but not by human power. The vision of the evenings and mornings that has been given to you is true, but seal up the vision, for it concerns the distant future." I, Daniel, was exhausted and lay ill for several days.

That is sort of how I felt when I was studying this chapter. I had a little glimpse of how Daniel must have felt. "Then I got up and went about the king's business. I was appalled by the vision; it was beyond understanding."

THE PROPHECY IS NOT BEYOND OUR UNDERSTANDING

This prophecy is not beyond our understanding — not because we are smarter than Daniel, but because we have seen its fulfillment. We not only know what the ram represented and what the goat represented, but we now know who the stern-faced man of intrigue was. There really is no question about the interpretation. But prophecy is not only meaningful for those who see its fulfillment — it is also meaningful for those who look ahead to its fulfillment.

Those who lived during the transition from the rule of Persia to the rule of Greece could get excited about the fact that they were getting closer to this event predicted by Daniel. He had given them many signs, and they were responsible to know them so they would not be caught off guard. Some of those signs were given in the form of imagery like the ram and the goat, but the imagery stood for something real that would take place.

The same is true for us regarding the Second Coming of Christ. He has told us many things to look for when his return is close. Some things are predicted using imagery, but that imagery stands for something real that will take place. When it happens, we will know. But woe to the person who is ignorant of all the prophecies. They will be caught off guard when some of the final events take place.

The Prophecy Is About Antiochus Epiphanes

Who was this "stern-faced . . . man of intrigue" who was about to come? The prophecy is about the coming of Antiochus IV, called Epiphanes.

Antiochus IV reigned over the Seleucid Empire from 175-164 B.C. Daniel said this would occur in the latter part of the reign of the four kings. It was about 150 years from the time of Alexander's death to the time of Antiochus. Daniel said it would be a while until he came.

As Daniel prophesied, this horn started small and grew in power. This man's father was Antiochus III. When his father died, Antiochus IV was not given the throne, but his older brother, Seleucus IV, was. Antiochus had royal blood, but there was no way he could be king. He went to Athens to study, and while he was there he grew in power, but ever so slowly. In fact, at one point he became the chief magistrate of Athens. While he was in Athens, his brother Seleucus died. Through political manipulation for which he became famous (he was "a master of intrigue," v. 23) he managed to get rid of his nephew and gain the throne. He started small but he grew in power.[6]

Other phrases (v. 9) tell us he grew in power "to the south" — that is, Egypt, "to the east" — that is, Syria, and "to the Beautiful Land" — that is, Israel. Antiochus finally set his sights on the Jewish people. Allan MacRae points out in his commentary on *Daniel* that neither the Ptolemies of Egypt nor the Seleucids of Syria had anything to do with Israel until this time. For 150 years the policy of these four kingdoms was "hands off of Israel." But Antiochus determined that he was going to bring Greek culture and customs to Israel and wean them away from their God and his Law.[7]

That is described for us in Daniel 8:10: "It [speaking of the little horn, Antiochus] grew until it reached the host of the heavens, and it threw some of the starry host down to the earth and trampled on them. It set itself up to be as great as the prince of the host [that is, the Son of God himself]; it took away the daily sacrifice from him, and the place of his sanctuary was brought low. Because of rebellion the host of the saints and the daily sacrifice were given over to it . . . truth was thrown to the ground."

We know from the record of history that Antiochus Epiphanes set himself up to be God in place of the Prince of princes. In fact, that is why they call him Epiphanes. He was Antiochus IV, but Epiphanes means "the manifest god." He put this phrase on all the coins — "Antiochus, the manifest God" — putting himself in the place of the Prince of princes.

The sentence "truth was thrown to the ground" found its fulfillment in the burning of Torah scrolls by Antiochus. This is recorded in I Maccabees 1:56, 57 in the Apocrypha, which describes events in the middle of the second century before Christ. Though not the inspired Word of God, the books of Maccabees give important historical events in the life of the Jewish people.

The books of the law that they found they tore to pieces and burned with fire.
Anyone found possessing the book of the covenant, or anyone who adhered
to the law, was condemned to death by decree of the king. (NRSV)

Daniel 8:24 says, "He will become very strong, but not by his own power. He will cause astounding devastation and will succeed in whatever he does. He will destroy the mighty men and the holy people. He will cause deceit to prosper, and he will consider himself superior. When they feel secure, he will destroy many and take his stand against the Prince of princes."

In I Maccabees 1:29-32 we find that Antiochus sent a contingent of soldiers to Jerusalem to pretend to make friends with the Jewish people. When he began in his deceitful way to make friends with the Jews, the soldiers seized control of Jerusalem and the temple. They fell upon the people and killed them, just as it says in the prophecy: "when they feel secure, he will destroy many" (Daniel 8:25). He was indeed "a master of intrigue." When the religious Jews resisted him, he began severe persecutions against them. The time of indignation and wrath had arrived as prophesied by Daniel 350 years before. It was a terrible day.

Furthermore, as the prophecy said, "He will . . . take his stand against the Prince of princes" (v. 25). Antiochus gave orders to force the Jews to worship pagan gods in the temple of Israel. He put a stop to the regular sacrifices, desecrated the temple by placing a statue of Jupiter in front of the sacred altar, and ordered the people to offer swine as a sacrifice to this heathen god. If they refused to worship him, they were put to death. The temple doors were closed, the sacrifices of the Jews were prohibited in 167 B.C., and the Jews could no longer worship in the temple.

God had prophesied the coming of that horrible day when the temple would be closed and the sacrifices of God's people stopped. But he also told them that it would only last 2,300 evenings and mornings. This could either be 2,300 days with the evening and morning being one day, or it could be 2,300 individual sacrifices, half in the morning and half in the evening. If the latter is the case, then it would be a total of 1,150 days or about three years. Someone looking ahead would have to consider both possibilities. As we look back with 20/20 hindsight, we find something very interesting.

While the temple was closed, many of the Jewish people fled from Jerusalem and went out into the wilderness. Soon there was a contingent of rebels living in the desert. One man rose to leadership, and he had five sons — the five sons of Maccabee. They started guerrilla raids in Jerusalem, attempting to win back control of the temple and start the sacrifices again. I don't know if they knew about the prophecy of Daniel 8 or not, but I think they might have. Whatever the case, history records that in 164 B.C. the high priesthood was reconsecrated. And approximately three years after the temple was closed, it was reopened. According to I Maccabees 4:52, they reinstated the sacrifice on the twenty-fifth day of the ninth month, the month Kislev, in the year 165 B.C.

The NIV footnote of Daniel 8:14 points out that Antiochus set up the pagan altar on Kislev 25, 168 B.C.[8] The sacrifices were begun on Kislev 25, 165 B.C., approximately 1,150 days later. God had delivered them from a terrible, horrible, no-good, very bad day just as he had promised.

Let it be an encouragement to you that when the Lord prophesies about the length of a time of persecution, he means it. Why doesn't he just say three years instead of 2,300 mornings and evenings? I don't know. Phrases like that are used in prophetic literature, but it doesn't mean that what is prophesied is not real. So when he tells those of us who may be alive when the Antichrist comes that a world leader will appear to have a fatal wound to the head and to come back to life (Revelation 13:1-4), that he will utter blasphemies for only forty-two months (that is, three and a half years) and then he will be put to an end, let that be an encouragement to you. If you are here during that three and a half years, then just like the Maccabee brothers in the midst of their three-year trial, hold on in the midst of that terrible day, because God has said it will end at the appointed time.

This is how it ended back then. The Maccabee brothers stormed the temple. When they got into the temple and restored it, they celebrated with a festival. During that festival, they lit a lamp. The oil usually lasted only a few days. They called this feast the Feast of Lights, or in the Hebrew *Channukah*. This is referenced in John 10:22 (NIV footnote) when Jesus went up to Jerusalem to celebrate Hannukah, the winter festival. Hannukah celebrates the historical account of the priests lighting the candle in the temple after it was reconsecrated. The candle was only supposed to last one day, but this time it burned for eight days.

Was this just a legend, or did God truly intervene? Amazing things do happen when God delivers his people from horrible days. In 1997 the super-typhoon Paka hit the island of Guam. During this storm that stalled over the island of Guam, Trans World Radio was the only radio station still transmitting in the midst of sustained winds of 200 mph. Their power was knocked out along with everyone else on the island. But they had a backup generator, and the man who was on the air vowed to keep talking until the fuel of the generator ran out. After some time on the air, he told his listeners that the fuel would run out at any time because there was only enough fuel to last five hours. God's people were praying all around the world, and the Lord kept that generator going for *thirteen hours*. One of the Trans World Radio missionaries on Guam at the time, Charlie Troxell, said, "There is no human explanation as to why the generator lasted that long." The missionaries of Trans World Radio know well that God can do such things.

Maybe that is what happened to those candles when the Temple of Jerusalem was reconsecrated. Whatever the case, this is why Hanukkah is celebrated with an eight-candle menorah. It is an eight-day festival that Jesus himself celebrated. To this day Hanukkah is celebrated on the twenty-fifth day of the ninth month, the month of Kislev, our month of December.

We have a wonderful Savior, Jesus our Lord. God restored the temple, and God restored his people. That same God, if he is your Heavenly Father, can and will take care of you. He is our King, and he will overthrow his enemies. The Westminster Shorter Catechism asks, "How does Christ execute the office of a king?" The answer is: "Christ executes the office of a king by subduing us to Himself and by ruling and defending us and in conquering all His and our enemies." Do you believe that?

Daniel 8:25 ends by saying, "He [Antiochus] will be destroyed, but not by human power." Toward the end of his reign Antiochus led an expedition toward the east, toward Babylon. While he was on that trip, he died. According to the historical record, he was not killed in battle by a sword nor by an assassin. He died from a nervous disorder that quickly took his life. He was "destroyed, but not by human power." God warned his people of this man's coming and promised that he would not last too long. God turned the curse into a blessing, because the people of God were stronger spiritually after their encounter with Antiochus Epiphanes.

God has a way of doing that for his children. We don't deserve it, but he does it. I do not know why it is so hard for us to remember the faithfulness of God and the love of our Heavenly Father in times of difficulty. But the next time you have a terrible, horrible, no-good, very bad day, remember that your God is the Wonderful Savior and the Sovereign King who wants the best for you, and he will work it out in his time. You can trust him. The late S. M. Lockridge wrote this encouragement.

> *No barrier can hinder Him*
> *From pouring out His blessing.*
> *He's enduringly strong;*
> *He's entirely sincere;*
> *He's eternally steadfast;*
> *He's immortally graceful;*
> *He's imperially powerful;*
> *He's impartially merciful.*
>
> *He's the greatest phenomenon that has*
> *Ever crossed the horizon of this world.*
> *He's God's Son. He's a sinner's Savior.*
> *He's the centerpiece of civilization.*
> *I'm trying to tell you, Church—*
> *You can trust Him!*

He does not have to call for help,
And you can't confuse Him.
He doesn't need you and He doesn't need me.
He stands alone in the solitude of Himself.

He's august and He's unique.
He's unparalleled; He's unprecedented;
He's supreme and preeminent.

He's the loftiest idea in literature.
He's the highest personality in philosophy.
He's the supreme problem of higher criticism.
He's the fundamental doctrine of true theology.
He's the cardinal necessity of spiritual religion.

He's the miracle of the age.
He's the superlative of everything good
　　that you can call Him.
I'm trying to tell you — you can trust Him!

He can satisfy all of our needs
And He can do it simultaneously.
He supplies strength for the weak.
He's available for the tempted and tried;
He sympathizes and He sees.

He guards and He guides.
He heals the sick. He cleansed the lepers.
He forgives sinners.
He discharges debtors;
He delivers captives.
He defends the feeble;
He blesses the young.
He guards the aged;
He rewards the diligent.
He beautifies the meek.
I'm trying to tell you — you can trust Him!

He's the key to knowledge.
He's the wellspring of wisdom.
He's the doorway of deliverance.
He's the pathway to peace.
He's the roadway to righteousness.

He's the highway to holiness.
He's the gateway to glory.
You can trust Him.

He's the Master of the mighty.
He's the Captain of the conquerors.
He's the Head of the heroes.
He's the Leader of legislators.
He's the Overseer of the overcomers.
He's the Governor of Governors.
He's the Prince of princes.
He's the King of kings.
He's the Lord of lords.
You can trust Him.

His office is manifold.
His promise is sure.
His life is matchless.
His goodness is limitless.
His mercy is everlasting.
His love never changes.
His Word is enough.
His grace is sufficient.
His reign is righteous.
His yoke is easy.
His burden is light.
I wish I could describe Him to you!

He's indescribable because
He's incomprehensible.
He's irresistible and He's invincible.
You can't get Him off your hands.
You can't get Him out of your mind.
You can't outlive Him
And you can't live without Him.

Pilate couldn't stand Him
When he found out he couldn't stop Him.
Pilate couldn't find any fault in Him.
The witnesses couldn't get their testimonies to agree.
Herod couldn't kill Him.
Death couldn't handle Him.
And thank God, the grave couldn't hold Him.

There was nobody before Him.
There will be nobody after Him.
He had no predecessor,
And He'll have no successor.
You can't impeach Him,
And He's not going to resign.
You can trust Him!

11

O Lord, Listen, Forgive, and Act

Daniel 9:1-19

In 1980 Peggy MacDonald walked around a piece of property in St. Louis County while it was still undeveloped ground — twenty-two acres of trees, rocks, and weeds. But she prayed that God would one day plant a church there, and years later Twin Oaks Presbyterian Church built on that very site. At that time she wrote in her diary:

> First, I asked God to do something powerful with numbers to make this land financially accessible to his people to do his work. As I walked the land, I talked with God and dreamed a little. I asked God to make this church a place where people could come and be made strong. A place where they didn't need to feel like they had everything together; a place where God and his people would help them put things together. The third part of my prayer was that this church not just be a refuge, but also a people who would reach out to the community with concern and say, "I'm coming to your house." Like Jesus when he found Zaccheus up a tree and said, "Come down, for I am going to your house." I prayed that this would be a church willing to reach out to people who were up a tree, perplexed and searching; they would not be too busy, but would be willing to say, "If you cannot come here, we will go to where you are."

She cried out to the Lord in that prayer in 1980 as she walked around and around that property. For the next ten years she drove by that property many times, but very little happened to that property in those ten years. The only thing she saw was that a corporation had cut down many trees in order to build condominiums on the site. I'm sure Peggy shrugged her shoulders more than once and thought, *Oh well, I guess it wasn't God's will to have a church built on this property.* Little did she know what Heaven was up to. Little did she know that she had laid hold of the power of God in that prayer, and Heaven was set in motion. The message of Daniel 9:1-19 is this: Since we can lay hold of the power of God through prayer, we must cry out to him. Using Daniel's prayer as a model, we will see that we must pray, "O Lord, listen! O Lord, forgive! O Lord, act!"

WE MUST CRY OUT, "O LORD, LISTEN" (9:17a)

"Now, our God, hear the prayers and petitions of your servant."

In 1 Kings 8:28-30 King Solomon spoke to God:

> *Give attention to your servant's prayer and his plea for mercy, O LORD my God. Hear the cry and the prayer that your servant is praying in your presence this day. May your eyes be open toward this temple night and day, this place of which you said, "My name shall be there," so that you will hear the prayer your servant prays toward this place. Hear the supplication of your servant and of your people Israel when they pray toward this place. Hear from heaven, your dwelling place, and when you hear, forgive.*

Eight times in the Psalms (NIV) the words, "Hear my prayer" are used. That was also the cry of Daniel as he sought the Lord.

The Background of the Prayer (9:1-3)

The *date* of the prayer is found in verse 1: "In the first year of Darius son of Xerxes (a Mede by descent), who was made ruler over the Babylonian Kingdom." The year would have been 538 B.C., the same year in which the events of Daniel 5 took place when Belshazzar was having his party and the handwriting appeared on the wall. That very night, King Darius the Mede conquered Babylon and killed Belshazzar.

The *reason* for the prayer is found in verse 2: "In the first year of his reign, I, Daniel, understood from the Scriptures, according to the word of the LORD given to Jeremiah the prophet, that the desolation of Jerusalem would last seventy years." Daniel was reading the words of the prophet Jeremiah. Now remember that Jeremiah was a contemporary of Daniel. Daniel knew that Jeremiah was a prophet, and he believed that what Jeremiah wrote were the very words of God. They were accepted as Scripture the moment they were written.

Some people think that the writings of the prophets and apostles were not accepted as coming from God until centuries after they were written. Such was not the case, as we see in 2 Peter 3:15, 16: "Paul . . . writes the same way in all his letters, speaking in them of these matters. His letters contain some things that are hard to understand, which ignorant and unstable people distort, as they do the other Scriptures." Peter and Paul were contemporaries. Paul's writings were immediately accepted as Scripture. As Paul wrote to the Thessalonians, "We also thank God continually because, when you received the word of God, which you heard from us, you accepted it not as the word of men, but as it actually is, the word of God" (1 Thessalonians 2:13).

Daniel read and understood that Israel's captivity in Babylon would last seventy years. He remembered that he was taken captive in the first wave of the captivity, about 606 B.C. Seventy years would bring the end of captivity and would be followed by the restoration of the people to the city of Jerusalem around 536 B.C. Jeremiah wrote:

> *This is what the LORD says: "When seventy years are completed for Babylon, I will come to you and fulfill my gracious promise to bring you back to this place. For I know the plans I have for you," declares the LORD, "plans to prosper you and not to harm you, plans to give you hope and a future. Then you will call upon me and come and pray to me, and I will listen to you. You will seek me and find me when you seek me with all your heart. I will be found by you," declares the LORD, "and will bring you back from captivity." (Jeremiah 29:10-14)*

What Daniel read in the Scriptures set him to praying, pleading the promises of God. "You said the desolation would only last seventy years. That is just two years away. Please listen to your servant's prayer, and restore the city and the sanctuary that bear your name."

We too need to plead the promises of Scripture. Most of our prayers ask God to give us more things, fix problems, or heal sickness. We do not always know God's will in those circumstances; so we cannot say for sure how he will answer. Paul writes to the Romans:

> *The Spirit helps us in our weakness. We do not know what we ought to pray for, but the Spirit himself intercedes for us with groans that words cannot express. And he who searches our hearts knows the mind of the Spirit, because the Spirit intercedes for the saints in accordance with God's will. (8:26, 27)*

This assures us that the Holy Spirit takes whatever we ask for and molds it into the will of God. So we know that his answer is what is best for us, though it is not always what we ask for.

But when we plead the promises of God, we know that what we are asking for is God's will. He has recorded it for us in the pages of Scripture. First John 5:14, 15 says, "This is the confidence we have in approaching God: that if we ask anything according to his will, he hears us. And if we know that he hears us — whatever we ask — we know that we have what we asked of him."

For example, Paul wrote, "For God did not give us a spirit of timidity, but a spirit of power, of love and of self-discipline" (2 Timothy 1:7). If we find ourselves frightened and weak, we can ask God to empower us to accomplish the task he has given us to do, and we know he will answer that prayer.

I once worked with a couple that was having marital problems. The husband said, "I just don't love my wife anymore." I told him that God commands us to love our wives (Ephesians 5:25). He knew that. I also reminded him that if he just considered his wife a neighbor, God commanded him to love his neighbor as himself (Matthew 22:39). He agreed with that.

Finally I said, "Let's suppose your wife has made you so angry that you look at her as your enemy. What does God command us concerning our enemies?" He responded with an inquisitive look as though he was wondering where I was going with this. I was, of course, thinking of Matthew 6:44.

I reminded him that God does not command us to do anything that he does not give us the grace to do. I read him the verse from 2 Timothy 1:7 and asked him to plead the promise of God to restore his love for his wife. God answered that prayer faster than I expected, and they are once again happily married. Let us plead the promises of God.

The *attitude* of prayer is found in Daniel 9:3: "So I turned to the Lord God and pleaded with him in prayer and petition, in fasting, and in sackcloth and ashes." The attitude of Daniel was one of earnestness and humility. His earnestness is seen in the words, "and pleaded with him in prayer." This was the attitude of Jesus in the Garden of Gethsemane as he pleaded with the Father to take the cup from him. "And being in anguish, he prayed more earnestly, and his sweat was like drops of blood falling to the ground" (Luke 22:44). This was the attitude of the church in Jerusalem as they prayed for Peter, who was in prison. "So Peter was kept in prison, but the church was earnestly praying to God for him" (Acts 12:5). This should be our attitude as we pray. So often earnestness is missing from our prayers. They seem so rote, so mechanical, without passion.

The writer of Hebrews gives us a hint that might help restore passion in our prayer life: "Remember those in prison as if you were their fellow prisoners, and those who are mistreated as if you yourselves were suffering" (13:3). The earnestness of prayer returns when we pray for people as though we were in their situation.

A young pastor was preparing a sermon in his study when there was a knock at his door, and someone told him that a child had been hit by a car in front of his church. He was informed that the ambulance was there, and the child was getting help. He looked up and said he would be right out after finishing his thought. Then his secretary came to the door and announced that it was his own daughter who had been hit by the car, and the pastor jumped up from his desk and ran to the street. Our identity with the need makes all the difference in the world.

I remember an incident n a prayer meeting years ago. A young lady had added her father's name to the prayer list. Some prayed for him; many just overlooked his name. One evening this young woman shared how her father was dying of cancer and that he did not know the Lord. Her story was told with passion and tears. Suddenly that became one of the main focuses of our prayer time. We rejoiced with her when he gave his heart to the Lord just days before he died. We need to pray earnestly.

The humility of Daniel is seen externally in the sackcloth and fasting. The attitude of humility is necessary in prayer, though the sackcloth and fasting are not required. Both of these external acts in Old Testament times were outward signs of a heart that was grieving over sin. When the people of Nineveh repented of their sins, the king declared a fast, and they all put on sackcloth, covering their heads with ashes (Jonah 3:5).

The problem is that it is easy for the external display to become a substitute for the internal reality. That is why Joel said, "'Even now,' declares the LORD, 'return to me with all your heart, with fasting and weeping and mourning.' Rend your heart and not your garments" (Joel 2:12, 13).

The same is true with fasting. Some people today think that fasting adds another twist to God's arm to get what they want in prayer. People come to this conclusion because of a mistranslation of Mark 9:29. In the text the disciples were unable to cast out the demon from the little boy. The King James Version says, "And he said unto them, This kind can come forth by nothing, but by prayer and fasting." It sounds as if prayer alone is not enough. But the proper translation is, "This kind can come out only by prayer." On that occasion the disciples failed to ask for divine assistance through prayer.

Isaiah further confirms this by pointing out that the true fast is not just going without food. He says that merely going without food won't make God notice you more or be more likely to answer your prayer. God looks at the heart.

> "Why have we fasted," they say,
> "and you have not seen it?
> Why have we humbled ourselves,
> and you have not noticed?"
> Yet on the day of your fasting, you do as you please
> and exploit all your workers.
> Your fasting ends in quarreling and strife,

> *and in striking each other with wicked fists.*
> *You cannot fast as you do today*
> *and expect your voice to be heard on high.*
> *Is this the kind of fast I have chosen,*
> *only a day for a man to humble himself?*
> *Is it only for bowing one's head like a reed*
> *and for lying on sackcloth and ashes?*
> *Is that what you call a fast,*
> *a day acceptable to the LORD?*
> *Is not this the kind of fasting I have chosen:*
> *to loose the chains of injustice*
> *and untie the cords of the yoke,*
> *to set the oppressed free*
> *and break every yoke?*
> *Is it not to share your food with the hungry*
> *and to provide the poor wanderer with shelter—*
> *when you see the naked, to clothe him,*
> *and not to turn away from your own flesh and blood?*
> *Then your light will break forth like the dawn,*
> *and your healing will quickly appear;*
> *then your righteousness will go before you,*
> *and the glory of the LORD will be your rear guard.*
> *Then you will call, and the LORD will answer;*
> *you will cry for help, and he will say: Here am I. (Isaiah 58:3-9a)*

The attitude of Daniel shows us that we should come into the presence of the Lord with an earnestness that storms the gates of Heaven, but a humility that realizes that he is sovereign and we are sinful. We do not even deserve to make these requests, much less feel like our fasting can twist his arm or our prayer can command the Lord what to do. Prayer is clearly the position of a beggar coming into the presence of a king.

The Basis of the Prayer (9:17, 18)

The basis of prayer is a concern for God's glory. "Now, our God, hear the prayers and petitions of your servant. For your sake, O Lord . . ." (9:17). Daniel makes this request not for his own sake, but for the Lord's. Maturing in prayer is seen when we are more concerned about the Creator's glory in our prayers than the creature's comfort.

The basis of prayer is an understanding of God's mercy. "We do not make requests of you because we are righteous, but because of your great mercy" (9:18b). Though James says the prayers of the righteous avail much (5:16), it is never on the basis of *our* righteousness that prayers are answered.

Daniel's prayer makes it very clear that we do not deserve any answers to our prayers. If we deserved answers to our prayers, then Daniel would have made his plea because of God's justice. Justice is getting what we deserve. Instead he made his plea according to God's mercy. We can only plead the mercy of God.

Over twenty years ago I was introduced to bank-by-phone. You simply dial in your payments, and the bank does the rest. It sounded like a great plan for me — until I made a terrible mistake one day. My former practice had been to write the checks to pay my bills in the evening, then take my paycheck to the bank the next day and drop my checks off in the mail. What I did not realize about the new way of doing things was that when you bank by phone, the payment is immediately subtracted from the account. Since I did not make my deposit until the next day, all fifteen payments bounced. At fifteen dollars per check, that totaled a lot of money for a poor assistant pastor.

I could not afford to pay my penalty. So I went to the bank and asked to talk with a vice-president. I explained the story to his secretary and told her that I realized I was completely in the wrong. I had no merit on my own that I could boast. I didn't have a lot of money in the bank, and I hadn't been a customer all that long. I told her that I was coming simply to "beg for mercy." In a few minutes a gentleman kindly ushered me into his office and told me to have a seat. He looked at me with a smile and said, "Tell me your story. I have never had anyone beg for mercy before. I like that." He mercifully forgave my debt.

By the mercies of God we can cry out, "O Lord, listen!" And once we have his ear, we can go on to the next step.

WE MUST CRY OUT, "O LORD, FORGIVE!" (9:15, 16)

Now, O Lord our God, who brought your people out of Egypt with a mighty hand and who made for yourself a name that endures to this day, we have sinned, we have done wrong. O Lord, in keeping with all your righteous acts, turn away your anger and your wrath from Jerusalem, your city, your holy hill. Our sins and the iniquities of our fathers have made Jerusalem and your people an object of scorn to all those around us.

When the Lord taught his disciples to pray, confession of sin was an important part of that prayer. Jesus taught us to pray, "Forgive us our debts, as we have also forgiven our debtors" (Matthew 6:12). Most of the prayers of Scripture follow the pattern described in the acrostic ACTS: Adoration, Confession, Thanksgiving based on truth from Scripture, and Supplication. This prayer of Daniel is no different. The adoration is found in verse 4, the confession is seen in verses 5-11a, the truth is remembered in verses 11b-15, and the supplication comes in verses 16-19.

We Must Confess Our Sinfulness (9:4-6)

O Lord, the great and awesome God, who keeps his covenant of love with all who love him and obey his commands, we have sinned and done wrong. We have been wicked and have rebelled; we have turned away from your commands and laws. We have not listened to your servants the prophets, who spoke in your name to our kings, our princes and our fathers, and to all the people of the land.

That confession of sin could be ours. Like us, Daniel lived among a people who were wicked, who had rebelled against the great and awesome God. They had turned away from his commands, ignoring and defying them, just as we have in America. They had shed innocent blood, distorted truth, and violated marriage covenants. Jeremiah wrote:

"I will hand them over to Nebuchadnezzar king of Babylon. . . . For they have done outrageous things in Israel; they have committed adultery with their neighbors' wives and in my name have spoken lies, which I did not tell them to do. I know it and am a witness to it," declares the LORD. (Jeremiah 29:21, 23)

America was founded on the principles of right and wrong revealed in the Word of God, but many have done outrageous things just like Israel. America is filled with adultery, murder, lies, and wickedness.

But notice that Daniel does not just confess the people's sins and make apologies for the sins of others, which is so easy to do. Rather, he included himself among those who sinned against the Lord. This man was thrown into the lions' den by King Darius for praying at his open window, because the other administrators could not find any wrongdoing in Daniel's life, present or past. (By the way, Daniel 9 may have been one of his prayers from that open window.) Yet this godly man says, "We have sinned and done wrong. We have been wicked and rebelled. We have turned away from your commands and laws. We have not listened to your servants the prophets."

It is not only the unbelievers in America who have sinned. We are all sinners and fall short of the glory of God. The Westminster Shorter Catechism says, "We sin daily in thought, word, and deed."[1] A prayer of confession used hundreds of years ago in the time of the Reformation says, "Deepen the sorrow within us for our sins."

The Pilgrims were a godly people, but when a drought struck their land, they turned to the Lord, humbly confessing their sins. Edward Winslow described the drought and their confession:

> There scarce fell any rain, so that the stalk of that [planting which] was first set, began to send forth the ear before it came to half growth, and that which was later, not like to yield any at all, both blade and stalk hanging the head and changing the color in such manner as we judged it utterly dead. Now were our hopes overthrown, and we [were] discouraged, our joy turned to mourning . . . because God, which hitherto had been our only shield and supporter, now seemed in His anger to arm Himself against us. And who can withstand the fierceness of His wrath?
>
> These and the like considerations moved not only every good man privately to enter into examination with his own estate between God and his conscience, and so to humiliation before Him, but also to humble ourselves together before the Lord by fasting and prayer. To that end, a day was appointed by public authority, and set apart from all other employments.[2]

We Must Also Confess the Righteousness of God (9:7, 8)

Lord, you are righteous, but this day we are covered with shame — the men of Judah and people of Jerusalem and all Israel, both near and far, in all the countries where you have scattered us because of our unfaithfulness to you. O LORD, we and our kings, our princes and our fathers are covered with shame because we have sinned against you.

Today we are covered with shame, for America, like Israel, is a pitiful place morally. In our shame we must confess that God is righteous in his judgments.

All Israel has transgressed your law and turned away, refusing to obey you. Therefore the curses and sworn judgments written in the Law of Moses, the servant of God, have been poured out on us, because we have sinned against you. You have fulfilled the words spoken against us and against our rulers by bringing upon us great disaster. Under the whole heaven nothing has ever been done like what has been done to Jerusalem. Just as it is written in the Law of Moses, all this disaster has come upon us, yet we have not sought the favor of the LORD our God by turning from our sins and giving attention to your truth. The LORD did not hesitate to bring the disaster upon us, for the LORD our God is righteous in everything he does; yet we have not obeyed him. (9:11-14)

The Lord is righteous when he brings disaster upon us for our shameful sin. Revelation 16:7 says, "Yes, Lord God Almighty, true and just are your judgments." Jeremiah writes:

> *Yes, this is what the LORD Almighty says: "I will send the sword, famine and plague against them and I will make them like poor figs that are so bad they cannot be eaten. I will pursue them with the sword, famine and plague and will make them abhorrent to all the kingdoms of the earth and an object of cursing and horror, of scorn and reproach, among all the nations where I drive them. (Jeremiah 29:17, 18)*

Why should we be surprised by destructive hurricanes in the Southeast? Why should we be surprised by deadly twisters in the Midwest? Why should we be surprised by disastrous floods in the Northeast and devastating fires in the Southwest? These are not quirks of nature. They are the judgments of God upon a nation covered with shame.

Does this mean that the people who experience this destruction are more wicked than others? No. Jesus encountered that question when he was here on earth.

> *Now there were some present at that time who told Jesus about the Galileans whose blood Pilate had mixed with their sacrifices. Jesus answered, "Do you think that these Galileans were worse sinners than all the other Galileans because they suffered this way? I tell you, no! But unless you repent, you too will all perish. Or those eighteen who died when the tower in Siloam fell on them — do you think they were more guilty than all the others living in Jerusalem? I tell you, no! But unless you repent, you too will all perish." (Luke 13:1-5)*

So the bad news is that God does punish sin with temporal judgments, and they are righteous judgments. But the good news is that he is also righteous in his forgiveness.

> *Lord, you are righteous. . . . The Lord our God is merciful and forgiving, even though we have rebelled against him; we have not obeyed the LORD our God or kept the laws he gave us through his servants the prophets. (Daniel 9:7, 9, 10)*

The Lord is righteous even in his forgiveness. He does not just turn his head, wink at our sin, and pretend that it did not happen. The Lord says he "does not leave the guilty unpunished" (Exodus 34:7). Because God is just, all sin will be punished. Either a person will pay the penalty for his own sin, or someone else must pay the penalty for him. But who would be gracious enough to pay the price of sin and bear the pain of Hell in our place? The answer, of course, is Jesus Christ.

But how could Jesus pay for my sin and God still preserve his justice? Paul answers that in Romans 3:25, 26:

> *God presented [Jesus] as a sacrifice of atonement, through faith in his blood. He did this to demonstrate his justice, because in his forbearance he had left the sins committed beforehand unpunished — he did it to demonstrate his justice at the present time, so as to be just and the one who justifies those who have faith in Jesus.*

Janet is a member of the congregation I pastor. She has a son named Matthew. When he was five years old, he had done something wrong and was going to be punished for his sin. He was concerned about his disobedience, and it made him wonder if he would go to Heaven when he died. His mother began to share the gospel with her little five-year-old. She explained how Jesus took our punishment upon himself. The idea went right over his head. Then Janet explained that she would now take the spanking that he deserved for his disobedience. Suddenly the message clicked, and he received Jesus Christ as his Lord and Savior.

So we can cry out, "O Lord, listen! O Lord, forgive!" Once we have his attention and know we are forgiven, then we can go further.

WE MUST CRY OUT, "O LORD, ACT!" (9:19)

> *O Lord, listen! O Lord, forgive! O Lord, hear and act! For your sake, O my God, do not delay, because your city and your people bear your Name.*

We need to boldly ask our Lord to act, but then we need to keep our eyes open looking for his answer. The church in Jerusalem was earnestly praying for the release of Peter. As soon as they began to pray, an answer was given. They did not know it yet, but an angel had been sent to remove the chains from Peter's arms and to open the gates of the prison. But when Peter arrived at the home of Mary, the mother of John, Rhoda ran to tell the praying group of believers that he was at the door. They told her she was out of her mind because Peter was in prison. They asked the Lord to act, but when he did, they did not believe it.

As soon as they began to pray, God began to answer. The same was true for Daniel. The angel Gabriel said, "As soon as you began to pray, an answer was given" (9:23). I believe that is what God does for his children *all the time*. As soon as we pray, an answer is on the way.

Isaiah 30:19 says, "How gracious he will be when you cry for help! As soon as he hears, he will answer you." Isaiah 58:9 says, "Then you will call, and the LORD will answer; you will cry for help, and he will say: here am I." And Isaiah 65:24 says, "Before they call I will answer; while they are still speaking I will hear."

But if God immediately answers the prayers of his children all the time, why does our experience seem to tell us otherwise? Most of the time there seems to be a long delay between our prayer and the answer. Think about this historical account. The angel came with the message of what would happen in the future, but the answer did not unfold completely for almost five hundred years. When the answer to his prayer finally came in its fullness, it came with many twists and turns, challenges and discouragements, as we will see in the next chapter. The only difference between us and Daniel is that the angel Gabriel came immediately and told him when and how it would happen.

When you pray, realize that God hears, forgives, and formulates an answer immediately. But though his answer is immediate, his action may take years to unfold, as it did in the case of Peggy MacDonald. In 1980 when she prayed over the property in West St. Louis County, I was in Muncie, Indiana, pastoring a small church. Immediately when she prayed, the Lord began to shake the heavens and set an amazing plan into motion. I was called to Covenant Presbyterian Church in St. Louis three years after she prayed. Two years later we were making plans to expand the facility. The congregation did not support the plans at first; so we were delayed for a year. It was hard to understand what the Lord was doing. I said, "Lord, why aren't you hearing our prayers to add on to this building?"

During the same year our congregation was struggling through some internal issues, and the Town and Country Municipality was changing its green space laws. As a result of the changes, 75 percent of all property in that area needed to be grass. That prevented us from being able to build the addition to the church to accommodate the growth we were experiencing. I said, "Lord, what are you doing? Why aren't you hearing our prayers?"

Nine years had passed since Peggy MacDonald first prayed over that land. Meanwhile, the Village of Twin Oaks had given the Vaterott Corporation permission to build condominiums on that site. Construction began with the clearing of the land, but they cleared too many trees and angered the residents of Twin Oaks. One man on the board of the Village of Twin Oaks was Charlie Brown of KMOX radio. He loved trees and felt that Vaterott was behaving in a reckless manner. The Village of Twin Oaks put their building plans on hold.

Meanwhile, we were looking for some land to build a new church since we could not expand our present location. We looked for two years! Numerous times I said, "Lord, why aren't you hearing our prayers?" Finally we put together a backup contract on the twenty-acre site in a prime location at a ridiculously low price of 38,000 dollars an acre. The land around our old church was selling for 200,000 dollars an acre. God had specifically answered Peggy MacDonald's prayer to do something amazing with numbers. He enabled us to raise over $2.4 million dollars in cash; so we had enough to buy the property and start the building.

He also answered her prayer that this would be a church that would help needy people. Twin Oaks Presbyterian has a strong divorce care ministry and a ministry to special-needs children and adults. In answer to her other prayer, it is a church that visits people in their homes through follow-up or door-to-door cold calls. In answer to her prayer the Lord has also laid it upon the hearts of our people to reach out to the poor in neighboring Valley Park.

Does prayer make a difference? You can be sure it does. Cry out to the Lord: "O Lord, listen! O Lord, forgive! O Lord, hear and act!" Then prepare to watch the hand of the sovereign God at work in your world. He does amazing things.

By the way, the first sermon I preached in the new building on that property was entitled, "The King's Court." The sermon was based on Psalm 100, which calls us to "Enter his gates with thanksgiving and his courts with praise." After the sermon one of the members asked me if I knew what the name of the condominiums that had been planned for that property were going to be called. I had no idea.

He smiled and said, "The King's Court." Our God has an amazing way of answering the prayers of his people. Do not hold back when you pray.

12

Good News, Bad News

DANIEL 9:20-27

You have heard those good news, bad news stories that comedians tell onstage. I never imagined one day I would know somebody that really experienced one. This is a true story. A friend of mine told me he had been driving to church on a rain-slick highway but lost control of his car.

"That's bad," I said.

"No, it was good, because I just skidded off the highway and didn't hit anything. Just then someone from church came by."

"Oh, that's good."

"No, that was bad, because she skidded in the same spot, lost control of her car, and hit mine. Right after that a patrol car pulled up in front of us."

"Oh, that's bad!"

"No, that was good, because he took us into his car, got us out of the rain, and allowed us to make some phone calls. Then a tow truck came around the curve."

"Oh, well, that is good."

"No, that was bad, because he lost control in the same spot and hit both of our cars. He totaled mine."

"Oh, that is bad."

"No, that is good, because my insurance got me a brand-new car that is much better than my old one."

Daniel 9 is a story of good news and bad news. Daniel was in his eighties in the first year of Darius, the king of Persia, when this scene took place. The city of Jerusalem and the Temple of the Lord lay in ruins over six hundred miles due west. Burdened over the thought of the city of God lying in ruins, Daniel prayed:

Now, our God, hear the prayers and petitions of your servant. For your sake, O Lord, look with favor on your desolate sanctuary. Give ear, O

God, and hear; open your eyes and see the desolation of the city that
bears your Name. We do not make requests of you because we are right-
eous, but because of your great mercy. O Lord, listen! O Lord, forgive! O
Lord, hear and act! For your sake, O my God, do not delay, because your
city and your people bear your Name. (9:17-19)

The moment Daniel started praying, the heavens were set in motion to
answer his prayer. Though his request would not begin to be answered for
ninety-three years, the Lord sent his angel Gabriel to tell Daniel what would
happen in the future. In Daniel 9:23, 24 Gabriel said:

As soon as you began to pray, an answer was given, which I have come to
tell you, for you are highly esteemed. Therefore, consider the message
and understand the vision: Seventy "sevens" are decreed for your people
and your holy city . . .

In this vision that Daniel received concerning the holy city of Jerusalem
and the sanctuary, Gabriel was basically saying, "Daniel, I have good news,
and I have bad news. *The good news* is that your prayer will be answered.
Jerusalem and the temple will be restored! *The bad news* is that the city will
be rebuilt in times of trouble. *But the good news* is that the Messiah will
soon come to that same city and temple that will be rebuilt!" Now that was
much more than he had asked for! And there was more. "But *the bad news*
is that the Messiah will have to die in that city! *But the best news of all* is
that when the Messiah dies, he will be the final sacrifice for sins, and no more
blood will need to be shed for the forgiveness of sins. He will be the perfect
sacrifice." Now that is immeasurably more than anything Daniel had asked
or even imagined! "But *the bad news is* that many will not know the prophecies, so they will reject his atoning sacrifice. As a result, the temple and
Jerusalem will be destroyed once more." Good news, bad news. That is the
summary of the vision that Daniel received, which we will now study.

The seventy "sevens" of Daniel 9 that were decreed for the people and
the sanctuary stand for seventy periods of seven years, or a total of 490 years.
This means that the events described in this passage were all fulfilled in the
first century. Not a word of Daniel 9 needs yet to be fulfilled!

THE PURPOSE OF THIS PROPHECY SHOWS THAT IT WAS COMPLETELY FULFILLED IN THE FIRST COMING OF CHRIST (9:24)

Seventy "sevens" are decreed for your people and your holy city to finish trans-
gression, to put an end to sin, to atone for wickedness, to bring in everlasting
righteousness, to seal up vision and prophecy and to anoint the most holy.

For the sake of argument, let me show you that it is at least possible that all this could have been fulfilled in the first century. Take the first couplet:

Seventy Sevens Are Decreed to Finish Transgression and Put an End to Sin

> But now he [Christ] has appeared once for all at the end of the ages to do away with sin by the sacrifice of himself. Just as man is destined to die once, and after that to face judgment, so Christ was sacrificed once to take away the sins of many people; and he will appear a second time, not to bear sin, but to bring salvation to those who are waiting for him. (Hebrews 9:26-28)

The writer of Hebrews says that Jesus came the first time to finish transgression and put an end to sin, "to do away with sin" through the sacrifice of his body on the cross. He will come a second time, not to bear sin, but to bring salvation to those who believe in Christ. These two purposes — to finish transgression and to put an end to sin — were fulfilled in the first coming of Christ.

Seventy Sevens Are Decreed to Atone for Sin and Bring in Everlasting Righteousness

> For this reason he [Christ] had to be made like his brothers in every way, in order that he might become a merciful and faithful high priest in service to God, and that he might make atonement for the sins of the people. (Hebrews 2:17)

> Listen to me, you who pursue righteousness and who seek the LORD. . . . My righteousness draws near speedily, my salvation is on the way . . . my salvation will last forever, my righteousness will never fail . . . my righteousness will last forever, my salvation through all generations. (Isaiah 51:1, 5, 6, 8)

The righteousness of Christ, which we receive by trusting in Jesus Christ alone for salvation, is an everlasting righteousness. It will not fail, and it will not fade. Jesus brought in "everlasting righteousness" (Daniel 9:24) by living in perfect obedience to the Law when he was here on earth two thousand years ago. Once you are clothed in his righteousness through faith in him, you cannot lose that standing before God. It is everlasting righteousness.

And no one disagrees that Jesus' death on the cross provided atonement for the sins of his people. Again these two purposes — to atone for sins and to bring in everlasting righteousness — were fulfilled in the first coming of Christ.

Seventy Sevens Are Decreed to Seal Up Vision and Prophecy

This is a little bit more difficult to understand, since there are two ways the word *seal* is used. It can either mean to authenticate, meaning to put a sign of approval on something, or it can mean to close up tight. The first way would be the way the word is used in Daniel 6:16, 17.

> *So the king gave the order, and they brought Daniel and threw him into the lions' den. The king said to Daniel, "May your God, whom you serve continually, rescue you." A stone was brought and placed over the mouth of the den, and the king sealed it with his own signet ring and with the rings of his nobles, so that Daniel's situation might not be changed.*

The signet ring sealed the den. There was no power in that ring. He did not wire the door shut. But the fact that he put his authenticating signature there said the decree could not be changed.

The written revelation of God is called the Bible. The Word of God was completed in the first century. The authenticating signature of the prophets and apostles was placed upon it, so that now it cannot be changed. We may not add to or subtract from God's written Word. Perhaps this is the meaning of that phrase.

Another way this Hebrew word is used is found in Daniel 8:26: "The vision of the evenings and mornings that has been given you is true, but seal up the vision, for it concerns the distant future." This is a slightly different form of the Hebrew word and is similar to the way it is used in Daniel 12:9, meaning that prophecy will be closed up, not to be opened again until the last days. In Daniel 12:8, 9 the prophet says:

> *I heard, but I did not understand. So I asked, "My lord, what will the outcome of all this be?" He replied, "Go your way, Daniel, because the words are closed up and sealed until the time of the end."*

Both forms of the Hebrew word are used here. The prophecies were authenticated and sealed up until the first century. I believe those seals were broken by Christ, the Lamb seated upon the throne in Revelation 5 — 6, chapters that revealed the Second Coming of Christ in more detail than Daniel had received. Either way, vision and prophecy were sealed up in the first century.

Seventy Sevens Are Decreed to Anoint the Most Holy

"To anoint" (Daniel 9:24) is the Hebrew word *Messiah* and the Greek word *Christ*. This could either be taken as anointing the most holy one or the most holy place. On the one hand, if it refers to anointing the most holy one, it could refer to the baptism of Jesus when he was anointed by John with water and anointed with the Holy Spirit by his Father.

> *Then Jesus came from Galilee to the Jordan to be baptized by John. But John tried to deter him, saying, "I need to be baptized by you, and do you come to me?" Jesus replied, "Let it be so now; it is proper for us to do this to fulfill all righteousness." Then John consented. As soon as Jesus was baptized, he went up out of the water. At that moment heaven was opened, and he saw the Spirit of God descending like a dove and lighting on him. (Matthew 3:13-16)*

On the other hand, there is no real basis for saying that the holy place had to be anointed. But even if it did, the holy place was destroyed in the first century (A.D. 70). So either way, this purpose was fulfilled in the *first* coming, not the second coming of Christ. Dr. Edward Young wrote: "When our Lord ascended into heaven and the Holy Spirit descended, there remained not one of the six items of Daniel 9:24 that was not fully accomplished."[1]

THE EXEGESIS OF THE PROPHECY SHOWS THAT IT WAS FULFILLED DURING THE FIRST COMING OF CHRIST

At least for the sake of argument, grant that these purposes, unclear though they may be, could all be fulfilled in the first century through the person and work of Jesus Christ.

That is just one piece of the puzzle. The most important question is whether the exegesis of the remaining three verses supports that conclusion.

The Decree to Rebuild Jerusalem (9:25)

> *Know and understand this: From the issuing of the decree to restore and rebuild Jerusalem until the Anointed One, the ruler, comes, there will be seven "sevens," and sixty-two "sevens." It will be rebuilt with streets and a trench, but in times of trouble.*

Gabriel begins with good news. "You were praying that God would do something with Jerusalem, which lies in ruins? I have good news! Jerusalem will be rebuilt in answer to your prayer." The word or decree to rebuild Jerusalem would be given by Artaxerxes, as seen in Ezra 7:11-26. The year was 457 B.C. What Daniel 9:25 is saying, as incredible as it may seem, is that from the date of the issuing of the decree in 457 B.C. until the Anointed One, the Messiah, comes, there would be seven sevens plus sixty-two sevens, a total of sixty-nine sevens. That is 483 years. This would mean that Gabriel pinpointed the Messiah being on this earth somewhere around A.D. 26. The year A.D. 26 is thought by many to be about the time of Jesus' baptism, his anointing, when the Holy Spirit descended on him (John 1:32). This was even better news than Daniel had asked for. Not only would the temple be rebuilt, but the Messiah, the true temple, would come. "I did not see a temple in the city, because the Lord God Almighty and the Lamb are its temple" (Revelation 21:22). And in addition to that, the Messiah would come into the prophesied second earthly temple built by Zerubbabel.

This verse prophesies the coming of "the Anointed One" and calls him "the ruler." That links him with the prophecy made by Micah two hundred years earlier. "But you, Bethlehem Ephrathah, though you are small among the clans of Judah, out of you will come for me one who will be ruler over Israel, whose origins are from of old, from ancient times" (Micah 5:2).

Some believe that the issuing of the decree was made by King Artaxerxes in the days of Nehemiah, which would be 445 B.C. This cannot be determined with absolute certainty, but using the solar calendar with the former date (457 B.C.) or the lunar calendar with the latter date (445 B.C.) you still arrive at the time that we know Christ was here on earth.[2] Others think the date should be 538 B.C. when Cyrus told the Jews to return at the end of the captivity. But his decree was to go back and rebuild the temple, not to rebuild the city of Jerusalem and its walls.

> *This is what Cyrus king of Persia says: "The LORD, the God of heaven, has given me all the kingdoms of the earth and he has appointed me to build a temple for him at Jerusalem in Judah. Anyone of his people among you — may his God be with him, and let him go up to Jerusalem in Judah and build the temple of the LORD, the God of Israel, the God who is in Jerusalem. (Ezra 1:2, 3)*

Daniel 9:25 says that until the Anointed One comes, there will be seven sevens and sixty-two sevens. It should be noted that there is no time that passes between the seven sevens and the sixty-two sevens even though it is split up. This just refers to sixty-nine consecutive weeks. Nothing in history or the text warrants any break between the two periods of time. We don't really know why Gabriel said seven and sixty-two instead of just adding them together to make sixty-nine, but it does *not* mean there is a hidden time period in there. This will become very important when we study the seventieth week, which also is set apart in verse 27.

Now the Jewish people have always been longing for the *Messiah* to come. They weren't looking for the Son of Man, they weren't looking for The Great Prophet, nor were they looking for the Mighty God. They were always looking for and longing for the Messiah. You might expect that word to appear hundreds of times in the Old Testament, since they were always looking for the Messiah. But it does not. The Hebrew for Messiah or Anointed One is only applied to the Christ twice in the Old Testament — here in Daniel 9 and in Psalm 2:2.

The reason the people were always waiting for and looking for the *Messiah* is because that was the only name of the One who was coming that had a time of arrival attached to it. None of the others did. It is this prophecy and this prophecy alone that gave rise to the Jewish people's looking for the Messiah. But even though the Lord told his people exactly when the Messiah would come, his people did not take it literally, or they did not know the prophecy; so they were not ready for him when he came the first time.

Now Daniel 9:25 was not all good news. There was some bad news too. Verse 25 goes on to say that the walls of Jerusalem would be rebuilt "in times of trouble." Read Nehemiah 4 — 6 sometime to see the difficulties that Nehemiah faced in rebuilding the walls. He had opposition from outside and inside. Yet in spite of all the difficulty, the walls were finished in fifty-two days. The prophecy of Daniel 9:25 was fulfilled when the walls of Jerusalem were finished in 445 B.C., almost a hundred years after Daniel received this answer to his prayer from Gabriel.

The Death of the Anointed One (9:26a)

"After the sixty-two 'sevens,' the Anointed One will be cut off and will have nothing."

Now this is even more bad news for Daniel. The phrase, "after the sixty-two sevens" means after the seven sevens plus the sixty-two sevens. In other words, Gabriel means the Anointed One will be cut off after a total of sixty-nine sevens, or 483 years. This means that sometime after the 483 years, the Anointed One, the Messiah, would be "cut off." Not during the 483rd year, but sometime after the 483rd year, the Messiah would die. Later, when we study Daniel 9:27, we will see how long after the 483rd year that was.

The twelve disciples missed this incredible prophecy. They must have been familiar with Daniel 9 because they used the term *Messiah*. But somehow they missed this prophecy, because they really did not think the Messiah would die. Read this encounter between Jesus and Peter:

> *Jesus and his disciples went on to the villages around Caesarea Philippi. On the way he asked them, "Who do people say I am?" They replied, "Some say John the Baptist; others say Elijah; and still others, one of the prophets." "But what about you?" he asked. "Who do you say I am?" Peter answered, "You are the Christ [the Messiah or Anointed One]." (Mark 8:27-29)*

Since Peter called him the Anointed One, you would conclude that he must have read and been familiar with Daniel 9:26, because it is one of the two places that word occurs in the Old Testament. So naturally, if Peter knows about the name Messiah, he must also know that the Messiah would be "cut off" or die. That is why Jesus immediately follows with this teaching:

> *Jesus warned them not to tell anyone about him. He then began to teach them that the Son of Man must suffer many things and be rejected by the elders, chief priests and teachers of the law, and that he must be killed and after three days rise again. He spoke plainly about this, and Peter took him aside and began to rebuke him. But when Jesus turned and looked at his disciples, he rebuked Peter. "Get behind me, Satan!" he said. "You do not have in mind the things of God, but the things of men." (vv. 30-33)*

When Jesus reminded Peter of the content of the prophecy, Peter could not accept it. Perhaps he did not really know the entire prophecy or did not take it literally. Whatever the reason, Peter was publicly rebuked for not knowing what the prophecy of Daniel meant. Many people make the same mistake regarding the prophecies of the Second Coming of Christ. Either they only vaguely know what the prophecy says, or they do not take it literally. Either way leads to not being prepared for his coming. We need to study prophecy carefully, know prophecy thoroughly, and take prophecy seriously. Peter did not.

The Destruction of Jerusalem (9:26b)

From the death of the Messiah, the angel Gabriel turned to even more bad news — the destruction of the city of Jerusalem and the temple. "The people of the ruler who will come will destroy the city and the sanctuary. The end will come like a flood: War will continue until the end, and desolations have been decreed."

These words prophesied the coming of the Romans under the leadership of Emperor Titus, "the ruler who will come." In A.D. 70 he destroyed the temple and the city of Jerusalem. The phrase, "the end will come like a flood" makes some people think of the end of the world. In reality it refers to the end of Jerusalem. The phrase describes the way Jerusalem was finally destroyed by Roman armies sweeping over the city "like a flood."

The phrase "war will continue until the end" refers to the fact that quite a few years passed between the time the temple was first destroyed in A.D. 70 and the final conquering of the Jews in A.D. 132. That was a long time. In the meantime, war continued as the Jews battled the Romans "until the end."

Here is Josephus' summary in *The Jewish Wars*. The Jews rebelled against the Romans in A.D. 66. War continued for the next four years. The Jews won a partial victory in A.D. 70, putting the Roman Cestius Gallus to flight. He had come from Syria to secure the city. But that small victory would cost the Jews dearly in the long run.

Vespasian began a campaign against Israel, but he was recalled to Rome. Consequently, his son Titus continued the task. He entered Jerusalem at its most crowded time — Passover. Reports of up to six hundred thousand Jewish people slaughtered were spread abroad. And the wars continued to the end, for the remaining Jews continued the resistance for some sixty years. The last stand of the Jews was at a large mountain by the Dead Sea known as Masada. Finally in A.D. 132 the Romans swept through like a flood, plowed the temple of the Lord under, and built an altar to Jupiter on that site. Vespasian set up an abomination that caused desolation in that holy place.[3]

At this point it would be helpful to explain the meaning of the last half of verse 27. Many people believe that the Antichrist is the abomination of desolation. Let me simply say to you that he is not. Comparing Daniel 9, Matthew 24, and Luke 21 shows that the Antichrist is not the abomination of desolation. The confusion can be cleared up by looking at several English translations and by direct translation from the Hebrew.

Here is the translation from the Hebrew that I worked on with Hebrew scholar Dr. V. Phillips Long of Regent College. Notice that the word "he" does not even occur in the Hebrew. "And on a wing [a corner of the altar] will be appalling detestable things even until complete destruction and what has been determined will be poured out on the desolating one."

The alternate reading in the NIV offers a translation for this difficult Hebrew text. The text could read, "And one who causes desolation [Titus] will come upon the pinnacle of the abominable temple until the end that is decreed is poured out on the desolate city [Jerusalem]." The end that is decreed and spoken of in this text is the end of the city of Jerusalem. One important internal exegetical support for such a translation is Hebrew parallelism. The first half of Daniel 9:26 refers to the Messiah, and the last half of verse 26 refers to the destruction of Jerusalem by Titus. As we will see, the first half of verse 27 refers to the Messiah, and the last half refers to the destruction of Jerusalem by Titus.

The Jewish publication of this text reads as follows: "At the corner of the altar will be an appalling abomination until the decreed destruction will be poured down upon the appalling thing."

One important principle of interpretation is that you do not build your theology on an obscure text. These alternate translations show that the Hebrew in this verse is very obscure. The King James Version says, "And for the overspreading of abominations he shall make it desolate, even until the consummation, and that determined shall be poured upon the desolate." This does not even make sense. Nevertheless, it is this verse alone that leads Pretribulation defenders to teach a seven-year period yet future when the

Antichrist will make a covenant with the Jewish people. There is no other verse in the entire Bible that says anything about a seven-year period in the future. This puts their interpretation on very shaky grounds.

The fact that the abomination spoken of in Daniel 9 was fulfilled in the first century can be seen by a comparison of the texts of Matthew 24 and Luke 21. These both refer to the same event, because the wording is exactly parallel. It is Luke that clarifies the fact for us that this refers to the destruction of Jerusalem and not to the Second Coming of Christ. Both texts move from the first-century destruction of Jerusalem into the teaching about the return of Christ.

Matthew 24:15-20	Luke 21:20-24
(15) So when you see standing in the holy Place "the **abomination that causes Desolation**" spoken of through the prophet Daniel — let the reader understand —	(20) When you see Jerusalem surrounded by armies [the abomination that causes desolation: Rome in A.D. 70], you will know that its desolation is near.
(16) **then let those who are in Judea flee to the mountains.** (17) let no one on the roof of his house go down to take anything out of the house. (18) Let no one in the field go back to get his cloak.	(21) **Then let those who are in Judea flee to the mountains,** let those in the city get out, and let those in the country not enter the city. (22) **For this is the time of the punishment in fulfillment of all that has been written.** [including Daniel]
(19) **How dreadful it will be in those days for pregnant women and nursing mothers!** (20) Pray that your flight will not take place in winter or on the Sabbath.	(23) **How dreadful it will be in those days for pregnant women and nursing mothers!** There will be great distress in the land and wrath against this people.
	(24) They will fall by the sword and will be taken as prisoners to all nations. Jerusalem will be trampled on by the Gentiles until the times of the Gentiles are fulfilled.

This last verse in Luke 21 shows that this passage is referring to the destruction of Jerusalem in A.D. 70. From A.D. 70 until the Six Days War in 1967, Jerusalem was trampled on by the Gentiles. The abomination that causes desolation spoken of by Daniel 9 refers to the events surrounding the destruction of Jerusalem and the setting up of the abominable Temple of Jupiter on the sacred site of the Temple of the Lord.

Is it important to pay attention to the little details of prophecy? Because of what happened to the Jews in Jerusalem we answer with a resounding yes. Jesus warned them in the verses above that when they saw the armies of Rome coming, those in the city should flee to the mountains in Judea, and those in the mountains should not run to the city. The Jews ignored that prophetic warning of Jesus. They ran into the city and stayed there. As a result, Josephus records, more than six hundred thousand Jews died, and perhaps many more.[4]

On the other hand, I have known women who were afraid to become pregnant because Matthew 24:19 says, "How dreadful it will be . . . for pregnant women and nursing mothers!" They are afraid that they will be pregnant when Jesus returns, and somehow that will be bad. When we realize that the prophecy of Matthew 24:19 was fulfilled in the destruction of Jerusalem, we can relax, and women can enjoy having children right up to the return of Christ with no worries.

The Covenant of the Anointed One (9:27a)

He will confirm a covenant with many for one "seven." In the middle of the "seven" he will put an end to sacrifice and offering.

I was told from my earliest years that this verse speaks of a seven-year period that is still future. People I trusted taught me that during this seven-year period the Antichrist would make a covenant or a peace treaty with the Jewish people. For three and a half years, he would be very friendly to them and help them rebuild the temple in Jerusalem so animal sacrifices could begin again. Then, after three and a half years, in the middle of the seven, the Antichrist would turn mean and put an end to their sacrificial system.

Then one day in 1980 I was reading Daniel 9 for my devotions. As I read, I began to wonder where in the world such an interpretation came from. It was as if scales fell off my eyes. I came to see that rather than presenting bad news about the Antichrist, Gabriel tells Daniel the good news about the Messiah. *And this is the best news of all.*

Who Made the Covenant?

The pronoun "he" begins verse 27. We all know that a pronoun needs an antecedent. The antecedent defines the pronoun. It does not take much to see that the Antichrist is not even mentioned in the context of Daniel 9. There are only two pronouns that "he" could refer to. One is the "ruler" of verse 26, but that ruler was a real Roman emperor who destroyed Jerusalem and the temple in A.D. 70.

The other noun is the other "ruler" mentioned in verse 25, the ruler who is called "the Anointed One" in both verses 25 and 26. That ruler is the Messiah. To me this is the most obvious antecedent, because the Messiah is the primary subject of all these verses. He is the One that the purpose in verse 24 is all about. He is the One who will atone for sin and bring in everlasting righteousness, not the Antichrist. The Messiah is the one who will finish transgression and put an end to sin, not the Antichrist. The "he" of verse 27 is the Messiah.

What Is the Covenant?

Gabriel says in Daniel 9:27, "He will confirm a covenant with many for one 'seven.'" Two different words are used in relationship to a covenant. One word means "to make a covenant," literally meaning "to cut a covenant." The Hebrew is *karat berit*. That would be used if indeed the Antichrist entered into a peace treaty, a covenant, with the Jews.

But that is not the Hebrew word used here. Instead verse 27 uses *gavar berit*, meaning that he will "confirm a covenant already in existence." The covenant of which he speaks is the Covenant of Grace. The Messiah came not to *make* a covenant but to confirm, ratify, *authenticate* the Covenant of Grace with his blood. That is very good news!

How and When Was the Covenant Ratified?

"In the middle of the seven [after three and a half years], he [the Messiah] will put an end to sacrifice and offering."

Jesus' public ministry was about three and a half years in length. At the end of that three and a half years, he was "cut off" (v. 26); that is, he was crucified on the cross of Calvary and died. When Jesus died, his death put an end to sacrifice and offering. Not one more drop of blood needed to be spilt.

The writer of Hebrews says, "Where these [sins and lawless acts, v. 17] have been forgiven, there is no longer any sacrifice for sin" (10:18). That is why Jesus cried from the cross, "It is finished" (John 19:30). The Old Testament sacrificial system was finished. Jesus put an end to sacrifice. Since the Jews did not recognize that, the Lord underscored the message by destroying the temple and forcing them to stop the sacrifices even in their unbelief. That is the message of the last half of verse 27 of Daniel 9.

Remember also that in verse 26 we saw that the Messiah would be "cut off" sometime after the sixty-ninth week. Now we find out that it was exactly three and a half years after the sixty-ninth week or the middle of the seventieth week. Now I hope you can see why there is no warrant for thinking that there is a period of time between the end of the sixty-ninth week and the beginning of the seventieth week. The whole prophecy was fulfilled in the approximate space of 490 years.

This is not complicated. I get excited when I share this exegesis with people. The other view about the Antichrist is really complicated since it inserts things into the text that are not even there and separates the seventieth week from the previous sixty-nine weeks by two thousand years when there is nothing in the text to suggest this. Now that is complicated! Daniel 9 is simply a prophecy about the first coming of Jesus Christ, specifically showing that he would die 486 years after Artaxerxes issued a decree to rebuild Jerusalem. If he gives us that kind of detail about his first coming, why should we be surprised when he tells us some timing details about the Second Coming. What great news this was! It is the best news of all!

THE CONCLUSION OF THE PROPHECY SHOWS THAT IT WAS FULFILLED DURING THE FIRST COMING OF CHRIST

What about the last three and a half years of the seventieth week of Daniel? Where did they go? Though Daniel 9 seems to leave that hanging, Revelation 12 picks it up. As we will see in Daniel 12, Daniel is trying to understand all these prophecies when the Lord speaks.

> *I heard, but I did not understand. [Some of you are probably saying that right now.] So I asked, "My lord, what will the outcome of all this be?" He replied, "Go your way, Daniel, because the words are closed up and sealed until the time of the end." (Daniel 12:8, 9)*

These words were closed and sealed up until the day that the Lamb seated on the throne was found worthy of opening the seals.

> *Then I saw in the right hand of him who sat on the throne a scroll with writing on both sides and sealed with seven seals. And I saw a mighty angel proclaiming in a loud voice, "Who is worthy to break the seals and open the scroll?" But no one in heaven or on earth or under the earth could open the scroll or even look inside it. I wept and wept because no one was found who was worthy to open the scroll or look inside. Then one of the elders said to me, "Do not weep! See, the Lion of the tribe of Judah, the Root of David, has triumphed. He is able to open the scroll and its seven seals." (Revelation 5:1-5)*

The seals were opened, and the content of the book of Revelation revealed information that Daniel did not receive. Revelation 12 tells us what happened in the last three and a half years of the seventieth week. They were fulfilled in the first century immediately after the ascension of Christ.

The Protection of the Church (Revelation 12:1-6)

Revelation 12 begins the second cycle of the book of Revelation. Cycle 1 begins in chapters 1 — 3 with seven real churches of the first century. Chapters 4 — 11 take us toward the Second Coming of Christ, ending at his return when the last trumpet sounds (the seventh trumpet) and "The kingdom of the world becomes the kingdom of our Lord and of his Christ" (11:15).

Cycle 2 begins in chapter 12, returning to the first century where chapters 1 — 3 started. What we read there describes the birth of Christ, his ascension, and the beginning years of the New Testament Church in wonderful but clear imagery. The dragon is Satan, the woman represents the chosen people of God, and the male child is Christ.

> *A great and wondrous sign appeared in heaven: a woman clothed with the sun, with the moon under her feet and a crown of twelve stars on her head. She was pregnant and cried out in pain as she was about to give birth. Then another sign appeared in heaven: an enormous red dragon with seven heads and ten horns and seven crowns on his heads. His tail swept a third of the stars out of the sky and flung them to the earth. The dragon stood in front of the woman who was about to give birth, so that he might devour her child the moment it was born. She gave birth to a son, a male child, who will rule all the nations with an iron scepter. And her child was snatched up to God and to his throne. The woman fled into the desert to a place prepared for her by God, where she might be taken care of for 1,260 days. (12:1-6)*

Now, 1,260 days is three and a half years. From the baptism of Christ until the death and ascension of Christ was three and a half years. That was the first half of the seventieth week of Daniel. The last half extends from the Ascension until the dispersion of the church in Jerusalem. For three and a half years the Lord took care of the church in Jerusalem. When John writes, "the woman fled into the desert to a place prepared for her by God," we need to remember this is imagery. The point is not that the Church went anywhere, but that God "[took] care of [her] for 1,260 days." That period of time when the Church was cared for in a unique way is recorded for us in Acts 1 — 7. The believers were meeting in homes every day. They found favor among even the unbelievers. They were seeing miracles. The Church was growing by the thousands. Then something bad happened.

The Persecution of the Church (Revelation 12:13-17)

The events that took place in Acts 8:1-4, when the Church was scattered, are described in wonderful imagery in these verses. Seeing how this imagery was fulfilled in real events can help us understand how to interpret prophetic imagery concerning the Second Coming of Christ in Daniel and Revelation.

> *When the dragon saw that he had been hurled to the earth, he pursued the woman who had given birth to the male child. The woman was given the two wings of a great eagle, so that she might fly to the place prepared for her in the desert, where she would be taken care of for a time, times and half a time, out of the serpent's reach. (Revelation 12:13, 14)*

These are different words of imagery to say the same thing as Revelation 12:6: The Church would be taken care of by God for three and a half years. That is what "a time, times and half a time" means. Then the persecution began.

"Then from his mouth the serpent spewed water like a river, to overtake the woman and sweep her away with the torrent" (12:15). The picture in this imagery is of the dragon trying to destroy the Church by drowning. He sweeps it away in a torrent. Satan walks away slapping his hands together saying, "There, that will take care of her." But did it?

I am reminded of the man who was involved in the clam industry. The enemy of the clam is the starfish because it opens the clam with its arms, then eats it. This man was bothered by some starfish that were destroying his clams; so he caught these starfish, cut them up in pieces, and threw them back into the ocean saying, "There that will take care of them." He did not know that a starfish has the ability to regenerate an entire new body from just one piece of its body. The man thought he had taken care of the problem, but he only made it worse.

Thus it was with Satan. He thought that persecution had destroyed the Church, when in reality, by the grace of God, he just scattered the Church so believers were able to take the gospel to the ends of the earth. "But the earth helped the woman by opening its mouth and swallowing the river that the dragon had spewed out of his mouth" (12:16). Obviously that did not make the dragon happy. "Then the dragon was enraged at the woman and went off to make war against the rest of her offspring — those who obey God's commandments and hold to the testimony of Jesus" (12:17).

We are the offspring of the woman, the Church, the chosen people of God, if we make the good confession and hold to the testimony of Jesus. We are engaged in this spiritual warfare to this day. The battle will climax, as we saw in Daniel 7, in Satan's last strategic move — becoming incarnate like Jesus did. Satan in human form is the one we call the Antichrist.

So the seventy weeks of Daniel were completed in the first century. They are history. We are now living in the wake of the conclusion of this prophecy. This spiritual warfare may seem like bad news. Yet as difficult as this may be at times, the very best news is just around the corner. Jesus Christ is coming again to destroy our enemy and to reign as King of kings and Lord of lords. That is immeasurably more than Daniel or we ever asked or even imagined!

13

The Man in the Golden Sash

DANIEL 10:1 — 11:1

In 1984 the church I was pastoring only had two evangelism teams, which went to homes on Tuesday evenings. We had very few visitors. But when we did have a visitor, I had the seminary student assistant set up an appointment by calling ahead. He would tell the family that either his team or the senior pastor's team would visit.

One evening my team was given the card of a family that the student assistant had set up in advance. I saw from the card that the husband was an athletic director in a nearby public school. My team drove to the house following the directions on the card. We walked to the door and knocked.

When the door opened, a large, muscular man stood there and stared at me for a moment. I said, "Hello, my name is Rodney Stortz, pastor of Covenant Presbyterian Church."

He then turned and shouted to his wife in another room, "Hey, honey, they sent the first string!"

Of course we did not have a first and second string in our evangelism ministry. In fact, I think all who are involved in evangelism should be considered first string. They are truly on the front lines of the spiritual battle.

On this day in Daniel's life you could truly say that God sent the first string. God the Father had already sent the angel Gabriel to Daniel twice. The first was recorded in chapter 7, and the next was recorded in chapter 9. This time, I believe, he sent his Son, the Second Person of the Trinity.

Before I show you from the text and other Scriptures why I say this, let me tell you about the context.

THE CONTEXT OF THIS VISION: THE THIRD YEAR OF CYRUS (10:1a)

"In the third year of Cyrus king of Persia . . ." Daniel calls this the third year of Cyrus. Since that monarch began to rule in Persia in 559 B.C., this could not mean that it was the third year of his reign in Persia. That would make the year 556 B.C. rather than 536 B.C. Instead Daniel is saying this was the third year of his reign after conquering Babylon. The man who conquered Babylon in 539 B.C. had two names. He was called Darius the Mede and Cyrus. Daniel 6:28 says, "So Daniel prospered during the reign of Darius, that is, the reign of Cyrus of Persia" (alternate translation found in the footnote of the NIV).

This was the king who had elevated Daniel to second in command in Babylon (6:3). He was also the king who later had Daniel thrown into the lions' den because of his practice of praying to the living God three times a day (6:16). Here is a short history of the first three years of the rule of Cyrus, king of Persia.

The First Year

In the first year of Cyrus, the decree was made to rebuild the temple in Jerusalem. According to Ezra 1, Cyrus made the decree to rebuild the temple in Jerusalem in the first year of his reign; that would be the summer of 538 B.C. This decree is not to be confused with the decree to rebuild Jerusalem spoken of in Daniel 9. Cyrus only issued a decree to rebuild the temple (Ezra 1:2). The decree to rebuild the walls of Jerusalem came from another Persian king, Artaxerxes. It was that second decree that marked the time for the beginning of counting the years until the coming of the Messiah (Daniel 9:25).

The Second Year

In the second year of Cyrus, the people began the sacrifices in Jerusalem. Cyrus made the decree to rebuild the temple in the first year of his reign, but the people did not leave for Jerusalem until the second year of his reign (537 B.C.). They were so excited about being able to worship and perform the sacrifices again that the first thing the people built under the leadership of Zerubbabel was the altar of God. In the seventh month of the year 537, they sacrificed their offerings for the first time and celebrated the feast of the seventh month, which is the Feast of Tabernacles. The Feast of Tabernacles was one of the three feasts that had to be celebrated by the people in Jerusalem. This was October of 537 B.C., and the building of the foundations of the temple had not yet begun.

The Third Year

On the third day of the first month of 536 B.C., in the third year of the reign of Cyrus, king of Persia, Daniel mourned for the situation in Jerusalem. He was thinking about the celebration of Passover that was to take place that month. This would be the first time the Passover had been celebrated in Jerusalem since the destruction of the temple in 586 B.C.— fifty years earlier. Passover was the second of three feasts that was to be celebrated by everyone in Jerusalem. During this time, Daniel went into a three-week period of mourning.

> *At that time I, Daniel, mourned for three weeks. I ate no choice food; no meat or wine touched my lips; and I used no lotions at all until the three weeks were over. On the twenty-fourth day of the first month, as I was standing on the bank of the great river, the Tigris . . . (10:2-4)*

Maybe Daniel was mourning because he could not be in Jerusalem for the first Passover celebration. Perhaps he was grieving because the foundation of the temple had not yet been started, even though the people had already been there almost a year. According to Ezra 3, they did get started the next month. Perhaps he was mourning because only fifty thousand people returned to Jerusalem. Daniel was ninety years old; so he was too feeble to return. But there were many others who did not want to go back because they were too comfortable in the Babylonian world.

He mourned until the twenty-fourth day, though the Passover and the following Feast of Unleavened Bread lasted from the 14th of the month until the 21st day of the month. On the twenty-fourth day, he looked up and saw a man standing there.

THE MAN OF THE VISION WAS THE SECOND PERSON OF THE TRINITY (10:5, 6)

> *I looked up and there before me was a man dressed in linen, with a belt of the finest gold around his waist. His body was like chrysolite, his face like lightning, his eyes like flaming torches, his arms and legs like the gleam of burnished bronze, and his voice like the sound of a multitude.*

Revelation 1:13-16 describes the very same person.

> *Among the lampstands was someone "like a son of man," dressed in a robe reaching down to his feet and with a golden sash around his chest. His head and hair were white like wool, as white as snow, and his eyes were like blazing fire. His feet were like bronze glowing in a furnace, and his voice*

was like the sound of rushing waters. . . . His face was like the sun shining in all its brilliance.

The Defense of This Being a Vision of the Pre-incarnate Christ

Daniel's experience was like that of the Apostle Paul when Jesus appeared to him on the road to Damascus. Acts 26:14 says that the men who were with Paul (then Saul) did not see the vision, and they fell to the ground. Daniel 10:7 says, "I, Daniel, was the only one who saw the vision; the men with me did not see it, but such terror overwhelmed them that they fled and hid themselves."

When the Apostle John saw Jesus, as recorded in the book of Revelation, he fell at Jesus' feet as though dead, and Jesus placed his hand on him saying, "Do not be afraid." Notice the similarities to Daniel's meeting with Jesus:

So I was left alone, gazing at this great vision; I had no strength left, my face turned deathly pale and I was helpless. Then I heard him speaking, and as I listened to him, I fell into a deep sleep, my face to the ground. A hand touched me and set me trembling on my hands and knees. He said, "Daniel, you who are highly esteemed, consider carefully the words I am about to speak to you, and stand up, for I have now been sent to you." And when he said this to me, I stood up trembling. Then he continued, "Do not be afraid, Daniel." (Daniel 10:8-12a)

When the prophet Ezekiel saw a vision of the glory of God, he too fell facedown on the ground, and notice what happened.

This was the appearance of the likeness of the glory of the LORD. When I saw it, I fell facedown, and I heard the voice of one speaking. He said to me, "Son of man, stand up on your feet and I will speak to you." As he spoke, the spirit came into me and raised me to my feet. (Ezekiel 1:28 — 2:2)

In a similar way Daniel experienced the strengthening of the Lord. The voice said:

"Stand up, for I have been sent to you." And when he said this to me, I stood up trembling. . . . Again the one who looked like a man touched me and gave me strength. "Do not be afraid, O man highly esteemed. Peace! Be strong now; be strong." When he spoke to me, I was strengthened. (Daniel 10:11, 18, 19)

Those words are the often quoted words of Jesus to his people: "Do not be afraid"; "peace"; "be strong." To me it seems rather obvious that this one who "looked like a man" was none other than the pre-incarnate Second Person of the Trinity.

The Problem of This Being a Vision of the Pre-incarnate Christ

Then he continued, "Do not be afraid, Daniel. Since the first day that you set your mind to gain understanding and to humble yourself before your God, your words were heard, and I have come in response to them. But the prince of the Persian kingdom resisted me twenty-one days. Then Michael, one of the chief princes, came to help me, because I was detained there with the king of Persia." (Daniel 10:12, 13)

The first day that Daniel set his mind on gaining understanding was the first day of his twenty-one-day fast. He continued in prayer until the Lord responded like he did in the past, but for three weeks nothing happened. Now we find out why. This one who "looked like a man," this one in the golden sash with eyes of blazing fire, was detained in battle for three weeks. He would have been there sooner, but an evil angel, the prince who hovers over the empire of Persia, resisted him. This is why Satan is called "the ruler of the kingdom of the air" (Ephesians 2:2).

Some do not think that such a delay could happen to the Second Person of the Trinity. So strong is the problem that one commentary I read agrees that Daniel saw Jesus in the opening of chapter 10 but says that in these verses he is speaking about another angel. That is a convenient way of handling this problem, but the text does not allow that. The whole chapter speaks about the same person. Most either make the whole chapter about an angel or say that just these verses refer to another angel. But there is another possibility.

Do you remember the historical account of the fall of Jericho found in the book of Joshua? On the night before the people began the battle of Jericho, Joshua went out all by himself, and suddenly there was a man before him with a drawn sword (Joshua 5). Joshua said, "Are you for us or for our enemies?" Do you remember the answer of the one who looked like a soldier? He said, "Neither, but as *commander of the army of the LORD* I have now come. . . . Take off your sandals, for the place where you are standing is holy."

This was God, not an angel. This was the Second Person of the Trinity, and *he described himself as the captain of the army of God.* He is the leader of all God's angels when they go into battle against Satan and his angels, "the powers of this dark world and . . . the spiritual forces of evil in the heavenly realms" (Ephesians 6:12).

In fact, that is what this vision is about. In Daniel 10:1b we read, "Its message was true and it concerned a great war." The word translated "war" is the same word, "armies" or "host," used by the Second Person of the Trinity when he described himself as Captain of the army of the Lord. This vision is about the spiritual warfare taking place in the heavenly realms, which we know very little about. Paul tells us to put on the whole armor of God because of this spiritual warfare. The warfare in the heavenly realms is being acted out on earth among human beings.

Revelation 12:4 says, "The dragon [Satan] stood in front of the woman [Mary] who was about to give birth, so that he might devour her child the moment it was born." That is what was happening in the heavenly warfare, but on earth this was being carried out by King Herod who killed all the infants in Bethlehem in an attempt to kill the one born King of the Jews.

Frank Peretti's books *This Present Darkness* and *Piercing the Darkness* give us a great picture of the spiritual war going on behind the scenes. Because I have experienced some difficult ones in my day, I appreciated Peretti's description of a congregational meeting of the church. Some people in the meeting were against the pastor, even though he was a godly man. The demons and the angels took their sides.

> Outside, even though it was still a half hour before the meeting, cars began to arrive, more than were usually there on Sundays. Several dark shadows kept a wary eye on everything from their perch atop the church roof, their stations around the building, or their appointed posts in the sanctuary. Lucius [a demon], more nervous than ever, paced and hovered about. What worried Lucius the most were the other spirits standing around, the enemies of the cause, the host of heaven.
>
> When Lucius saw the Colemans come in the front door, he was agitated. In the past, they had never been very strong against the defeats and discouragements Lucius ordered, and their marriage had just about dissolved. Then they aligned themselves with Praying Busche [the pastor], hearing his words and becoming stronger all the time. Before long they and others like them would be a real threat.
>
> But their arrival didn't cause Lucius as much agitation as the huge messenger of God who accompanied them. As the Colemans found a seat, Lucius swooped down and accosted the new intruder. The angel said nothing. He only riveted his eyes on those of Lucius and stood firm. Triskal and Krioni [angels] entered with pastor Hank and his wife Mary.[1]

A vote was being taken to see if the congregation would retain the godly pastor Hank. The congregation was evenly divided between those who supported his Biblical preaching and those who did not. When the vote was taken, two men from the opposing sides were chosen to count the votes. Guilo, the head angel, watched the count.

> He bent over the two men to have a look. Gordon Mayer was counting first, silently, then handing the ballots to John Coleman. But he stealthily hid a few yea ballots in his palm. Guilo checked to see how closely the demons were watching, then made a stealthy move himself, touching the back of Mayer's hand. A demon saw it and struck Guilo's hand with bared talons. But Guilo's move had succeeded in foiling Mayer's effort. The ballots dropped out of Mayer's hand and John Coleman saw them.[2]

THE BATTLE OF THE VISION WAS TRUE SPIRITUAL WARFARE (10:20 — 11:1)

> So he said, "Do you know why I have come to you? Soon I will return to fight against the prince of Persia, and when I go, the prince of Greece will come; but first I will tell you what is written in the Book of Truth. (No one supports me against them except Michael, your prince. And in the first year of Darius the Mede, I took my stand to support and protect him.)

These verses show us the battle of the army of the Lord. The Second Person of the Trinity was doing battle with the Prince of Persia, probably Satan himself, over the soul of Cyrus, Darius the Mede. This heavenly battle would eventually find its way into the events of world history when Greece, in God's time, would conquer Persia, as we will see in Daniel 11.

But the thing that bothers people the most is that the Second Person of the Trinity was delayed about three weeks by the Prince of Persia. If he is God, could he not have destroyed Satan in a moment? Yes, but we don't understand the ways of God. Remember the historical account of the Second Person of the Trinity wrestling with Jacob all night to a draw. How could Jacob have the strength to match God in a wrestling match? I don't know, but that is what God decided should happen.

The Second Person of the Trinity who did battle in the Old Testament is now seated at the right hand of God in Heaven. Paul writes in Ephesians 1:20-22:

> [God] raised [Jesus] from the dead and seated him at his right hand in the heavenly realms, far above all rule and authority, power and dominion, and every title that can be given, not only in the present age but also in the one to come. And God placed all things under his feet and appointed him to be head over everything for the church.

From this place of authority, he stands for his people in important battles, he speaks important messages to his people, and he strengthens his people at important times.

The Lord Stands for His People in Important Battles

"And in the first year of Darius the Mede, I took my stand to support and protect him" (Daniel 11:1). Listen to what the prophet Isaiah had to say about Darius the Mede, also known as Cyrus the Great.

> This is what the LORD says to his anointed, to Cyrus, whose right hand I take hold of to subdue nations before him and to strip kings of their armor, to open doors before him so that gates will not be shut: I will go before you and will level the mountains; I will break down gates of bronze and cut through bars of iron. I will give you the treasures of darkness, riches stored in secret places, so that you may know that I am the LORD, the God of Israel, who summons you by name. For the sake of Jacob my servant, of Israel my chosen, I summon you by name and bestow on you a title of honor, though you do not acknowledge me. I am the LORD, and there is no other; apart from me there is no God. I will strengthen you, though you have not acknowledged me, so that from the rising of the sun to the place of its setting men may know there is none besides me. I am the LORD, and there is no other. . . . I will raise up Cyrus in my righteousness: I will make all his ways straight. He will rebuild my city and set my exiles free, but not for a price or reward, says the LORD Almighty. (Isaiah 45:1-6, 13)

The Lord stood up for his people by using Cyrus the Great, showing that the battle belongs to the Lord. In the spiritual war, he worked in the heart of Cyrus, his anointed leader of Persia, in order to deliver his people. This is how history records God's stand for his people:

> In the first year of Cyrus king of Persia, in order to fulfill the word of the LORD spoken by Jeremiah, the LORD moved the heart of Cyrus king of Persia to make a proclamation throughout his realm and to put it in writing: This is what Cyrus king of Persia says: "The LORD, the God of heaven, has given me all the kingdoms of the earth and he has appointed me to build a temple for him at Jerusalem in Judah. Anyone of his people among you — may his God be with him, and let him go up to Jerusalem in Judah and build the temple of the LORD, the God of Israel, the God who is in Jerusalem." (Ezra 1:1-3)

The Lord will stand for you and will fight the spiritual battles for you as well, but you do need to ask. This anonymous poem expresses that well.

I got up early one morning,
And rushed right into the day;
I had so much to accomplish,
That I didn't have time to pray.

Problems just tumbled about me,
And heavier came each task.
Why doesn't God help me? I wondered.
He answered, "You didn't ask."

I wanted to see joy and beauty,
But the day toiled on, gray and bleak.
I wondered why God didn't show me.
He said, "But you didn't seek."

I tried to come into God's presence;
I used all my keys at the lock.
But God gently and lovingly chided,
"My child, you didn't knock."

I woke up early this morning,
And paused before entering the day.
I had so much to accomplish
That I had to take time to pray!

What about those times when it seems like God doesn't answer our prayers or fight our battles? Has he forgotten us? No. I love the historical account of Stephen after he preached in Jerusalem. The Jews became so angry that they began to stone him. The Lord could have intervened in that battle and saved Stephen's life, but he chose not to. But he gave Stephen a glimpse of the Lord standing for his people. Luke writes:

But Stephen, full of the Holy Spirit, looked up to heaven and saw the glory of God, and Jesus standing at the right hand of God. "Look," he said, "I see heaven open and the Son of Man standing at the right hand of God." (Acts 7:55, 56)

The Lord Speaks Important Messages to His People

In the third year of Cyrus king of Persia, a revelation was given to Daniel. . . . Its message was true and it concerned a great war. The understanding of the message came to him in a vision. (Daniel 10:1)

The messages of God found in his revealed Word are true, and "the truth will set you free" (John 8:32). In Daniel 10:21, his Word is called "the Book of Truth." The truth will set you free from the guilt of sin if you believe his message that Jesus died on the cross for your sins. The truth will set you free from the consequences of sin if you believe his Word and obey it. And the truth will set you free from worry if you remember that God is working everything together for the good of his people.

The Lord showed that he controls the future by telling Daniel in 539 B.C. that after Cyrus died, there would be three more kings before a powerful and wealthy king would arise (Daniel 11:2). The first of these three kings was Cambyses (530-522 B.C.). Cambyses had his younger brother Smerdis killed so he could secure his throne. While Cambyses was at war, a man who looked like his brother took over the throne in Persia. Because of being a look-alike, he was called Pseudo-Smerdis. Cambyses came home to kill him, but he died on the journey. So Gaumata or Pseudo-Smerdis became king for seven months in 522 B.C., and then he died. The son-in-law of Cyrus, Darius Hystaspes, became king in his place, reigning from 522-486 B.C.

Just as the Lord had truthfully prophesied, a fourth king came to power who was far richer and greater in power than the previous three. This one was none other than the husband of Queen Esther, King Xerxes. You may remember that in the third year of his reign, Xerxes hosted a six-month world's fair to display his power and his incredible wealth. Daniel said that this fourth king would "gain power by his wealth" (11:2).

After he deposed Queen Vashti because she would not display her beauty lewdly, Xerxes went into battle for three years, to try to put down the rebellion of the Greeks. Daniel 11:2 says, "He will stir up everyone against the kingdom of Greece." After three years of battle, Xerxes was defeated by the Greeks in the crucial battle of Salamis in 480 B.C.

Xerxes reigned until he was assassinated by the chief of the palace guards in 465 B.C. His second son Artaxerxes ruled in his place. If Xerxes was Artaxerxes' father, who was his mother? Could it possibly have been Esther?

After Xerxes died, was Esther the queen mother when Nehemiah was the cupbearer of Artaxerxes? We do not know for sure, but we do know that the Lord was working all these things together to deliver his people from the hand of the evil Haman. His Word was true about these four kings, and his Word is true when it says, "We know that in all things God works for the good of those who love him, who have been called according to his purpose" (Romans 8:28). No matter how difficult things are for you in your life right now, let this truth set you free from worry. He is working in your life right now to deliver you.

The righteous cry out, and the LORD hears them;
he delivers them from all their troubles.

The LORD is close to the brokenhearted
and saves those who are crushed in spirit.
A righteous man may have many troubles,
but the LORD delivers him from them all. (Psalm 34:17-19)

The Lord Strengthens His People at Important Times

While he was saying this to me, I bowed with my face toward the ground and was speechless. Then one who looked like a man touched my lips, and I opened my mouth and began to speak. I said to the one standing before me, "I am overcome with anguish because of the vision, my Lord, and I am helpless. How can I, your servant, talk with you, my lord? My strength is gone and I can hardly breathe." Again the one who looked like a man touched me and gave me strength. "Do not be afraid, O man highly esteemed," he said. "Peace! Be strong now; be strong." When he spoke to me, I was strengthened and said, "Speak, my lord, since you have given me strength." (Daniel 10:15-19)

The Lord speaks to us as we read and hear his written Word, and he speaks to us when we worship him. Through his Word and worship he strengthens us to prepare us for the battles we may face in life. When you come to worship the Lord in faith, you never leave as the same person. You are changed and strengthened, having met with the Lord himself. People have such a cavalier attitude toward worship. The least illness or tiredness keeps them home. Sickness that does not keep them home from work or school will frequently keep them home from worship. They do not realize what they are sacrificing when they miss worship.

A treasurer in a church I pastored would meet people at the door as they came for worship. He would greet them with a smile and a handshake at both morning worship services. That made me start thinking. If that treasurer would give a hundred-dollar bill to each person who walked through that door every Lord's day, people would drag themselves out of bed to get to worship. They would come home from the lake early on the weekend to get to worship. Sadly, they would do that for only a hundred-dollar bill. In reality we get so much more from worship. We would spend the money that week, and it would be gone. But the Lord strengthens his people for battle through his Word in worship.

Do you not know? Have you not heard? The LORD is the everlasting God, the Creator of the ends of the earth. He will not grow tired or weary, and his understanding no one can fathom. He gives strength to the weary and increases the power of the weak. Even youths grow tired and weary, and young men stumble and fall; but those who hope in the LORD *will renew their strength. They will soar on wings like eagles; they will run and not grow weary, they will walk and not be faint. (Isaiah 40:28-31)*

The Lord has given us the promise, "Never will I leave you; never will I forsake you" (Hebrews 13:5). The Father has sent the first string to help us in our battles. He will stand with you, he will speak to you, and he will strengthen you for whatever you face in life.

14

His Story Written in Advance

DANIEL 11:2-20

Some scholars, particularly those who do not believe in the miracle of predictive prophecy, are convinced that these chapters of Daniel had to have been written in 150 B.C. because they are so historically accurate down to the minute details. For these scholars, this is the only acceptable explanation of Daniel's incredible accuracy. The problem is that Daniel lived from approximately 620 B.C.-530 B.C., and the book claims to have been written by Daniel himself, an eyewitness of this period of Babylon's history (7:15; 8:1, 15; 9:2, 22; 10:7). Either the author lied about who he was, or Daniel predicted the future in vivid detail. If he lied about who he was, why should we believe anything else he wrote? I believe that Daniel is the author of this book and that the Spirit of God in him could predict the future. God can be specific about events in the future because he planned the future. So if he breaks into human history to tell us what will happen, those events must be very important to study and understand.

Now the events predicted in Daniel 11:2-20 were future to Daniel, but they are past for us. If these verses in Daniel have already been fulfilled, why should we take the time to study them? What good will that do us? One benefit is that it helps build our trust in the sovereignty of God, being convinced that he "works out everything in conformity with the purpose of his will" (Ephesians 1:11). This chapter shows that God is sovereign over the events of human history.

There is another very important benefit that is sometimes overlooked. As we compare the wording of these prophecies in Daniel 11 to records of ancient history, we will learn some very important rules for understanding prophecy. Historically scholars seemed to have arbitrarily decided on principles they would use to interpret prophetic writings. For example, the early immoral life of Augustine of Hippo shaped the principles of interpretation he used for certain parts of Scripture. He had fallen into a life of sexual immorality and debauchery, fathering a child out of wedlock. After he committed his life to Christ, he was very sensitive to the dangers of carnal living. So when he studied the Song of Songs, he could not believe that the Holy Bible would be discussing human sexuality and the sensual parts of the human anatomy, which he considered evil. Consequently he drew on the Alexandrian Fathers' allegorical interpretation of Scripture to interpret the Song of Solomon.

The allegorical method of interpretation spiritualizes the whole Bible. Everything in the Bible stands for something else. For example, the children of Israel crossing the Jordan into the Promised Land is considered a picture of Christians passing through death into Heaven. This was very promising for Augustine when he approached the Song of Solomon because he could avoid the sexual overtones of the book. He has been credited with making popular the view that the Song of Songs is really about Christ's love for his Church. So for Augustine, the two breasts of the Shulammite were the Old and New Testaments. Now we may laugh at such an understanding of the Bible, but it has been popular for many centuries, and though it is losing influence, many still hold to it.

Augustine did a similar thing with Biblical prophecy, particularly the prophecies concerning the Second Coming of Christ. At the beginning of his walk with Christ, he was a Premillennialist.[1] The official stand of the early church for the first three centuries was premillennial. A premillennialist believes that Christ will physically descend in the clouds with the sound of the trumpet; the dead will then be raised imperishable, and the remaining believers will be changed into their immortal bodies. We will all be caught up to meet the Lord in the air and escort him back to this earth to establish his reign for a thousand years — a millennium. Christ will return before the Millennium; hence the word *premillennial*. We will then reign with him on this newly re-created earth and enjoy its pleasures.

This did not sit well with St. Augustine. As Nathaniel West reminds us, Augustine called the Millennium

> partly spiritual . . . partly ceremonial. . . . Such was the theory of the great Augustine, by which the future Millennium, the hope of the martyrs, to be realized at the Second Coming of Christ, was "spiritualized" into a present politico-religious fact, and whose name did more to fasten it upon the church for thirteen centuries than all other names beside.[2]

So when it came to the prophecies of the Second Coming of Christ, he borrowed again from the Alexandrian Fathers and used the allegorical interpretation. It appears to me from this quote that Augustine was not driven by exegesis but by preference.

One does not find many prophecies of the first coming of Christ fulfilled allegorically or spiritually. There are some figures of speech like Isaiah 11:1, "A shoot will come up from the stump of Jesse." But even that figure of speech was fulfilled literally in that Jesse's line of kings was cut off like a stump before the Messiah came, and Jesus was a descendant of those kings.

Augustine's allegorical interpretation of prophecy shaped the thinking of the Church for the next fifteen hundred years. When the sixteenth- and seventeenth-century Reformers rediscovered the gospel, they leaned heavily on the writings of Augustine. They appeared to adopt his view of the Second Coming with very little question. For example, John Calvin, in his commentary on Isaiah, gives an interesting interpretation of the prophecy of a future day on earth when the wolf will lie down with the lamb.

> Though Isaiah says that the wild and tame beasts will live in harmony, that the blessing of God may be clearly and fully manifested, yet he chiefly means what I have said, that the people of Christ will have no disposition to do injury, no fierceness or cruelty. They were formerly like lions or leopards, but will now be like sheep and lambs; for they will have laid aside every cruel and brutish disposition.[3]

> He now declares plainly, that men themselves, having laid aside the depravity which naturally dwells in them, will be inclined, of their own accord, to do what is right. He speaks of believers who have been regenerated to a new life. It is, therefore, a distinguishing mark of the genuine members of the Church, that they are free from all desire of doing injury to others.[4]

Having worked in the church for over twenty-five years, I must say that if this is as good as it gets, then I am very discouraged. Even regenerate saints can at times be very hurtful. As I say often to our pastoral staff, "We must love the sheep, but remember sheep have teeth and they will bite."

PROPHECY IS HISTORY WRITTEN IN ADVANCE

Rather than being arbitrary as to how we interpret prophecy, I think it is important to see how the prophecies of the Old Testament were fulfilled and use the same principles as we study the prophecies of Christ's Second Coming. One such principle is that some Biblical prophecy is "his story,"

God's story, written in advance. Biblical prophecy is many times history written in advance. It is true that the prophetic descriptions of history are rather cryptic in nature, as you will see. You may scratch your head, wondering what in the world Daniel is talking about. Even Daniel when he wrote these prophecies and those who heard them in his day could not decipher precisely what it all meant. But as these events were being fulfilled, it was easy for those who knew Daniel's prophecies to see God fulfilling those prophecies.

Again, some prophecy is history written in advance. Knowing this principle will keep you from unfruitful speculation about prophecies of the Second Coming. We may not always be able to understand the prophecy until it is history. But if you understand this principle, it will force you to know what those prophecies are. If the people in Daniel's day had studied and had known these prophecies, they would know year after year, decade after decade, century after century what was happening. In the same way, you will know the events surrounding the return of Christ if you know the prophecies. It is amazing how many people hold very firmly to positions about the Second Coming who have never read or studied the prophecies of the Old Testament. Though they have never even read them, yet they still have strong opinions about the future.

PROPHECY IS WRITTEN FOR FUTURE GENERATIONS

The second important principle of prophetic interpretation that comes from a study of these verses is that prophecy is written for future generations. David Chilton, author of *Paradise Restored*, is a postmillennialist. A postmillennialist believes that the Church of Jesus Christ, through the help of the Holy Spirit, will Christianize the whole world, including all the governments of the world. Only after the Church has Christianized the world will Jesus Christ come back again. Chilton teaches that the entire book of Revelation was fulfilled in the first century with the destruction of Jerusalem in A.D. 70. Part of his reasoning is that God would not write the book of Revelation to seven churches of the first century if it had to do with something that would occur at least two thousand years in the future.

Anyone who studies Daniel 11 knows that is faulty reasoning because at times God gives prophecies to people who will not live to see their fulfillment. He gives the prophecy in one generation even though it will not be fulfilled for generations to come. The prophecies of Daniel 11 were written in 536 B.C. They only began to be fulfilled in 530 B.C., and verses 21-35 were not fulfilled until 150 B.C. The end of Daniel 11 and the beginning of chapter 12 will not be fulfilled until at least after the year A.D. 2003.

In a similar way, Peter writes:

*Concerning this salvation, the prophets, who spoke of the grace that was
to come to you, searched intently and with the greatest care, trying to find
out the times and circumstances to which the Spirit of Christ in them was
pointing when he predicted the sufferings of Christ and the glories that
would follow. (1 Peter 1:10, 11)*

Can you picture the prophets? They were writing all these things about
the coming Messiah, and they were trying so hard to figure out what it
would be like. What does it mean that a child will be born and he will be
called Immanuel? What does it mean that a virgin will give birth to a son?
What does it mean that the Messiah will be cut off? They were trying to figure this out, but they could not do it. Peter ends by saying, "It was revealed
to them that they were not serving themselves but you, when they spoke of
[these] things" (v. 12).

The same is true of the Second Coming of Christ. Some of the prophecies of Christ's return were given to Daniel and the Old Testament prophets,
while some were given to John and the New Testament apostles; but they
were all revealed for you or at least for those who will be alive when Christ
comes back. Such principles of interpretation are important to understand
before delving into prophecy.

THE PURPOSE OF THE PROPHECY OF DANIEL 11

The purpose of Daniel 11 is to prepare God's people for two great crises to
come. The first crisis was the persecution of God's people by Antiochus
Epiphanes. This first crisis came about in the year 170 B.C., recorded for us
in Daniel 11:21-35. We will study this crisis in the next chapter. The second
great crisis will be the persecution of God's people by the Antichrist
Epiphany. This is my own play on words, meaning "the appearance of the
Antichrist." This second crisis will occur just prior to the return of Christ
and is recorded for us in Daniel 11:36 — 12:3. These verses show that the
resurrection of the righteous dead, the Rapture, occurs after the Tribulation
under the Antichrist's rule. We will study this second crisis in the next chapter as well.

The Kings of Persia and Greece (11:2-4)

Chapters 10 — 12 of Daniel form one continuous passage. The chapter
divisions that were added around the thirteenth century are rather unfortu-
nate, and they can be confusing. I do appreciate the attempt at clarification
made by the *New International Version* with three subheadings. Daniel 10:1
— 11:1 has the subheading, "Daniel's Vision of a Man." We studied that in
the previous chapter.

The next heading introduces Daniel 11:2-35 and is entitled, "The Kings of the South and the North." This section is an incredible prediction of the events of the Syrian kings (the kings of the north) and the Egyptian kings (the kings of the south). The first three verses set the stage for the kings of the north and the kings of the south with an overview of the kings of Persia and the first king of Greece. This history written in advance covers the years 530 B.C.-150 B.C.

The next division occurs between verses 35 and 36. The NIV calls this section, "The King Who Exalts Himself." This section covers Daniel 11:36 — 12:4 and is really just one unit, though the NIV throws in one more subtitle that is unnecessary, as you will see. The king who exalts himself is the Antichrist, who will rule just prior to the return of Christ and the resurrection/rapture of the saints.

In Daniel 11:2-20, the prophet gives an overview of history that will lead up to the first crisis. Verse 2 speaks of three kings of Persia, then a fourth. The point of this verse is not to say that there are only four kings in the history of Persia. That is why the text says there will be "three more kings." The main point of this verse is to show something very important about the fourth king.

The three kings of Persia mentioned here were Cambyses (530-522 B.C.), Pseudo-Smerdis or Gaumata (522 B.C.), and Darius I (522-486 B.C.). Darius I was the father of Xerxes (Ahasuerus), who became the husband of Queen Esther. Xerxes (486-465 B.C.) is the fourth king of verse 2: "who will be far richer than all the others. When he has gained power by his wealth, he will stir up everyone against the kingdom of Greece."

The book of Esther opens with Xerxes hosting a six-month fair to display his wealth and military power in the third year of his reign (484 B.C.). "For a full 180 days he displayed the vast wealth of his kingdom and the splendor and glory of his majesty" (Esther 1:4). That was followed by a weeklong banquet in the citadel of Susa. He was demonstrating and boasting of his military power, because he was about to march his vast army to the west and shore up his kingdom.

At that banquet the king became drunk and ordered his wife Vashti to display her beauty to the people and nobles. The queen refused to come to the banquet hall. Xerxes was so furious about being humiliated by his wife on such an occasion that he had Vashti deposed. The wise men of the kingdom then told the ruler:

Therefore, if it pleases the king, let him issue a royal decree and let it be written in the laws of Persia and Media, which cannot be repealed, that Vashti is never again to enter the presence of King Xerxes. Also let the king give her royal position to someone else who is better than she. Then when the king's edict is proclaimed throughout all his vast realm, all the women will respect their husbands, from the least to the greatest. (Esther 1:19, 20)

The military campaign to the west lasted three years (483-480 B.C.). Xerxes was drawn into a battle with the Greeks. He crossed the Aegean Sea and sailed toward Greece. Xerxes lost that battle, and this was the beginning of the end of the power of Persia. Just as Daniel had prophesied in chapters 2, 7, and 8, Babylon would be followed by Persia, and Persia would be followed by Greece as a world power.

King Xerxes came home to Persia a defeated general and a defeated man. He longed for the solace of his beautiful wife Vashti, but his irrevocable decree would not allow him to see her. He ordered that a search be made of his entire kingdom to find a new queen. After a year a Jewish girl named Hadassah was chosen. He gave her the name Esther. In the palace, Esther may have had a strong influence on his son who became the next king of Persia. That king's name was Artaxerxes, who employed a cupbearer named Nehemiah.

Persia dominated the world for the next 150 years, until the time of Alexander the Great (336-323 B.C.). This was accurately predicted in Daniel 11:3, 4.

A mighty king will appear, who will rule with great power and do as he pleases. After he has appeared, his empire will be broken up and parceled out towards the four winds of heaven. It will not go to his descendants, nor will it have the power he exercised, because his empire will be uprooted and given to others.

The reign of Alexander the Great was also prophesied, in Daniel 8:5-8. The imagery is different, but the message is still the same.

As I was thinking about this, suddenly a goat with a prominent horn between his eyes came from the west, crossing the whole earth without touching the ground. He came toward the two-horned ram I had seen standing beside the canal and charged at him in great rage. I saw him attack the ram furiously, striking the ram and shattering his two horns. The ram was powerless to stand against him; the goat knocked him to the ground and trampled on him, and none could rescue the ram from his power. The goat became very great, but at the height of his power his large horn was broken off, and in its place four prominent horns grew up toward the four winds of heaven.

This mighty king appeared on the scene after his father Philip of Macedonia died in 336 B.C. He swiftly conquered many of the kingdoms of the known world, including Persia, by 330 B.C. The last kingdom to be conquered was Babylon, now weakened under Persian rule. It was his desire to rebuild the city of Babylon the Great, though he was certainly unaware that

God had said through the prophet Jeremiah that the city of Babylon would never be rebuilt.

> *So desert creatures and hyenas will live there, and there the owl will dwell.*
> *It will never be inhabited or lived in from generation to generation. As*
> *God overthrew Sodom and Gomorrah along with their neighboring towns*
> *. . . so no one will live there; no man will dwell in it. (Jeremiah 50:39, 40)*

Alexander the Great tried to rebuild Babylon, but he died in 323 B.C. When he died, he left his mentally challenged half-brother Philip III and his son Alexander IV in charge. These two were under the guidance of Perdiccas. All three were eventually murdered: Perdiccas in 321 B.C., Philip III in 317 B.C., and Alexander IV in 311 B.C. The kingdom was then parceled up among four generals. That is the meaning of his kingdom being "broken up and parceled out toward the four winds of heaven" and that "it will not go to his descendants."

Two of the nations were very weak, while the other two became world powers. The two world powers fought each other for the next 150 years. Their battles and their struggles for power were predicted in the verses that follow. One of those rulers is called "the king of the North," a phrase you will see over and over again in these verses. The kingdom of the north is the kingdom of Syria.

The kingdom of Syria extended from Damascus to Jerusalem, northward into Asia Minor, and westward to Macedonia. Macedonia was one of these four ruling kingdoms, but it was very weak. Syria also extended into Iraq and Iran. That is the territory of the king of the North to keep in mind as the prophecy unfolds. This territory was ruled by the Selucid dynasty.

The other kingdom was called the kingdom of the south. Daniel 11:5 says, "The king of the South will become strong, but one of his commanders will become even stronger than he and will rule his own kingdom with great power." This was Ptolemy Lagos, who gained control of the land of Egypt.

Immediately after Alexander's death, Ptolemy proved himself to be quite shrewd. When the generals assigned members of their group to rule the various sections of the empire, he controlled Egypt, thus securing a region that is easy to defend since there are deserts on three sides. Only by sea could it be easily attacked. As long as Ptolemy could maintain a strong navy, he would be almost impregnable.

Ptolemy Lagos won the trust of the Egyptian people by following Alexander's lead in declaring himself a successor to the ancient Pharaohs and worshiping at the shrines of the Egyptian gods. The kingdom of Egypt was ruled by the Ptolemies for almost three centuries. Their kingdom extended west into northern Africa and south all the way to Lake Victoria.

Now, what does the prophecy mean, "The king of the South will become strong, but one of his commanders will become even stronger than he and will rule his own kingdom with great power"? One of Ptolemy's generals in 316 B.C. was Seleucus. He became even stronger than Ptolemy Lagos and returned to Babylon to establish his own kingdom, which became the kingdom of the north, Syria.

Daniel 11:6-20 is concerned with the history of these two powerful kingdoms. The purpose of these verses is to give an overview of history in advance so the people of God would be prepared for the coming of the first major crisis recorded in Daniel 11:21-35. This passage divides into three sections: the events surrounding Laodice and Bernice (vv. 6-9), the career of Antiochus III (vv. 10-19), and the reign of Seleucus IV (v. 20).

Laodice and Bernice (11:6-9)

After some years, they [the king of the North and the king of the South] will become allies. The daughter of the king of the South will go to the king of the North to make an alliance, but she will not retain her power, and he and his power will not last. (11:6a)

After many years of hostility between these two kingdoms, they desired to promote a lasting peace and become allies. Antiochus II, the grandson of Seleucus I, was ruling Syria, the kingdom of the north. Ptolemy II was ruling in Egypt, the kingdom of the south. To seal the alliance, Ptolemy gave his daughter Bernice in marriage to Antiochus II. The marriage was accompanied with great celebration as Bernice came to the Seleucid capital of Antioch. Antiochus put his first wife Laodice away and sent her and her sons to Ephesus in Asia Minor. But Bernice did not retain her power as queen because Antiochus II grew tired of her after a son was born. He went to Ephesus to live with Laodice, but he was poisoned by her to insure her children's right to the throne of Syria.

In those days she will be handed over, together with her royal escort and her father and the one who supported her. One from her family line will arise to take her place. (11:6b, 7a)

Bernice was handed over to Laodice, who had Bernice and her infant son murdered. Laodice had most of her leading supporters killed too. At the same time, the father of Bernice, Ptolemy II, died. One from her own family arose to take his place. This was Ptolemy III, the brother of Bernice. Greatly angered by the murder of his sister, he attacked the Seleucid realm by land and by sea.

He will attack the forces of the king of the North and enter his fortress; he will fight against them and be victorious. He will also seize their gods, their metal images and their valuable articles of silver and gold and carry them off to Egypt. For some years he will leave the king of the North alone. Then the king of the North will invade the realm of the king of the South but will retreat to his own country. (11:7-9)

Seleucus II, the son of Laodice, was in power at the time. He fled back to Asia Minor while the army of Ptolemy III plundered his kingdom and carried the spoils back to Egypt. The last sentence describes an unsuccessful counterattack by Seleucus II.

Antiochus III and Seleucus IV (11:10-19)

His sons will prepare for war and assemble a great army, which will sweep on like an irresistible flood and carry the battle as far as his fortress. Then the king of the South will march out in a rage and fight against the king of the North, who will raise a large army, but it will be defeated. When the army is carried off, the king of the South will be filled with pride and will slaughter many thousands, yet he will not remain triumphant. For the king of the North will muster another army, larger than the first; and after several years, he will advance with a huge army fully equipped. In those times many will rise against the king of the South. The violent men among your own people will rebel in fulfillment of the vision, but without success. (11:10-14)

The sons of the king of the North, Seleucus II, who had an unsuccessful attack on Egypt, prepared for war and assembled a great army. Seleucus II had two sons. The older, Seleucus III, began to assemble forces to attack Egypt but was killed in a revolt four years after becoming king. He was succeeded by his younger brother, Antiochus III, who swept on "like an irresistible flood" and carried the battle "as far as his fortress" (11:10). He completely defeated the king of the South, Ptolemy III (Euergetes). Antiochus reestablished control over most of the land they had formerly held and kept Egypt at bay through almost thirty-six years of constant fighting.

The last sentence of this section refers to a revolt by a faction of Jewish men in the land of Israel. They gave their support to Antiochus in hopes of gaining freedom from Egypt. Their vision of better conditions for Israel under Antiochus failed because it was ultimately his son who brought such horrible pain and destruction upon the people of God.

The Egyptian forces at that time tried to retain control of Israel, and this resulted in one of the great battles in the career of Antiochus III, at Gaza. In 198 B.C. Antiochus gained control of Israel, which the Ptolemy Dynasty had controlled for more than a century. Daniel 11:15, 16 says:

Then the king of the North will come and build up siege ramps and will cap-
ture a fortified city. The forces of the South will be powerless to resist;
even their best troops will not have the strength to stand. The invader will
do as he pleases; no one will be able to stand against him. He will estab-
lish himself in the Beautiful Land [that is, Israel] and will have the power
to destroy it.

Despite thirty-six years of military victories, Antiochus III was not able to completely conquer Egypt; so he decided to use diplomacy. Daniel 11:17 says:

He will determine to come with the might of his entire kingdom and will
make an alliance with the king of the South. And he will give him a daugh-
ter in marriage in order to overthrow the kingdom, but his plans will not
succeed or help him.

What he did and what is prophesied in these verses is that Antiochus the Great decided to give his daughter in marriage to the king of Egypt, hoping that she would influence her husband to support her father's purposes. The king of Egypt was Ptolemy V; the daughter that Antiochus gave was named Cleopatra, who became the first influential Egyptian to bear that famous name. She gave her loyalty to her husband instead of standing with her father.

Discouraged with his attempts in Egypt and not satisfied with the amount of land he already controlled, Antiochus turned his attention to the coastlands, a word used in Scripture to designate all the lands across the Mediterranean Sea to the west of Israel. This is recorded for us in verse 18: "Then he will turn his attention to the coastlands and will take many of them, but a commander will put an end to his insolence and will turn his insolence back upon him."

As he attacked the coastlands, he was turned back by the forces of a rising new superpower. Few had heard much about this future world power called Rome, the fourth kingdom of Daniel 2, "strong as iron — for iron breaks and smashes everything" (v. 40). The Roman armies defeated Antiochus the Great at the famous battle of Thermopolae and completely overcame him at Magnesia. The Roman commander demanded that he surrender his navy, give up most of his land in Asia Minor, pay a huge indemnity, and give Rome tribute for the next twelve years. The Roman commander also chose twenty men as hostages. One was Antiochus' younger son, Antiochus IV, later known as Antiochus Epiphanes.

With his kingdom reduced and his treasury depleted, Antiochus the Great made his eldest son, Seleucus IV, co-regent and went to the eastern part of his kingdom in search of funds. Daniel 11:19 says, "After this, he will turn back toward the fortresses of his own country but will stumble and fall, to be seen no more." When Antiochus III tried to rob the treasury of a small temple in the east, the guardians of the temple attacked him and killed him, and he was seen no more.

The reign of Seleucus IV (187-176 B.C.), the successor of Antiochus III, is referred to in verse 20: "His successor will send out a tax collector to maintain the royal splendor. In a few years, however, he will be destroyed, yet not in anger or in battle." In comparison to the thirty-six years of his father's reign, the eleven years of his own reign seemed like "a few years." He sent out a tax collector to try to replenish the money his father had lost, but to no avail. His chief minister conspired against him and killed him. He was destroyed, and "not in anger or in battle."

THE SIGNIFICANCE OF THIS FULFILLED PROPHECY FOR US

First, this fulfilled prophecy shows us that God is sovereign in the affairs of men and of nations. No one comes to power except those God places in that position of authority. Paul says in Romans 13:1, "Everyone must submit himself to the governing authorities, for there is no authority except that which God has established. The authorities that exist have been established by God." Daniel 11:2-20 shows this to be true. Therefore, we must honor and submit ourselves to the government that is over us, no matter who that governing authority is. That does not mean we cannot use godly and just means to challenge and change the governing leadership. But it must be done with grace. In that light, these prophecies also show the frailty of those who appear to be powerful men and women.

> He brings princes to naught and reduces the rulers of this world to nothing. No sooner are they planted, no sooner are they sown, no sooner do they take root in the ground, than he blows on them and they wither, and a whirlwind sweeps them away like chaff. (Isaiah 40:23, 24)

Second, this fulfilled prophecy strikes a deathblow to openness of God theology. Toward the end of the twentieth century a new movement among evangelicals called "the Openness of God" was promoted by Greg Boyd of Bethel College, Clark Pinnock, and others. This theology is derived from nineteenth-century Process Theology. They teach that since the essence of God is love, he could not plan or know the future because that would rob his creatures of their freedom. They teach that God does not know any more about the future than you or I. John Jefferson Davis challenges this theology:

> This claim that God lacks a comprehensive knowledge of the future simply does not square with the reality of predictive prophecy of Scripture. It

stretches the lines of credibility to support that God and the Biblical writers are only making shrewd guesses when highly detailed predictions about future events are being made.

Third, this fulfilled prophecy instructs us in understanding similar New Testament prophecies regarding the Second Coming of Christ. One short example is Jesus' teaching on his return in Luke 21:20-28.

When you see Jerusalem being surrounded by armies, you will know that its desolation is near. Then let those who are in Judea flee to the mountains, let those in the city get out, and let those in the country not enter the city. For this is the time of punishment in fulfillment of all that has been written. How dreadful it will be in those days for pregnant women and nursing mothers! There will be great distress in the land and wrath against this people. They will fall by the sword and will be taken as prisoners to all the nations. Jerusalem will be trampled on by the Gentiles until the times of the Gentiles are fulfilled. There will be signs in the sun, moon and stars. On the earth, nations will be in anguish and perplexity at the roaring and tossing of the sea. Men will faint from terror, apprehensive of what is coming on the world, for the heavenly bodies will be shaken. At that time they will see the Son of Man coming in a cloud with power and great glory. When these things begin to take place, stand up and lift up your heads, because your redemption is drawing near.

Imagine living in the days when Antiochus II divorced Laodice and married Bernice. The events of the day make what is happening unmistakable, since the Lord has told you in advance. In those days some of the prophecies of Daniel 11 had been fulfilled, but some were yet future. You study such prophecies because they are warning you of a great crisis that is coming, but you do not know when.

This is how it is with Luke 21. Some of this prophecy has already been fulfilled. Luke 21:20-24a was fulfilled in the destruction of Jerusalem in A.D. 70.

After the prediction that some Jews would fall by the sword and others would be taken as prisoners to all the nations, Jesus added this incredible prediction: "Jerusalem will be trampled on by the Gentiles until the times of the Gentiles are fulfilled" (v. 24b). I have seen that take place in my lifetime. The Jews have not only returned to the land of Israel, but in 1967 they captured Jerusalem. Today it is the Jewish capital of Israel. Jesus predicted this would happen because he controls the affairs of men.

We have no idea how much time will pass between verses 24 and 25, but the next main event on the prophetic clock of Luke 21 is described in these words:

There will be signs in the sun, moon, and stars. On the earth, nations will be in anguish and perplexity at the roaring and tossing of the sea. Men will faint from terror, apprehensive of what is coming on the world, for the heavenly bodies will be shaken. (vv. 25, 26)

These words describe what will happen in ecological disasters during the Great Tribulation predicted in the trumpets of Revelation 8 — 11. Like the people living during the fulfillment of the prophecies of Daniel 11, we cannot imagine exactly what all these things mean as we look into the future. But when these things begin to happen, they will be just as clear to us as the events of the fourth through second centuries before Christ were to those who knew the prophecies of Daniel 11. They observed those prophecies and prepared themselves for the coming of a great crisis.

So too we should look for these signs and prepare ourselves for the return of our Savior, for he says, "At that time they will see the Son of Man coming in a cloud with power and great glory. When these things begin to take place, stand up and lift up your heads, because your redemption is drawing near" (Luke 21:27, 28).

I would encourage you to list the prophecies of the trumpets found in Revelation 8 — 11, so that you know the sequence of what is coming during the Tribulation. These four chapters follow a pattern similar to Daniel 11 but are rarely studied. The imagery is not always clear, but then neither was Daniel 11. The prophecies only made sense when they were fulfilled. Then it was all clear as a bell.

The reason it is important to do this is because of Jesus' warning in Luke 21 to those who do not know what to expect:

Be careful, or your hearts will be weighed down with dissipation, drunkenness and the anxieties of life, and that day will close on you unexpectedly like a trap. For it will come upon all those who live on the face of the whole earth. (vv. 34, 35)

When the events of the Great Tribulation begin, they will be terrifying. If you do not know what is happening, because you are unfamiliar with the prophecies, your heart will become "weighed down with dissipation, drunkenness and the anxieties of life." But if you know what to expect, you will not be afraid. Instead you will be excited, looking up, for your redemption draws near.

Several years ago I had my first CT scan. Not only do the technicians make you drink a quart of chalky liquid, but they inject a dye into your veins. The equipment the doctors use for this procedure looks like a space gun out of *Star Wars*. The doctor told me that thirty seconds after the dye was injected, I would feel a burning sensation in my throat. That would be accompanied by a bad taste, and the burning sensation would extend through my body until it reached my bladder. Then he left the room to start the procedure.

Sure enough, all he said came true exactly as he told me. If he had not explained these things to me in advance, I would have feared something had gone terribly wrong when I felt the burning sensation in my throat. I would have panicked, trying to get his attention if possible. But he prepared me, so my heart would not get weighed down with anxiety. So it will be for those who know the prophecies and live to see the Great Tribulation. Take heart — your Redeemer draws near.

15

The Two Great Crises

DANIEL 11:21 — 12:4

In the previous chapter I gave you a taste of how the prophecies of Daniel 11 were fulfilled down to the very details of marriages and murders, as well as the rise and fall of world leaders. The prophecies of Daniel 11:2-20 were written to prepare God's people for the coming of a great crisis in the land of Israel — the coming of a man of intrigue known as Antiochus Epiphanes. Although Antiochus was not of great importance in world history, he was of tremendous importance in the history of God's people, and in the history of redemption, which is what the Bible is all about. But this man has already been introduced to us in Daniel 8. Why would he have to be described again in Daniel 11?

I believe there are two reasons. First, Daniel 11 adds the dimension of giving a chronology so that the people of God would know when the time of his persecution was close. Second, he is introduced in Daniel 11 for the specific purpose of drawing a parallel between the persecution under Antiochus Epiphanes (Daniel 11:21-35) and the persecution under Antichrist Epiphany (Daniel 11:36-45). Some scholars believe that the last ten verses are simply a recapitulation of the previous fifteen verses. I will show you from the text why this cannot be true.

You will see in this chapter that the vision of Daniel given by Christ himself draws a parallel between these two men by, first, explaining their character, second, presenting their career, and third, describing the crisis that God's people would face. In both cases the Lord calls for a particular response from God's people to the crisis.

THE CRISIS OF ANTIOCHUS EPIPHANES (11:21-35)

The first great crisis that the people of God had to face took place under the rule of Antiochus IV. Those who knew their God were able to firmly resist. "His armed forces will rise up to desecrate the temple fortress and will abolish the daily sacrifice. Then they will set up the abomination that causes desolation. With flattery he will corrupt those who have violated the covenant, but the people who know their God will firmly resist him" (11:31, 32).

His Character (11:21-24)

They were called to resist a very powerful, contemptible, deceitful man of intrigue. Let me explain to you the character of Antiochus Epiphanes. He is described in Daniel 11:21: "He [Seleucus IV] will be succeeded by a contemptible person who has not been given the honor of royalty."

Antiochus is described as "a contemptible person." His contemporaries considered him a rather erratic type of man. While he gloried in his title of Epiphanes, "the manifest god," many preferred to call him Epimanes, which means "a madman." Though praised to his face, he was generally despised.[1]

You may remember from the last chapter that Antiochus IV, the younger son of Antiochus the Great, was taken captive to Rome along with nineteen other men. He wanted the throne of his father, but he was "not . . . given the honor of royalty"; but his brother was. When Antiochus IV found out that his brother was on the throne, he escaped Rome and made his way back to his own country of Syria.

The authorities in the Seleucid kingdom had no desire to make him king. So he made a deal with the king of Pergamum, who furnished him with money and supplies enabling him to enter Syria, where he took over the kingdom by clever maneuvering and by killing all who would oppose him.

Daniel put it this way: "He will invade the kingdom when its people feel secure, and he will seize it through intrigue" (11:21). He came back as the long-lost brother who arrived to help his royal brother secure his kingdom. He came with the appearance of being a friend, taking his brother and his kingdom completely by surprise because they were not expecting anything like this. Daniel adds, "Then an overwhelming army will be swept away before him; both it and a prince of the covenant will be destroyed. After coming to an agreement with him, he will act deceitfully, and with only a few people he will rise to power" (11:22, 23). That is when he killed his brother, and with the handful of men he brought back from Rome, he took the throne.

Daniel 11:24 describes more of his character: "When the richest provinces feel secure, he will invade them and will achieve what neither his fathers nor his forefathers did. He will distribute plunder, loot and wealth among his followers." One of the things that Antiochus Epiphanes loved to do was to loot the treasuries of the temples, because he considered himself a god. He would then go through the streets, taking the silver and gold and throwing it to his followers. He would laugh as the people threw themselves upon the ground collecting the pieces of gold and silver. His best friends always received the best gifts. Antiochus was a deceitful, incredibly arrogant king. This section ends by saying, "He will plot the overthrow of fortresses — but only for a time." His days and his actions were numbered by the Lord from the very start.

His Career (11:25-30)

The career of Antiochus is described beginning in verses 25, 26.

With a large army he will stir up his strength and courage against the king of the South. The king of the South will wage war with a large and very powerful army, but he will not be able to stand because of the plots devised against him. Those who eat from the king's provisions will try to destroy him; his army will be swept away, and many will fall in battle.

Here is what happened according to the historical record. Antiochus' sister, Cleopatra, had been the Queen of Egypt since her husband died. Then when she died, her teen-aged son, Ptolemy VI, became the King of Egypt. The advisers of this young man gathered a large army with the intentions of trying to conquer Israel and southern Syria. When he heard this, Antiochus IV quickly marched against Egypt. He defeated the Egyptian army and took possession of his nephew, Ptolemy VI. "Those who eat from the king's provisions will try to destroy him," and they made the Egyptian ruler's brother Ptolemy VII king instead.

Instead of using force to restore his nephew Ptolemy VI to power, Antiochus decided to use diplomacy. He sat down with him and said, "Let's make a treaty." The man of intrigue said, "Let us join these two nations together." But when they sat down at the table, Antiochus had a plan, and Ptolemy VI had a different plan. So they deceived each other. Verse 27 says, "The two kings, with their hearts bent on evil, will sit at the same table and lie to each other, but to no avail, because an end will still come at the appointed time." Dr. Allan MacRae wrote:

The youthful Egyptian king would try to persuade his uncle that if the invaders would leave Egypt its people would rally around the legitimate king and he would then rule Egypt in friendly fashion, and would give Antiochus whatever he might desire. The uncle would falsely declare that his only purpose was to secure the legitimate rights of his nephew. Thus the two kings would "sit at the same table and lie to each other." As predicted, the schemes of both men failed. Antiochus, thinking himself a master of strategy, put trust in the lying promises of his nephew and withdrew his forces from Egypt. As soon as he had done so, the nephew made peace with his brother (Ptolemy VII), leaving Antiochus without any power in Egypt. . . . Yet the plans of Ptolemy VI also failed, for the supporters of Ptolemy VII did not give their full support to Ptolemy VI but insisted that the two brothers reign as joint kings, thus leaving Egypt in a state of weakness.[2]

The kings and leaders of this world will connive and twist, deceive and lie in order to try to get their own way. But God sits in heaven, laughing: "You are not going to accomplish your purposes; my plan will be fulfilled."

Now Daniel 11:28 says, "The king of the North [that is, Antiochus] will return to his own country with great wealth, but his heart will be set against the holy covenant. He will take action against it and then return to his own country." On his way back to Syria, Antiochus stopped in Jerusalem. With "his heart . . . set against the holy covenant" of God's people, he declared certain laws changed and then left. He was attempting to bring the Jewish people in line with Hellenistic patterns.

When he returned home, he realized that his nephew had deceived him. Daniel 11:29 says, "At the appointed time he will invade the South again." The appointed time was God's appointed time for Antiochus to act. Angry at being deceived by his nephew, he went to Egypt to invade it again. This time the outcome would be different from what it was before. Daniel 11:30 says, "Ships of the western coastlands will oppose him, and he will lose heart."

Antiochus assembled his navy and sailed the Mediterranean Sea along the coast of Israel until he came to Egypt. When he docked his ships in the harbor of Pelusium, near Alexandria where his nephews were, he was met by another navy. He looked on the ship and saw a familiar flag. These were his friends from Rome. The man from Rome who approached his camp was Gaius Linus, his dear friend. They had spent years together in Rome while Antiochus was in exile. Antiochus was glad to see him, hoping to enlist his help against the Egyptians; but Gaius was not smiling. He took out a piece of paper, and on it was written a decree coming from the Senate of Rome. The Senators told Antiochus Epiphanes to leave his hands off Egypt, destroy his navy, and go home.

Antiochus told Gaius he wanted some time to think about the proposal. Gaius promptly took a stick and drew a circle around Antiochus. Gaius said, "You may take all the time you want to think about it, but you are not leaving this circle until you give me an answer, and there is only one answer that is acceptable."[3] Seeing the determination of the Roman envoy, Antiochus decided to do what the Roman Senate had asked. He got back on his ship, disassembled his navy, and ordered his troops to leave Egypt at once.

The Crisis (11:30-35)

Antiochus tried to conceal his anger. Can you imagine this proud man, who thinks he is a god, being humiliated in front of all of his soldiers? He was furious, and he was looking for a place to vent his anger. He then remembered his stop in Jerusalem and what he considered to be the arrogant confidence of the Jewish people. He went back to Jerusalem. Verse 30 tells us, "Then he will turn back and vent his fury against the holy covenant. He will return and show favor to those who forsake the holy covenant."

The soldiers of Antiochus drew their swords and promised favors of gold and silver to all who would forsake the covenant. But to those who would not forsake it, they gave immediate beatings, imprisonment, or death. Soldiers were sent out with orders to kill women who had their boys circumcised and to compel every Jew to sacrifice to Zeus. The regular ceremonies and sacrifices of the temple were stopped, and an altar of Zeus was placed above the altar of the Lord, so polluting the sanctuary that no pious Jew would worship there. But many Jewish people gave in to the pressure instead of facing persecution, because Antiochus showed favor to those who forsook the holy covenant.

As Daniel had prophesied about Antiochus, "His armed forces will rise up to desecrate the temple fortress and will abolish the daily sacrifice. Then they will set up the abomination that causes desolation. With flattery he will corrupt those who have violated the covenant, but the people who know their God will firmly resist him" (11:31, 32).

Antiochus could be a winsome, charismatic man. He flattered people to win their favor. He gave silver and gold to those who denied their belief in the God of Abraham, and thousands of Jews did so, bowing their knee to Antiochus and Zeus. But thousands defied him and were killed by the sword, and others, as prophesied, resisted by force.

One of those who resisted was an old priest named Mattathias. When the king's soldiers tried to force everyone in his home town of Modin to sacrifice to Zeus, Mattathias forcibly resisted them and pulled down the pagan altar. He and his five sons then fled into the desert where other groups were hiding. Not only did the old priest firmly resist the soldiers, but he also instructed others.

Daniel wrote, "Those who are wise will instruct many" (v. 33). Wisdom is associated in the Scriptures with the Word of God. "For the LORD gives wisdom, and from his mouth come knowledge and understanding" (Proverbs 2:6). Surely part of Mattathias' instruction was to show how God had predicted this very oppression of Antiochus IV, so the people would be encouraged, because ultimately they would be victorious over Antiochus.

With these refugees, Mattathias led guerrilla operations against the Syrian armies. When he died, his son, Judas Maccabeus, became the leader of their army of rebels. This young man demonstrated unusual military ability. As prophesied in verses 33, 34, "for a time they will fall by the sword or be burned or captured or plundered. When they fall, they will receive a little help." Even though they received virtually no help from their Jewish brothers who had been deceived, they held out hope for victory because Daniel had promised these losses would be just "for a time."

The last phrase of verse 34 was a warning to the wise: "and many who are not sincere will join them." When the Maccabees began to achieve military victories, some who were "not sincere" joined their cause. Some who joined the cause did not do so for the sake of God and his kingdom. Instead, they joined them for nationalistic or selfish reasons.

The battle against the Syrian forces would be difficult. Antiochus would continue to use flattery, trying to gain support for his cause even from among the faithful. At times it worked. Daniel says in verse 35, "Some of the wise will stumble, so that they may be refined, purified and made spotless until the time of the end, for it will still come at the appointed time." Some of the wise in the resistance stumbled and fell, just as Peter, the disciple, one day would. But like Peter, they would be refined and restored; they would be purified and come out stronger than they were before. In Luke 22:31 Jesus said to Peter, "Simon, Simon, Satan has asked to sift you as wheat. But I have prayed for you, that your faith may not fail. And when you have turned back, strengthen your brothers."

The last phrase of Daniel 11:35 had to be the most encouraging of all, "until the time of the end, for it will come at the appointed time." "The end" in the Scriptures does not always refer to the end of the world. Here is one case where it specifically refers to the end of the reign of Antiochus that would come at "the appointed time." These words were given so that the resistance would not lose heart in the midst of battle and persecution.

The Conclusion for Today

What a nugget of gold is found in the phrase, "but the people who know their God will firmly resist him" (11:32). Antiochus was not the first, nor would he be the last world leader to persecute God's people or to attempt to lead them astray. The ones who will be able to resist this opposition are those who "know their God." There have been times in every age and every country when it was very hard to be a Christian. Only those who know God will "firmly resist."

The apostle Paul said, "I want to know Christ and the power of his resurrection" (Philippians 3:10). Is that your heart's passion? Now is the time to grow in your knowledge of God through reading and studying his Word. Don't wait for the crisis to begin. In 1990 American troops were involved in Operation Desert Storm to liberate Kuwait from Iraqi invaders. For months the soldiers trained in the desert in full gear in anticipation that one day they might be engaged in battle. When the war finally started, they were ready. It would have been too late to start training the day before the battle.

Today is the day to focus your attention on knowing God. Congressman Jim Talent, a member of my congregation, ran for Governor of Missouri but lost in the 2000 elections. He had been ahead in the polls for weeks prior to election day. The whole evening of election day he was ahead in the count. Soon after midnight the tide began to turn. Around 3 in the morning, after he had given his concession speech, he lay in bed talking to the Lord. "Lord, I don't mean to be disrespectful, but I have a question — if I had to lose the election, why did I have to lose this way?"

Two days earlier in our worship service we had read Paul's words in Philippians 3:10 about knowing Christ, and the Lord brought those words to Jim's mind in a unique way. It was as if the Lord said, "Do you want to know me, Jim?" The answer was, "Yes!" "Do you want to know the power of my resurrection?" The answer was, "Yes!" The Lord said, "Then you must share in the fellowship of my sufferings. I lost an 'election' too. The other man's name was Barabbas. The polls looked good on Sunday when everyone was cheering and waving palm branches, but by Friday I could not get one vote. Even my friends abandoned me." Jim concluded that if it took losing the election to help him know the Lord better, the painful, humbling experience was worth it. He considered everything a loss compared to the surpassing greatness of knowing Christ Jesus his Lord (see Philippians 3:8).

Can you say that? Do you want to know Christ? Now is the time to grow in your knowledge of Christ, because only those who know their God will be able to firmly resist the evil. Those who know their God are described as being wise and, according to Daniel 11:33, ought to be involved in teaching and discipling others in knowing him through his Word. The day may come when you will be asked to fall by the sword or to be burned or captured or plundered. When you fall, you may receive little help from other Christians. Will you be ready? I hope so, because some of you reading these words might be alive when the second great crisis comes upon God's people.

THE CRISIS OF ANTICHRIST EPIPHANY (11:36 — 12:4)

We come now to the second great crisis that the people of God will have to face. During the first great crisis, which took place under the rule of Antiochus IV, those who knew their God were able to firmly resist.

> His armed forces will rise up to desecrate the temple fortress and will abolish the daily sacrifice. Then they will set up the abomination that causes desolation. With flattery he will corrupt those who have violated the covenant, but the people who know their God will firmly resist him. (11:31, 32)

During the second great crisis, which the people of God will face under the Antichrist, those who win souls will shine like stars. "Those who are wise will shine like the brightness of the heavens, and those who lead many to righteousness, like the stars for ever and ever" (12:3).

There is a gap of more than two thousand years between verses 35 and 36 of Daniel 11. How dare I speak of such a gap when I reject such a gap in Daniel 9, which so many people believe in? Here is my reasoning: First, Daniel 9 says 490 years have been appointed. There is no exegetical reason to believe in a gap when Daniel says that 490 years have been appointed. Why should he say there are 490 years if, because of the break in the middle, there are 2,490 years appointed? But there is no such timetable for Daniel 11.

Second, when you read Daniel 11:36-45, you will notice that the king of the North and the king of the South are no longer fighting against each other. Instead, they are fighting against someone else. For example, Daniel 11:40, 41 says:

> *At the time of the end the king of the South will engage him in battle, and the king of the North will storm out against him with chariots and cavalry and a great fleet of ships. He will invade many countries and sweep through them like a flood. He will also invade the Beautiful Land. Many countries will fall, but Edom, Moab and the leaders of Ammon will be delivered from his hand.*

There is somebody else on the scene here, and it is not the king of the North or the king of the South.

Third, Daniel makes it very clear that this ruler comes to power at the time of the resurrection, the Second Coming of Jesus Christ.

> *At that time Michael, the great prince who protects your people, will arise. There will be a time of distress such as has not happened from the beginning of nations until then. But at that time your people — everyone whose name is found written in the book — will be delivered. Multitudes who sleep in the dust of the earth will awake: some to everlasting life, others to shame and everlasting contempt. (12:1, 2)*

Michael is called "the archangel" in Jude 9, and 1 Thessalonians 4:16 says, "For the Lord himself will come down from heaven, with a loud command, with the voice of the archangel and with the trumpet call of God, and the dead in Christ will rise first."

Finally, there is an interesting parallel between Antiochus Epiphanes (the "manifest god") and the Antichrist Epiphany, the "appearance" of Satan. The parallel way Daniel presents these two men shows that Antiochus is clearly a foretaste of the Antichrist. Daniel, in the same way he speaks of Antiochus, presents the character, the career, and the crisis of the Antichrist.

His Character (11:36-39)

The character of the Antichrist is similar to the character of Antiochus.

The king will do as he pleases. He will exalt and magnify himself above every god and will say unheard-of things against the God of gods. He will be successful until the time of wrath is completed, for what has been determined must take place. (11:36)

Speaking of the Antichrist, Paul says:

Don't let anyone deceive you in any way, for that day will not come until the rebellion occurs and the man of lawlessness is revealed, the man doomed to destruction. He will oppose and exalt himself over everything that is called God or is worshiped, so that he sets himself up in God's temple, proclaiming himself to be God. (2 Thessalonians 2:3, 4)

Daniel says the Antichrist will be successful in this until the time of his wrath is completed. Paul tells us when that will be. "And then the lawless one will be revealed, whom the Lord Jesus will overthrow with the breath of his mouth and destroy by the splendor of his coming" (2 Thessalonians 2:8).

Some think that these verses are a reiteration of the description of Antiochus. Daniel 11:37 shows this cannot be Antiochus. "He will show no regard for the gods of his fathers or for the one desired by women, nor will he regard any god, but will exalt himself above them all." This cannot be Antiochus because he did regard the gods of his fathers. In fact, he built temples for the gods of his fathers. The Antichrist will show no regard for the gods of his fathers or for the god desired by women. We have no idea right now what that means, but it will be interesting to see when history unfolds this prophecy.

We have no clue as to what verse 38 refers to either when it says, "Instead of them, he will honor a god of fortresses; a god unknown to his fathers he will honor with gold and silver, with precious stones and costly gifts." We must put such prophecies in our mind's file, because when the Antichrist appears, these will be clues we need to confirm that he is here. He will not tell us who he is; in fact, he will try to deceive us, using flattery like Antiochus did with the Jews. Anyone who read Daniel 11:21-35 fifty years before it happened would not have had a clue what Daniel was talking about. But when the prophecies were fulfilled, the wise understood.

Even some of the wise stumbled and fell for a short time (Daniel 11:35) because Antiochus was so deceptive. In the same way, Jesus, speaking of the great tribulation before his return, said, "At that time if anyone says to you, 'Look, here is the Christ!' or, 'There he is!' do not believe it. For false Christs and false prophets will appear and perform great signs and miracles to deceive even the elect — if that were possible. See, I have told you ahead of time" (Matthew 24:23-25). The Antichrist will claim to be Christ, and he will be convincing. Some of the elect who do not know the prophecies well will be deceived for a time, but when they come to their senses, they will be restored like the people in the days of Antiochus (cf. Daniel 11:35). Paul writes:

> The coming of the lawless one will be in accordance with the work of Satan displayed in all kinds of counterfeit miracles, signs and wonders, and in every sort of evil that deceives those who are perishing. They perish because they refused to love the truth and so be saved. For this reason God sends them a powerful delusion so that they will believe the lie and so that all will be condemned who have not believed the truth but have delighted in wickedness. (2 Thessalonians 2:9-12)

His Career (11:40-45)

Now consider the career of the Antichrist, beginning in verse 42:

> He will extend his power over many countries; Egypt will not escape. He will gain control of the treasures of gold and silver and all the riches of Egypt, with the Libyans and Nubians in submission. But reports from the east and the north will alarm him.

Believers will know when reports from the east and the north alarm this man, and they will be able to say, "I told you so!" Reading on, "and he will set out in a great rage to destroy and annihilate many. He will pitch his royal tents between the sea and the beautiful holy mountain" (NIV margin). "The beautiful holy mountain" is Jerusalem, and "the sea" is the Mediterranean Sea. Watch for the day when a man who is a world leader pitches his tent right there in the place that is called the Valley of Megiddo, in Hebrew *harmagido*, Armageddon. When he starts pitching his tent there, you can start looking up. In that day, Daniel 12:3 says, "Those who are wise will shine like the brightness of the heavens, and those who lead many to righteousness, like the stars for ever and ever."

This will be the crisis of the last days. I really believe it could happen in our lifetime. Israel is now back in the Promised Land, the world is basically at peace, there are ecological disasters on the horizon, and all those things were prophesied. The most important thing that God's people can do in the last days is to let their light shine in the darkness. Keep in mind as the world keeps getting darker that the darker the darkness, the brighter is the light. What we will need to do during that time is to proclaim the good news of Jesus Christ because those days will be the best of times and the worst of times. Let me show you why.

In those days many will run to and fro and accumulate knowledge. Daniel 12:4 says, "But you, Daniel, close up and seal the words of the scroll until the time of the end. Many will go here and there to increase knowledge." We are in an information age right now that is unprecedented in the history of the world. We are increasing in knowledge daily. We travel, going to and fro, all over the globe. You know what it is like taking your kids from soccer to basketball to piano lessons; we are running all over the place. When my oldest daughter Katie was just a teenager, she had been overseas in Ireland and England three times! The Lord says about the last days that people will be running here and there, and they will increase in knowledge.

Second, in the last days Michael is going to protect God's people in distress. Daniel 12:1 says, "At that time Michael, the great prince who protects your people, will arise. There will be a time of distress such as has not happened from the beginning of nations until then." This is just like Matthew 24, when Jesus says there is going to be a great distress, a great tribulation, unequaled from the beginning of the world until now and never to be equaled again. These two passages are talking about the same event. Jesus said that if those days are not cut short, no one would survive; but for the sake of the elect, these days will be shortened. If the elect are not on earth, if they are in heaven during the Great Tribulation, why would it have to be shortened for their sake, for our sake? It is because we are going to be here. It is because Jesus says that immediately after the Tribulation the sun will be darkened, and the moon will not give its light, and the stars will fall from the sky, and the sign of the Son of Man will appear in the sky. Notice that it goes on to say, "But at that time your people — everyone whose name is found written in the book — will be delivered" (Daniel 12:1).

In the last days, thirdly, many will be saved. Daniel 12:3 says, "Those who are wise will shine like the brightness of the heavens, and those who lead many to righteousness, like the stars for ever and ever." The days of the Tribulation, the last days of the world, are going to be the best of times for the Church of Jesus Christ because there will be unparalleled growth. I recently heard of a man who once embraced a premillennial view of the Second Coming but has now rejected that view in favor of Postmillennialism. The main reason he gave was that he does not like the idea that the Church will get worse and become apostate. He says that he would like to see the church and the world end more positively.

The truth is that the message of both the Scripture and Premillennialism are very positive about the Church in the end times. The Scriptures teach that the Church will go through the Tribulation, and the Church of Jesus Christ will grow faster than it ever has before. One reason is seen in Romans 11:25, which tells us that Jews will become part of the Church in huge numbers. Paul says, "I do not want you to be ignorant of this mystery, brothers, so that you may not be conceited. Israel has experienced a hardening in part until the full number of the Gentiles has come in." This will be the greatest time in the history of the Church. There will be more people coming to Christ than at any other time in the history of the Church. That is why Daniel 12:3 says, "Those who are wise will shine like the brightness of the heavens, and those who lead many to righteousness, like the stars for ever and ever."

In light of "the wise . . . shin[ing] like the brightness of the heavens," remember that Proverbs 11:30 says, "He who wins souls is wise." Our purpose as we approach the last days ought to be to lead people to a saving knowledge of Jesus Christ. That is exactly what Daniel is telling us. When you get to this point in history, "those who are wise will shine like the brightness of the heavens, and those who lead many to righteousness, like the stars for ever and ever."

At the time of Christ when Israel rejected their Messiah, that meant that the nations of the whole world could now be reconciled to God. The gospel went out to the whole world. Paul says, "If their [Israel's] rejection is the reconciliation of the world, what will their acceptance [when they come to Christ] be but life from the dead?" (Romans 11:15), which is exactly what Daniel says here in verses 1, 2: "But at that time your people — everyone whose name is written in the book — will be delivered. Multitudes who sleep in the dust of the earth will awake: some to everlasting life, others to shame and everlasting contempt."

The Lord has told us much detail in Daniel 11 about the last days. Details about the Second Coming of Christ found in the book of Revelation are written just like Daniel 11. If you don't know how to interpret them, then go back to Daniel 11:2-35 and see how that enigmatic and cryptic description of history was fulfilled in vivid detail. Those to whom the prophecy was future did not know what was being predicted, but anyone who learned the prophecies and were alive when they were fulfilled knew exactly what they were talking about. Later anyone looking back could show verse by verse and phrase by phrase exactly what had happened. The same is true about the Second Coming of Christ. Let me give a parallel example from the book of Revelation.

This calls for a mind with wisdom. The seven heads are seven hills on which the woman sits. They are also seven kings. Five have fallen, one is, the other has not yet come; but when he does come, he must remain for a little while. The beast who once was, and now is not, is an eighth king. He belongs to the seven and is going to his destruction.

The ten horns you saw are ten kings who have not yet received a king-dom, but who for one hour will receive authority as kings along with the beast. They have one purpose and will give their power and authority to the beast. They will make war against the Lamb, but the Lamb will overcome them because he is Lord of lords and King of kings — and with him will be his called, chosen and faithful followers.

Then the angel said to me, "The waters you saw, where the prostitute sits, are peoples, multitudes, nations and languages. The beast and the ten horns you saw will hate the prostitute. They will bring her to ruin and leave her naked; they will eat her flesh and burn her with fire. For God has put it into their hearts to accomplish his purpose by agreeing to give the beast their power to rule, until God's words are fulfilled. The woman you saw is the great city that rules over the kings of the earth. (Revelation 17:9-18)

Some try to look into their crystal ball and guess to whom these seven kings among whom five are fallen refer. But that would be as impossible to guess as a person living in Daniel's day could predict that Daniel 11:21-35 referred to Antiochus Epiphanes. No one could do that. But those who had studied the prophecies and were watching the events of history unfold knew exactly what was happening.

Our approach should be like that of the faithful Jews who knew the specific prophecies by heart and were watching the events of history unfold. They knew when the prophecies were fulfilled, and they were ready. They were ready when the first crisis came, and they were ready when the Messiah came. These were people like Simeon who "was waiting for the consolation of Israel" (Luke 2:25), and Joseph of Arimathea who was "waiting for the kingdom of God" (Mark 15:43). Know the prophecies, read them, and study them, because the events of the last days are about to come to our door.

Why is it so important to know what the Lord says about the details of the Second Coming? First, it is important because "All Scripture is God-breathed and is useful for teaching, rebuking, correcting and training in righteousness, so that the man of God may be thoroughly equipped for every good work" (2 Timothy 3:16, 17). There are no throwaway passages of Scripture. Jesus himself said, "See, I have told you ahead of time" (Matthew 24:25). It must be important since he let us know in advance what is going to take place.

The second reason knowing the details is important is that it keeps us focused on the return of Christ. Far too many people do not even think of his return, much less live in light of it. Those who live in light of his return every day will have a radically different outlook on what is important in life.

Jesus said to them, "I tell you the truth, at the renewal of all things, when
the Son of Man sits on his glorious throne, you who have followed me will
also sit on twelve thrones, judging the twelve tribes of Israel. And every-
one who has left houses or brothers or sisters or father or mother or chil-
dren or fields for my sake will receive a hundred times as much and will
inherit eternal life." (Matthew 19:28, 29)

Let's suppose you were moving to Houston in four years, and you were
told that for every dollar you sent to a certain bank in Houston, the bank
would match it with a hundred dollars. Would you not send most of your
money ahead to Houston? I would send everything I did not need for living! Knowing that would change the way I choose to live my life in St.
Louis while I await my move to Houston. So it is with everyone who longs
for the return of Christ.

16

The End

DANIEL 12:5-13

The last six chapters of the book of Daniel have brought confusion to the minds of God's people and division to the Church of Jesus Christ. I do not think it needs to be that way. God revealed these chapters to prepare and encourage God's people, not to confuse and divide.

By now it should be evident to the reader that the key to understanding these last chapters is to see that the focus is mainly on two great crises that were going to come upon God's people. The first was the crisis brought about by Antiochus around 168 B.C. The second crisis will be the one brought about by the Antichrist sometime in the future. These warnings were written both to prepare God's people for the future and to remind them that he is sovereign. The Lord himself is in control of all these events. He knows all the details of the future, because he planned them. Even in our darkest hour we can trust his plan because he is our Father, and he loves us. As the Apostle Paul wrote, "In all things God works for the good of those who love him" (Romans 8:28). These prophecies reveal to us that God has a planned future for his people; so we can trust him in the difficult crises of life.

Daniel tells his readers about these two crises in three couplets found in four of the last six chapters. Typical of apocalyptic literature, notice how the order is reversed:

Daniel 7:7-27	The kingdom of **Antichrist**
Daniel 8:9-27	The kingdom of **Antiochus**
Daniel 9:24-27	**An interlude of good news:** After the reign of **Antiochus,** the Messiah will come to die and deliver his people from sin.

| Daniel 11:21-35 | The kingdom of **Antiochus** in more detail |
| Daniel 11:36-45 | The kingdom of **Antichrist** in more detail |

| Daniel 12:1-4 | **An interlude of good news:** After the reign of **Antichrist,** the Messiah will come to reign and resurrect his people from death. |

| Daniel 12:7-9 | The kingdom of **Antichrist** |
| Daniel 12:10-12 | The kingdom of **Antiochus** |

The mistake people make most often is to think that Daniel 12 is either speaking only of Antiochus or only of the Antichrist. The conclusion of the book of Daniel, found in Daniel 12:5-13, can best be understood when we realize that these two crises are reviewed one last time in response to two questions.

First the Lord speaks about the kingdom of the Antichrist in verse 7 in answer to Daniel's first question in verse 6. Then the Lord speaks about the kingdom of Antiochus in verses 10-12, in answer to Daniel's second question found in verse 8.

That may sound complicated at first until we realize that Jesus responded in a similar way to his disciples when they asked him two questions about the future of the temple, recorded in Matthew 24.

The first question asked by the disciples was, "When will the temple be destroyed?"

"Do you see all these things?" he asked. "I tell you the truth, not one stone here will be left on another; every one will be thrown down." As Jesus was sitting on the Mount of Olives, the disciples came to him privately. "Tell us," they said, "when will this happen . . . ?" (Matthew 24:2, 3, emphasis added)

The second question was, "What will be the sign of your coming?"

As Jesus was sitting on the Mount of Olives, the disciples came to him privately. "Tell us," they said, ". . . what will be the sign of your coming and of the end of the age?" (Matthew 24:3, emphasis added)

Jesus answers their second question first, in Matthew 24:4-14. Those verses end with these words of Jesus: "And this gospel of the kingdom will be preached in the whole world as a testimony to all nations, and then the end will come." He then answers their first question in Matthew 24:15-20:

So when you see standing in the holy place "the abomination that causes desolation," spoken of through the prophet Daniel — let the reader under-

stand — then let those who are in Judea flee to the mountains. Let no one on the roof of his house go down to take anything out of the house. Let no one in the field go back to get his cloak. How dreadful it will be in those days for pregnant women and nursing mothers! Pray that your flight will not take place in winter or on the Sabbath.

Now how can I say with such certainty that Matthew 24:15-20 speaks of the time of the destruction of Jerusalem and the temple by the Romans, when so many other fine Christians believe this speaks of the Second Coming of Christ? The answer to that is found in the parallel text in Luke 21:20-24. Luke uses the same terminology as Matthew and ends with the description of the fall of Jerusalem.

When you see Jerusalem being surrounded by armies, you will know that its desolation is near. Then let those who are in Judea flee to the mountains, let those in the city get out, and let those in the country not enter the city. For this is the time of punishment in fulfillment of all that has been written. How dreadful it will be in those days for pregnant women and nursing mothers! There will be great distress in the land and wrath against this people. They will fall by the sword and will be taken as prisoners to all the nations. Jerusalem will be trampled on by the Gentiles until the times of the Gentiles are fulfilled. *(Luke 21:20-24, emphasis added)*

Jesus then returns to question 2 in the very next verse in Matthew 24. Verses 21-31 say:

For then there will be great distress, unequaled from the beginning of the world until now — and never to be equaled again. If those days had not been cut short, no one would survive, but for the sake of the elect those days will be shortened. At that time if anyone says to you, "Look, here is the Christ!" or, "There he is!" do not believe it. For false Christs and false prophets will appear and perform great signs and miracles to deceive even the elect — if that were possible. See, I have told you ahead of time.

So if anyone tells you, "There he is, out in the desert," do not go out; or, "Here he is, in the inner rooms," do not believe it. For as lightning that comes from the east is visible even in the west, so will be the coming of the Son of Man. Wherever there is a carcass, there the vultures will gather. Immediately after the distress of those days "the sun will be darkened, and the moon will not give its light; the stars will fall from the sky, and the heavenly bodies will be shaken." At that time the sign of the Son of Man will appear in the sky, and all the nations of the earth will mourn. They will see the Son of Man coming on the clouds of the sky, with power and great glory. And he will send his angels with a loud trumpet call, and they will gather his elect from the four winds, from one end of the heavens to the other.

Then Jesus returns to the disciples' first question in Matthew 24:32-35. In Matthew 24:34 he says, "I tell you the truth, this generation will certainly not pass away until *all these things* [see v. 2] have happened." The first question the disciples asked was, "When will the temple be destroyed?" Jesus said that the temple would be destroyed within forty years, one generation. Jesus made that prediction around A.D. 30, and the temple was destroyed in A.D. 70. His prophecy was accurate. Though he was specific about when the first event would occur, he was not so specific about the second question regarding his coming again.

In answer to question 2, Jesus said in Matthew 24:36, "No one knows about *that day or hour*, not even the angels in heaven, nor the Son, but only the Father" (emphasis added).

In a similar way in Daniel 12:5-13, the one who is speaking, the one who is answering the two questions, is none other than the pre-incarnate Second Person of the Trinity. He is the man clothed in white linen who is standing above the waters of the river talking with the two angels. Jesus answers the two questions in a way similar to the way he answered the disciples' two questions in Matthew 24. One of the questions had to do with something that was not too far in the future, and the other was very far in the future when Jesus Christ would come back again.

THE BEGINNING OF THE END

Now as we study these nine verses of Daniel 12, there is one important theme to keep in mind: the end. In these nine verses, the word "end" is found six times in the Hebrew, though it occurs only four times when it is translated into English (in the NIV and other translations). There is no question that Daniel is focusing on the concept of "the end" as he comes to the end of his book. Let's study the significance of why the Lord speaks so much about the end in this final chapter. The Lord speaks of the end of the rule of the Antichrist, he speaks about the end of the rule of Antiochus, and he speaks about the end of the life of Daniel.

HOW LONG UNTIL THE END OF THE RULE OF THE ANTICHRIST? (12:5, 6)

The first question is found in verses 5, 6.

Then, I Daniel, looked, and there before me stood two others, one on this bank of the river and one on the opposite bank. One of them said to the man clothed in linen [that is Jesus, as we saw in Daniel 10], who was above the waters of the river, "How long will it be before these aston-ishing things are fulfilled [the Hebrew word translated "fulfilled" is the word "end"]?"

Now this question is not easy to translate (interpret) from the Hebrew, and it is not any easier to understand. The question seems purposefully vague. Dr. V. Phillips Long, Professor of Old Testament and Hebrew at Regent College, confirms that since the meaning of the first question is vague, it is best understood by the way the question is answered. We may not understand the question, but one thing is for sure — Jesus did. The answer to this question, which is found in verse 7, indicates that the man was asking, "How long after these astonishing things start will these aston-ishing things end?"

Now the astonishing things referred to here in verse 6 are those found at the end of Daniel 11 and the beginning of chapter 12. Let me remind you of what these astonishing things are.

The astonishing things starting in verse 36 of Daniel 11 describe the coming of a very mean and obtrusive king whom we call the Antichrist. He will say unheard of things against the God of gods. He will exalt himself above all gods. He will invade countries and sweep through them like a flood. He will invade the Holy Land. He is going to do some astonishing things. The astonishing things get even more astonishing in 12:1.

At that time Michael, the great prince who protects your people, will arise. There will be a time of distress such as has not happened from the begin-ning of nations until then. But at that time your people — everyone whose name is found written in the book — will be delivered. Multitudes who sleep in the dust of the earth will awake: some to everlasting life, others to shame and everlasting contempt.

These things are astonishing! A future king will magnify himself above all gods, and a future day will see the dead raised to life! Here an angel says, "Tell me, please, how long will it be from the start of these things to the end of these things?" We know that he is not asking the question, "How long will it be from the days of Daniel until these astonishing things hap-pen?" That has been at least 2,500 years, and Jesus does not say anything like that in his answer. Here is how Jesus answers the question, how long? The rule of the Antichrist will end after three and one half years.

The man clothed in linen [who is Jesus], who was above the waters of the river, lifted his right hand and his left hand toward heaven, and I heard him swear by him who lives forever, saying, "It will be for a time, times

*and half a time. When the power of the holy people has finally been bro-
ken, all these things will be completed." (12:7a)*

I can see Daniel with a confused look in his eye saying, "Oh no, not
that again! What in the world is 'a time, times and a half a time'?" We saw
that exact phrase before, in 7:25. Remember that Daniel 7 speaks of the kingdom of the Antichrist. There are very clear parallels between 7:21-27 and
11:36-45. What is more, those two passages parallel Revelation 13. There are
incredible parallels using in many cases the exact same terminology.

For example, Daniel 7:21 says, "As I watched, this horn [that is, the
Antichrist] was waging war against the saints and defeating them."
Remember, Jesus said in Daniel 12 that "when the power of the holy people
has been finally broken, all these things will be completed." The power of the
people of God would be put to the test because the Antichrist will be making war against the saints — Jewish and Gentile Christians who make up
the church. They will be beaten down; they will die.

Daniel 7:24 says, "The ten horns are ten kings who will come from this
kingdom. After them another king will arise, different from the earlier ones;
he will subdue three kings." In other words, there are going to be ten kings
ruling when the Antichrist will come. He will kill three of the kings, and
then he will rule. Verse 25 says: "He will speak against the Most High and
oppress his saints and try to change the set times and the laws. The saints will
be handed over to him for a time, times and half a time."

Irenaeus lived in the second century. He was discipled by a man whose
name was Polycarp, and Polycarp was discipled by John, who wrote the book
of Revelation. I find it interesting to read what Irenaeus has to say about the
Antichrist since he was so close to John. He wrote:

John affirmed the teaching of Daniel in his apocalypse, concerning the ten
kings who shall arise. In Revelation 17:12, he teaches us what the ten horns
shall be, which were also seen by Daniel. It is manifest, therefore, that of
these potentates, of these kings, the Antichrist shall slay three, and shall subject the rest to his power, and he himself shall be the eighth among them.

Even Irenaeus, discipled by Polycarp, who was discipled by John, said
an Antichrist is coming. He said you will know when he is here because ten
kings will be ruling, and he will slay three of them and then take over all of
them.

Let me explain why I think "a time, times and half a time" means three
and a half years. In Revelation 12:6 John says, "The woman fled into the
desert to a place prepared for her by God, where she might be taken care of
for 1,260 days." Now Revelation 12 says that the dragon, who is Satan,
wanted to kill the Christ-child, but he failed. Christ was snatched up into

heaven, and after he was snatched up into heaven, God took care of his church for three and a half years. We know this from our study of the book of Acts. From the time of the ascension of Jesus Christ until God dispersed the church in the persecution of Acts 8 was three and a half years. Three and a half years are 1,260 days. During that time the church remained safe in Jerusalem. God protected and nurtured the church in those early years as it grew, preparing the church for persecution.

Now there is a parallel to verse 6, a repetition of the same incident, in Revelation 12:14. John describes the same situation but uses different words. "The woman was given the two wings of a great eagle, so that she might fly to the place prepared for her in the desert [the same thing John says in verse 6], where she would be taken care of for a time, times and half a time, out of the serpent's reach." "A time, times and a half a time" is the same thing as 1,260 days or three and a half years. That three and a half years in Revelation 12 is talking about the three and a half years from the ascension of Christ until the church was scattered in persecution. Daniel, on the other hand, is talking about the three and a half years the Antichrist will perse- cute the church during the Tribulation.

Let me show you how specific Bible prophecy is. Revelation 13:1, 2 says:

> And the dragon stood on the shore of the sea. And I saw a beast coming out of the sea. He had ten horns and seven heads, with ten crowns on his horns, and on each head a blasphemous name. [The ten horns are the same thing Daniel talked about.] The beast I saw resembled a leopard, but had feet like those of a bear and a mouth like that of a lion. The dragon gave the beast his power and throne and great authority.

Who else in the history of the world gave his power and his authority and his throne to someone else? God the Father gave his Son his power, his authority, and his throne. The Antichrist is not the opposite of Christ — he is the counterfeit of Christ. He will try to do everything that Jesus did. The dragon — Satan — will give to his son, Satan incarnate, his power, his authority, and his throne.

Then, according to verse 3, this counterfeit "seemed to have had a fatal wound, but the fatal wound had been healed. The whole world was aston- ished and followed the beast." You will know when the Antichrist begins his reign, because it will appear that a world leader has died and come back from the dead, just like Christ died and rose again on the third day. But the Antichrist is a counterfeit. Only those who know the Scriptures will know he is not the Lord.

Verses 4, 5 say, "men worshipped the dragon because he had given authority to the beast, and they also worshipped the beast and asked, 'Who is like the beast? Who can make war against him?' The beast was given a mouth to utter proud words and blasphemies and to exercise his authority for forty-two months."

Forty-two months is three and a half years. An angel asked the question, "How long are these astonishing things going to take place?" These astonishing things are the events we read about in Daniel 11 and in Revelation 13. They will last three and a half years.

John writes in Revelation 13:7, "He was given power to make war against the saints and to conquer them." Remember, Daniel 12:7 says that this tribulation is going to continue until "the power of the holy people has been finally broken." He will make war against the saints and conquer them. He will be given authority over every tribe and people and language and nation. The Antichrist will be a leader over the whole world, something we have never, ever had before. But we have seen the world "shrink" so much in our day that for the first time in history we can see how this could possibly happen. Centuries ago people would have considered such an idea laughable. John continues:

> All inhabitants of the earth will worship the beast — all whose names have not been written in the book of life belonging to the Lamb that was slain from the creation of the world. He who has an ear, let him hear. If anyone is to go into captivity, into captivity he will go. If anyone is to be killed with the sword, with the sword he will be killed. This calls for patient endurance and faithfulness on the part of the saints. (Revelation 13:8-10)

This intense persecution will last three and a half years. It will be the best of times; it will be the worst of times. It will be the best of times because the gospel of the kingdom will expand faster than it ever has before. Matthew 24:14 says, "This gospel of the kingdom will be preached in the whole world as a testimony to *all* nations, and then the end will come" (emphasis added). It will be the best of times because the Jews will come into the Church in mass conversions — not by the hundreds, not by the thousands, but by the tens and hundreds of thousands. It will be the best of times.

But it will be the worst of times because Christians will be led into captivity and killed with the sword. This rule of the Antichrist will last three and a half years.

The Rule of the Antichrist Will End with the Resurrection of Believers (12:1)

After speaking of the rule of the Antichrist in chapter 11, Daniel 12:1 says:

> At that time Michael, the great prince who protects your people, will arise. There will be a time of distress such has not happened from the beginning

of nations until then. But at that time, your people — every one whose name is found written in the book — will be delivered.

The phrase "at that time" is used twice. The first time it indicates that the rule of the Antichrist will be the Great Tribulation — a time of distress such as has not happened from the beginning of the nations until now. The second time the phrase is used is a little more vague. Will the believers be delivered before this three-and-a-half-year tribulation begins or after it is over? Daniel 12:1 alone cannot answer that question clearly. We need to use the principle of comparing Scripture with Scripture.

Other Scriptures make the order clear. For example, Daniel 7:21, 22 shows that the rule of the Antichrist will end with the return of Christ.

As I watched, this horn [the Antichrist] was waging war against the saints and defeating them, until the Ancient of Days came and pronounced judgment in favor of the saints of the Most High, and the time came when they possessed the kingdom.

He is waging war against the saints, Jewish and Gentile Christians; then Jesus returns. Matthew 24:29, 30 also makes this clear.

Immediately after the distress of those days, "the sun will be darkened, and the moon will not give its light; stars will fall from the sky, and the heavenly bodies will be shaken." At that time the sign of the Son of Man will appear in the sky, and all the nations of the earth will mourn. They will see the Son of Man coming on the clouds of the sky, with power and great glory. (emphasis added)

When Jesus was caught up in the clouds at the Ascension, the angels said he was going to come back in the same way. That is what Jesus says in verse 31: "He will send his angels with a loud trumpet call, and they will gather his elect from the four winds, from one end of the heavens to the other." This gathering together is the Rapture, the saints being caught up to meet the Lord in the air, and it will happen, verse 29, "immediately after the distress of those days."

The letters of Paul confirm the same order — for example, in 2 Thessalonians 2:1, "Concerning the coming of our Lord Jesus Christ and our being gathered to him." Here again is the same Greek word *episunago*, which describes the Rapture. This means that Paul is introducing a lesson on the Rapture. He continues:

We ask you, brothers, not to become easily unsettled or alarmed by some prophecy, report or letter supposed to have come from us, saying that the

day of the Lord has already come. Don't let anyone deceive you in any
way, for that day will not come until the rebellion occurs and the man
of lawlessness is revealed, the man doomed to destruction. (vv. 2, 3,
emphasis added)

That is the Antichrist. Paul says, "Don't let anyone deceive you . . . for
that day will not come until . . . the man of lawlessness is revealed [the
Antichrist]." Sadly, many in the evangelical church have been deceived. They
have bought into the mistaken view that Christ is coming back before the
Antichrist is revealed and the Tribulation starts. Paul responds with a
resounding, "No!" He continues in verses 4, 5:

He will oppose and exalt himself above everything that is called God or is
worshiped, so that he sets himself up in God's temple, proclaiming him-
self to be God. Don't you remember that when I was with you I used to
tell you these things?

The whole concept of opposing God is also seen in Daniel 7 and 11, as
well as in Revelation 13. The early church fathers believed and taught the
same thing. Irenaeus wrote, "These kings shall give their kingdom to the
beast and *will put the church to flight*, and after that the Antichrist will be
destroyed by the coming of the Lord." It is interesting that in the second
century Irenaeus taught that the Church will be on earth during the time of
the Antichrist and that he will make the church flee.

Read the words of another church father, written in A.D. 120, only twenty
years after the Apostle John left this earth.

There shall appear a deceiver of the world who will look like the Son of
God and shall do signs and wonders and the earth shall be given over into
his hands, and he will commit iniquities which have never been seen since
the world began. Then shall the creation of mankind come to the fiery
trial and many shall be offended and lost, but those who endure in their faith
will be saved by this curse itself. And then there shall appear these signs.
First the sign of the Son of Man in heaven, then the sign of the trumpet,
and thirdly, the resurrection of the dead.

As Paul writes in 2 Thessalonians 2:8-10:

The lawless one will be revealed, whom the Lord Jesus will overthrow
with the breath of his mouth and destroy by the splendor of his coming.
The coming of the lawless one will be in accordance with the work of
Satan displayed in all kinds of counterfeit miracles, signs and wonders, and

in every sort of evil that deceives those who are perishing. They perish
because they refused to love the truth and so be saved.

Now is the time to prepare to take a bold stand, as Daniel did in
Babylon. Those reading this book may be alive in the days of the Antichrist,
whose kingdom is figuratively called "Babylon" in the book of Revelation
(17 — 18). The stand that Daniel took for righteousness and the stand that
Daniel's three friends took in the face of the fiery furnace is one that you
may one day have to take. For in the day that the Antichrist rules the whole
world, he will

> *force everyone, small and great, rich and poor, free and slave, to receive a*
> *mark on his right hand or on his forehead, so that no one could buy or*
> *sell unless he had the mark, which is the name of the beast or the number*
> *of his name. (Revelation 13:16, 17)*

Are you prepared to be a Daniel? Will you be like Shadrach, Meshach,
and Abednego, refusing to bow to the image of the Beast, refusing to receive
his mark? Now is the time to put on the full armor of God and walk in the
power of God's Spirit through meditating on his Word. The Lord's words to
Joshua are appropriate for spiritual warfare.

> *Do not let this Book of the Law depart from your mouth; meditate on it*
> *day and night, so that you may be careful to do everything written in it.*
> *Then you will be prosperous and successful. Have I not commanded you?*
> *Be strong and courageous. Do not be terrified; do not be discouraged, for*
> *the LORD your God will be with you wherever you go. (Joshua 1:8, 9)*

Remember that the Lord is with you, and he will give you the grace
you need at the moment you need it. Many Christians are afraid of failing
under the intense pressure of persecution. At the risk of underestimating the
importance of preparing ourselves, we must not forget the grace of God
who will sustain his people.

Corrie ten Boom tells the story of talking with her father about her fear-
ing his death. She could not imagine being able to cope with her father dying.
He said to five-year-old Corrie, "When we take a ride on the train, when do
I give you your ticket?"

She answered, "You give me the ticket just as we are getting on the train."

"That's right, Corrie. And your heavenly Father will give you the
strength and grace you need just at the moment you need it and not a minute
sooner." God will sustain his people in the face of persecution and death.
"And when the power of the holy people has been finally broken, all these
things will be completed" (Daniel 12:7).

Daniel was confused by what he heard, so he wrote, "I heard, but I did not understand" (12:8). I hope and pray that is not how you are feeling right now. I hope I have added light from the New Testament. Daniel did not have that light, so he was still confused, and that prompted him to ask a second question.

WHAT ABOUT THE END OF THE RULE OF ANTIOCHUS?

The second question of Daniel 12 has to do with Antiochus. Here is where I deviate from many other commentators. Most writers conclude that Daniel 12 is either speaking only about the Antichrist or only about Antiochus. The key to understanding the meaning of the numbers at the end of the chapter is to realize that Daniel 12 speaks about both.

The reason we know this to be true is based on the answer to the second question, not because of the wording of the second question, which again is vague. The translation of the second question in the NIV is, "My lord, what will be the outcome of all this be?" (v. 8).

As with the first question, the translation of this question is difficult. There are only four Hebrew words: "Lord, what end things." It is as if Daniel was so confused about the outcome of the crisis of the Antichrist that he decided to ask a question about the other crisis, the one that was covered before. Basically he is saying, "My Lord, what will be the end of *the other things?*" The word translated "outcome" in the NIV is not the best translation. Here we again have the Hebrew word "end." The angel had asked about the end of the crisis of the Antichrist; now Daniel asks about the end of the crisis of Antiochus.

The Wicked Will Continue to Be Wicked

The answer to Daniel's question has two parts. After essentially telling Daniel in verse 9, "Go away and don't worry about it," he gives the first part of his answer in verse 10: "Many will be purified, made spotless and refined, but the wicked will continue to be wicked." Now that may not seem to be much of an answer to the question, "What will the end of these things be?" But as with the first question, asked by the angel, the clear answer can help us better understand the intent of the vague question. This answer is clear, first, because it is easily translated from the Hebrew.

The other reason the answer is clear is because we have heard these exact words before. They can be found in the passage that spoke of the crisis of Antiochus in 11:21-35. That passage ends with these words, "Some of the wise will stumble, so that they may be *refined, purified and made spotless* until the time of the end [of the crisis of Antiochus], for it will still come at the appointed time." It is for this reason that I think the Lord is talking about the end of the crisis with Antiochus.

In addition, Daniel 12:10 says, "But the wicked will continue to be wicked." That will be true at the end of the crisis of Antiochus, but not at the end of the crisis of the Antichrist. When that period of time is over, the wicked will be destroyed at the return of Christ and eventually cast into Hell for eternity.

Those Who Are Wise Will Understand

The second part of the answer to his question is found in the last half of verse 10: "None of the wicked will understand, but those who are wise will understand." In answer to the question, "What is going to be the end of these things?" the Lord says, "The wise will understand," because it is already recorded in the Scriptures. Be wise and search the Scriptures, for then you will know. Here is the detail the Lord gives in verses 11, 12:

From the time that the daily sacrifice is abolished and the abomination that causes desolation is set up, there will be 1,290 days. Blessed is the one who waits for it and reaches the end of the 1,335 days.

Daniel 9 records for us the time that the daily sacrifice was abolished and the abomination that causes desolation was set up. That took place during the days of Antiochus Epiphanes. This is history to us. The Lord says, "Those who are wise, those who have read the Scriptures, those who know the prophecies will understand when it happens. But you don't need to understand it now, Daniel. Just go your way. Those who live through the days of Antiochus and are wise will understand."

The New Testament says the same will be true about the return of Christ and the coming of the Antichrist. The wise will know when it will happen, because they have the Word of God. First Thessalonians 5:1 says, "Now, brothers, about times and dates we do not need to write to you, for you know very well that the day of the Lord will come like a thief in the night." Some teachers say this means that Jesus could come back tonight. They say, "You don't know when Jesus is coming back. He will come like a thief and surprise all of us." From what I have shown you from Scripture, you understand that Jesus could not come back tonight. He will not come back until three and a half years after the Antichrist is revealed by appearing to die and to come back to life. Jesus cannot come back tonight.

Paul continues in verse 3, "While people are saying 'peace and safety,' destruction will come on them suddenly, as labor pains on a pregnant woman, and they will not escape." There will be people in the world who will be surprised at his coming even after the three and a half years. They will be saying, "peace and safety," thinking all is well. This will be the best of times and the worst of times. It will be the best of times for the world because the whole world will be at peace. There will be one ruler, and everybody will honor him. But it will be the worst of times for Christians because Christians all over the world will be persecuted.

But not everyone will be surprised. Notice the very next phrase: "But you, brothers, are not in darkness so that this day should surprise you like a thief." The return of Christ need not surprise you like a thief, because the Lord has told you exactly what will happen. He told you what to look for. He told you how to recognize the Antichrist, and he told you that three and a half years after that, Jesus will come for his people at the Rapture.

Now some of you may question this, because Jesus said, "No one knows the day or the hour of his coming" (Matthew 24:36). How can we know when it is three and a half years away? Three and a half years is a round number; it may not be exactly three and a half years. We do not know the exact day or the exact hour. A woman does not know the day or the hour of the birth of her baby, but she knows when she is in the ninth month. She knows when the time is close. And those who are wise will understand and know when the time is close because they have the Scriptures. We are not in darkness. So study the prophecies! God took the time to write them down for us to know, so that we will not be surprised like a thief.

GO YOUR WAY, DANIEL

We have studied two questions about "the end." One had to do with the end of the crisis of the Antichrist, and the other with the end of the crisis of Antiochus. The third question is not asked, but it is implied. My paraphrase of that question is this: "What will be the end of the life of Daniel?"

Daniel 12:13 says, "As for you, go your way till the end." The Lord is not talking about the end of the reign of the Antichrist or the end of the world, because Daniel would not live to see that day. When the Lord Jesus uses the word "end" here for the fifth time, He is speaking of the end of Daniel's life. He tells Daniel two things in the face of the reality of his own death.

You Must Live

The first message is this: "Until your death, Daniel, you must live." The Lord says in verse 13a, "As for you, go your way till the end." And in verse 9 he says, "Go your way, Daniel, because the words are closed up and sealed until the time of the end."

In the first phrase the Lord says, "Daniel, I have given you prophecies that are beyond your comprehension. I want you to take that prophecy, realizing that you will not understand it, and seal it (with seven seals) until the time of the end." What is absolutely magnificent is that when we read the book of Revelation and come to chapter 5, we see John, the writer of Revelation, weeping because he is standing before a book that is sealed. It has been sealed for centuries, and he wants to know what is in the book. He is weeping because he thinks no one has the power or the authority to open the seals. An angel walks over to John and says in essence, "Do not weep! See, the Lamb who is seated on the throne has the power and the authority to break the seals" (vv. 5-7). He breaks the seals that have sealed up the prophecies that were first revealed in the book of Daniel. The book of Revelation repeats a lot of what is recorded in Daniel, but it tells us much more about the coming of the Lord.

So in essence the Lord told the prophet, "Daniel, I don't want you to worry about the future right now. I want you to 'go your way.'" The phrase "Go your way" (Daniel 12:13) means to live your life. Keep on doing what you are doing. Don't quit your job, and don't sell your possessions. Live your life to the full. This was true for Daniel, and it is true for you.

Martin Luther was once asked what he would do if he knew Jesus Christ was going to return the next day. His answer was, "I would plant a tree." A tree takes decades to grow. Martin Luther was saying it does not matter if Jesus is coming back tomorrow, a hundred years from now, or a thousand years from now. We must go our way and live our life. That is what God is calling us to do. We must keep busy in the kingdom. Jesus said in Matthew 24, after he taught his disciples about his return,

> You also must be ready. . . . Who then is the faithful and wise servant, whom the master has put in charge of the servants in his household . . . ? It would be good for that servant whose master finds him doing so when he returns. I tell you the truth, he will put him in charge of all of his possessions. But suppose that servant is wicked and says to himself, "My master is staying away a long time," and he then he begins to beat his fellow servants and to eat and drink with the drunkards. The master of that servant will come on a day when he does not expect him and at an hour he is not aware of. He will cut him to pieces and assign him a place with the hypocrites. (vv. 44-51)

Go your way, live your life, and keep serving Christ. When Jesus comes back, will he find you busy in the kingdom? Or will you be one who is beating his fellow servants, eating and drinking with the drunkards, carousing around, thinking, *He is not coming back*? Don't be foolish, but be wise and live your life for the Lord and his kingdom.

Die Your Death

The Lord said to Daniel in essence, "Until your death you must live, but after your death you will rest." Daniel 12:13 ends by saying, "You will rest, and then at the end of the days you will rise to receive your allotted inheritance." You will rest, you will rise, and then you'll receive.

Rest from All Your Labors

Revelation 14:13 says, "Then I heard a voice from heaven say: 'Write: Blessed are the dead who die in the Lord from now on.' 'Yes,' says the Spirit, 'they will rest from their labor, for their deeds will follow them.'" Today is not the time of rest. We must not seek to live at ease in this world. That time is coming after we die. It is not now. We need to be like Caleb, who at age eighty-five said, "Give me the hill country!"

Some people in my church, after retiring from their secular career, went into full-time Christian work. They either devoted themselves to the work of the local church or went out as missionaries into a foreign field. They are exciting examples of those who are committed to the Lord. Far too many Christians retire from everything when they get older. They even retire from the work of the kingdom and spend most of their time traveling or taking a break from church. Our rest from all our labors comes *after* we die.

Rest and Then You Will Rise

> *Brothers, we do not want you to be ignorant about those who fall asleep, or to grieve like the rest of men, who have no hope. We believe that Jesus died and rose again and so we believe that God will bring with Jesus those who have fallen asleep in him. According to the Lord's own word, we tell you that we who are still alive, who are left till the coming of the Lord, will certainly not precede those who have fallen asleep. For the Lord himself will come down from heaven, with a loud command, with the voice of the archangel and with the trumpet call of God, and the dead in Christ will rise first. After that, we who are still alive and are left will be caught up together with them in the clouds to meet the Lord in the air. And so we will be with the Lord forever. (1 Thessalonians 4:13-17)*

One of the members of my congregation, Justine Siefert, is dying of cancer as I write this chapter. She probably has only four to six weeks to live. Whenever I visit with her, she is filled with questions about what to expect when she dies. I read her Revelation 7:9-17, which gives us the clearest picture of what we will see first upon reaching heaven. One of her concerns is that she will be alone when she gets there, because no one really close to her has gone to heaven yet. I reminded her of two women in our congregation who had died in the previous year and will be waiting to greet her.

But she is genuinely concerned about missing her family. I told her that time will go so fast in heaven as we gaze upon the magnificent beauty of the Lord that it will seem like just a moment from the time we first enter Heaven until our souls return with Jesus to meet our renewed bodies in the air. Then we will be with the Lord and with our saved loved ones for all eternity on a renewed earth with no more suffering, no more sorrow, and no more sin. That always brings a smile to her face. We will rest; then we will rise.

Rise and You Will Receive

The message to Daniel is a message to us. Go your way. When you die you will rest from your labors. But one day after you have rested, you will rise again. And when you rise again, Daniel will be there, and you'll receive your allotted inheritance with him.

> *Praise be to the God and Father of our Lord Jesus Christ! In his great mercy he has given us new birth into a living hope through the resurrection of Jesus Christ from the dead, and into an inheritance that can never perish, spoil or fade — kept in heaven for you. (1 Peter 1:3, 4)*

Some of you have had the experience of receiving an inheritance. When you receive it, you get very excited. But all the inheritances we could ever receive on this earth will perish, spoil, fade, or get spent. The inheritance that Jesus gives us will not. If you are a believer in Jesus Christ, you have an inheritance in Heaven waiting for you.

If you have ever given an inheritance or a gift to someone, you know the excitement you feel when you have found the perfect gift for someone. You cannot wait to give it to that person. Jesus Christ has found the perfect gift for you, an incredible inheritance beyond your comprehension, and he can't wait to give it to you. He said to his Father while praying in the Garden of Gethsemane, "Father, I want those you have given me to be with me where I am, and to see my glory" (John 17:24). Jesus cannot wait to show you his glory, your inheritance, your mansion. After you die, you will rest; then you will rise; and then you'll receive an inheritance.

At many of the Christian funerals I perform, I love to end with the words of Joni Eareckson Tada from her book, *Heaven, Your Real Home.*

> In C. S. Lewis's *Last Battle*, the concluding book in the *Chronicles of Narnia*, there was not the usual "and they lived happily ever after." Instead, on the last page of this book, after scores of exhilarating adventures and journeys in all the previous books, C. S. Lewis wrote that now he had come to the beginning of the real story. All the previous chapters of adventures in Narnia had only been the cover and the title page. The real Chapter One was about to begin, a story no one on earth had ever read, which would go on forever and ever with each chapter better than the last.[1]

Notes

CHAPTER ONE: NO COMPROMISE

1. Bryan Chapell, *Standing Your Ground* (Grand Rapids, MI: Baker Book House, 1989), pp. 19, 20.
2. Jay Braverman, *Jerome's Commentary on Daniel: A Study of Comparative Jewish and Christian Interpretations of the Hebrew Bible* (Washington. D.C.: Catholic Biblical Association of America, 1978), pp. 67, 68.
3. Tremper Longman III, *Daniel*, NIV Application Commentary (Grand Rapids, MI: Zondervan, 1999), p. 50.
4. R. Kent Hughes, *Romans*, Preaching the Word (Wheaton, IL: Crossway Books, 1991), p. 45.
5. Quoted in Donald K. Campbell, *Daniel: Decoder of Dreams* (Wheaton, IL: Victor Books, 1977), p. 10.
6. A. Leo Oppenheim, *Ancient Mesopotamia: Portrait of a Dead Civilization* (Chicago: University of Chicago Press, 1964), pp. 183-197.
7. Chapell, *Standing your Ground*, p. 23.
8. Ibid., p. 32.
9. Ibid., pp. 28, 29.

CHAPTER THREE: REVEALER OF MYSTERIES

1. *History of Rome* (New York: Funk and Wagnalls), pp. 382, 383.
2. Ibid., p. 383.
3. Ibid., p. 390
4. Tremper Longman III, *Daniel*, NIV Application Commentary (Grand Rapids, MI: Zondervan, 1999), p. 82.

CHAPTER FOUR: FAITH STANDING BEFORE THE FIRE

1. Philip Yancey, *Where Is God When It Hurts?* (Grand Rapids, MI: Zondervan, 1977), p. 104.
2. Ibid., pp. 109, 110.
3. *Trinity Hymnal* (Atlanta: Great Commission Publications, 1991), p. 108.
4. Ibid.
5. Ibid.
6. Anonymous, *He Maketh No Mistake* (available from various sources; e.g., www.webedelic.com/church/mistaket.htm).
7. Bryan Chapell, *Standing Your Ground* (Grand Rapids, MI: Baker Book House, 1989), pp. 88, 89.
8. *Trinity Hymnal*, p. 108.

CHAPTER FIVE: PRIDE COMES BEFORE THE FALL

1. C. S. Lewis, *Mere Christianity* (New York: Simon and Schuster, 1980), p. 109.
2. *International Standard Bible Encyclopedia* (1949), 4:2127, 2128.
3. Kenneth Barker, ed., *NIV Study Bible* (Grand Rapids, MI: Zondervan, 1985), p. 1307.
4. H. C. Leupold, *Exposition of Daniel* (Columbus, OH: Wartburg Press, 1949), pp. 208-214.
5. Lewis, *Mere Christianity*, pp. 109, 111.
6. Ibid., p. 111.

CHAPTER SIX: THE HANDWRITING ON THE WALL

1. Tremper Longman III, *Daniel*, The NIV Application Commentary (Grand Rapids, MI: Zondervan, 1999), p. 143.
2. Donald K. Campbell, *Daniel: Decoder of Dreams* (Wheaton, IL: Victor Books, 1977), p. 58.
3. Ibid.
4. Longman, *Daniel*, p. 136.
5. Ibid., p. 138.
6. Ibid., p. 154.
7. Ibid., p. 139.
8. Ibid.
9. Ibid., p. 140.
10. A. Wolters, "The Riddle of the Scales in Daniel 5," *Hebrew Union College Annual* 62 (1991):155.
11. Ibid.
12. Longman, *Daniel*, p. 142.

CHAPTER SEVEN: FAMILY SEDANS OF THE FAITH

1. Max Lucado, *God Came Near: Chronicles of the Christ* (Portland: Multnomah Press, 1987), pp. 133, 134.
2. *Expositor's Bible Commentary*, ed. Frank E. Gaebelein, 10 vols. (Grand Rapids, MI: Zondervan, 1976-1992), 7:76.
3. Ibid., pp. 76, 77.
4. Based on original research by the author.
5. Lucado, *God Came Near*, p. 136.

CHAPTER EIGHT: WHAT IS THE MEANING OF ALL THIS?

1. Kathleen Norris, *Amazing Grace: A Vocabulary of Faith* (New York: Riverhead Books, 1998), p. 318.
2. Ibid.
3. Ibid.
4. *The Expositor's Bible Commentary*, ed. Frank E. Gaebelein, 10 vols. (Grand Rapids, MI: Zondervan, 1976-1992), 7:85, 86.
5. Ibid., p. 86.
6. Ibid.

CHAPTER NINE: THY KINGDOM COME

1. Charles H. Spurgeon, *Spurgeon's Sermons on the Second Coming*, ed. David Otis Fuller (Grand Rapids, MI: Zondervan, 1943), Preface.
2. Ibid., p. 6.
3. Ibid.
4. Ibid., p. 7.
5. Ibid., p. 18; also see *Spurgeon at His Best*, ed. Tom Carter (Grand Rapids, MI: Baker Book House, 1988), p. 183.
6. *Spurgeon's Sermons on the Second Coming*, p. 110.

CHAPTER TEN: A STERN-FACED MAN OF INTRIGUE

1. Judith Viorst, *Alexander and the Terrible, Horrible, No Good, Very Bad Day* (New York: Macmillan, 1972), pp. 1, 4, 10, 11, 23, 25.
2. Gerhard Hasel, "The First and Third Years of Belshazzar (Daniel 7:1; 8:1)," *Andrews University Seminary Studies* 15 (1976):153.
3. Tremper Longman III, *Daniel*, The NIV Application Commentary (Grand Rapids, MI: Zondervan, 1999), p. 202.
4. Ibid., pp. 202, 203.
5. C. F. Keil, *Biblical Commentary on the Book of Daniel* (Grand Rapids, MI: Eerdmans, 1949), p. 310.
6. Longman, *Daniel*, p. 206.
7. Allan A. MacRae, *The Prophecies of Daniel* (Singapore: Christian Life Publishing, 1991), p. 144.
8. *The NIV Study Bible*, p. 1312.

CHAPTER ELEVEN: O LORD, LISTEN, FORGIVE, AND ACT

1. Westminster Shorter Catechism (Publishing Committee of the Free Church of Scotland, 1967), p. 309.
2. Peter Marshall and David Manuel, *The Light and The Glory* (Old Tappan, NJ: Fleming H. Revell, 1977), pp. 141, 142.

CHAPTER TWELVE: GOOD NEWS, BAD NEWS

1. Edward Young, *The Messianic Prophecies of Daniel* (Grand Rapids, MI: Eerdmans, 1954), p. 83.
2. *NIV Study Bible*, p. 684.
3. William Whiston, *The Complete Works of Flavius Josephus* (Chicago: Donohue, Henneberry and Co., 1895), pp. 572, 573, 699-705.
4. Ibid., p. 686.

CHAPTER THIRTEEN: THE MAN IN THE GOLDEN SASH

1. Frank E. Peretti, *This Present Darkness* (Wheaton, IL: Crossway Books, 1986), pp. 96, 97.
2. Ibid., p. 103.

CHAPTER FOURTEEN: HIS STORY WRITTEN IN ADVANCE

1. Saint Augustine, *The City of God* (New York: Dutton and Company, 1947), p. 288.
2. "History of the Premillennial Doctrine," in Nathaniel West, ed., *Premillennial Essays of the Prophetic Conference Held in the Church of the Holy Trinity* (Chicago: Revell, 1879), p. 351.
3. John Calvin, *Commentary on the Book of the Prophet Isaiah* (Grand Rapids, MI: Wm. B. Eerdmans, 1948), p. 348.
4. Ibid., p. 386.

CHAPTER FIFTEEN: THE TWO GREAT CRISES

1. Allan A. MacRae, *The Prophecies of Daniel* (Singapore: Christian Life Publishing, 1991), pp. 228, 229.
2. Ibid., 232.
3. Ibid., 234.

CHAPTER SIXTEEN: THE END

1. Joni Eareckson Tada, *Heaven: Your Real Home* (Grand Rapids, MI: Zondervan, 1995), p. 63.

Scripture Index

General Index

Index of Sermon Illustrations

Professing Christian almost loses his business, repents of his immoral lifestyle, but after a while goes back to his sins, 83

Corruption prevalent in U.S. Congress, 91

Author as boy accepts pay for circulars he didn't deliver, gets caught, 91-92

Pastor encourages author who has liver cancer with 2 Corinthians 1, congregation prays, author recovers from surgery, 95

Judith Viorst writes of a little boy's "terrible, horrible, no-good, very bad day," 129

Woman dying of cancer has many questions about Heaven, 232

Jesus Our Substitute
Five-year-old can't understand Jesus' taking our punishment, until mother says she will get the spanking her son deserves, 155

Judgment of God
In late 1980s Saddam Hussein was rebuilding Babylon, but Operation Desert Storm wiped it all out, 105

Edward Winslow speaks for the Pilgrims: drought upon us because we are under God's wrath, 153

Love of God
Bedridden miner answers Satan's doubts with a look at the cross — "doesn't Jesus love me!" 59-60

S. M. Lockridge poem on trusting the all-sufficient God, 141-144

Corrie ten Boom's father tells her (she dreads her father's death) that just as he gives her the ticket as they are boarding the train, God gives us the grace we need just at the time we need it, 227

Joni Eareckson Tada shares C. S. Lewis's comments on how this life is just the cover and title page, but life in Heaven will be many chapters, each better than the last, 233

Loving the World
Young couple work, work, work to fill nice house with things, grow cold to the things of God, 67-68

Materialism
Young couple work, work, work to fill nice house with things, grow cold to the things of God, 67-68

Little boy saying bedtime prayer prays for a bike loudly enough for his father to hear, 93

Mercy of God
Author asks bank for mercy when he misunderstands how bank-by-phone works, overdraws his checking account, 151

Persecution
Albania takes away citizens' Christian names, in case curiosity about their names takes them to the Bible, 18

Pro-life sidewalk counselor arrested on false charges, 29-30

Just as a man's attempt to kill a starfish produced more starfish, persecution of the church spreads the gospel and brings others to Christ, 173

Prayer
Author and church circle pray over his cancer; God gives healing and strength, 30-31

Author experiences worse pain than ever before but gets through it, later discovers his church was praying for him at that time, 55-56

Little boy saying bedtime prayer prays for a bike loudly enough for his father to hear, 93

Vincent and Margaret Crossett, missionaries, were chased out of Mainland China but prayed for forty years for the little church there, which during that time grew to four thousand strong, 95

Pastor encourages author who has liver cancer with 2 Corinthians 1, congregation prays, author recovers from surgery, 95

Peggy MacDonald prays over undeveloped ground, prays that a caring church would exist there, 145, 156-157

Group begins to pray for woman's father more earnestly when she tearfully shares that her father is dying from cancer, 149

Edward Winslow speaks for the Pilgrims: drought upon us because we are under God's wrath, need to pray 153

Poem on not taking time to pray, ask, seek, knock, 183

Pride
C. S. Lewis: "There is one vice of which no man in the world is free," 61, 67, 68

Young couple work, work, work to fill nice house with things, grow cold to the things of God, 67-68

Chuck Colson full of pride as he served the President of the United States, became involved in Watergate, went to prison, found God, 68-69

In late 1980s Saddam Hussein was rebuilding Babylon, but Operation Desert Storm wiped it all out, 105

Reliability
Don Sutton had no no-hitters, won few major awards, but was a reliable pitcher for twenty-one seasons, 89

Return of Christ
Just as a pregnant woman does not know the exact time her baby will be born but knows

About the
Book Jacket

The design of the book jacket brings together the talents of several Christian artists. The design centers around the beautiful banner created by artist Marge Gieser. It is photographed here on the jacket at about one-twentieth of its original size.

Concerning the symbolism used in the banner for *Daniel: The Triumph of God's Kingdom* Marge Gieser writes:

> "A kingdom that shall stand forever" is symbolized by the massive columns and architectural detail. The Lamb of God is also shown standing, carrying the resurrection banner. The Lamb standing signifies Jesus' victory over death. The white banner stands for Christ's body. The staff is shaped like a cross, reminding us of His death on the cross. The banner also bears a cross, always colored red. The nimbus around the Lamb's head stands for divinity.

The other artist contributing his talents to the creation of the jacket was David LaPlaca, art direction.